THE ADDISON-WESLEY NETWORKING BASICS SERIES

L2TP

The Addison-Wesley Networking Basics Series

The Addison-Wesley Networking Basics Series is a set of concise, hands-on guides to today's key technologies and protocols in computer networking. Each book in the series covers a focused topic and explains the steps required to implement and work with specific technologies and tools in network programming, administration, and security. Providing practical, problem-solving information, these books are written by practicing professionals who have mastered complex network challenges.

Thomas Clark, *Designing Storage Area Networks: A Practical Reference for Implementing Fibre Channel SANs*, 0-201-61584-3

Geoff Mulligan, *Removing the SPAM: Email Processing and Filtering*, 0-201-37957-0

Richard Shea, *L2TP: Implementation and Operation*, 0-201-60448-5

John W. Stewart III, *BGP4: Inter-Domain Routing in the Internet*, 0-201-37951-1

Brian Tung, *Kerberos: A Network Authentication System*, 0-201-37924-4

Andrew F. Ward, *Connecting to the Internet: A Practical Guide about LAN-Internet Connectivity*, 0-201-37956-2

Visit the Series Web site for new title information:
http://www.awl.com/cseng/networkingbasics/

THE ADDISON-WESLEY NETWORKING BASICS SERIES

L2TP

Implementation and Operation

Richard Shea

Addison–Wesley
An Imprint of Addison Wesley Longman, Inc.
Reading, Massachusetts • Harlow, England • Menlo Park, California
Berkeley, California • Don Mills, Ontario • Sydney • Bonn
Amsterdam • Tokyo • Mexico City

The publisher offers discounts on this book when ordered in quantity for special sales. For more information, please contact:

AWL Direct Sales
Addison Wesley Longman, Inc.
One Jacob Way
Reading, Massachusetts 01867
(781) 944-3700

Visit A–W on the Web: www.awl.com/cseng/

Library of Congress Cataloging-in-Publication Data

Shea, Richard, 1972
    L2TP : implementation and operation / Richard Shea.
        p.   cm. — (The Addison-Wesley networking basics series)
    Includes bibliographical references and index.
    ISBN 0-201-60448-5
    1. L2TP (Computer network protocol) I. Title. II. Series.
    TK5105.572 .S54   1999
    004.6'2—dc21   99–37615
                                                          CIP

ISBN 0-201-60448-5
Text printed on recycled paper
1 2 3 4 5 6 7 8 9 10—CRW—0302010099
First printing, September 1999

Contents

Preface

Remote access has become more and more popular as organizations rely increasingly on their data networks. The increasing popularity of telecommuting and the numbers of individuals who are mobile are two strong factors in this trend. In order for organizations to provide traditional remote access, they must research and plan their use and make sizeable capital investments in infrastructure. To begin with, an organization needs to predetermine call capacity because the number of calls that can be simultaneously terminated is a factor in deciding what level of remote access device and how many T1 lines are purchased. The organization's call capacity must be increased to allow for the remote access connections to be made. Remote access connections are generally made via dedicated T1 lines (or T3 lines for very large organizations) connected to the remote access equipment. Next there is the purchase of the remote access equipment consisting of a device that terminates T1 or T3 lines on one side and has a connection to the organization's private network (typically Ethernet) on the other side.

Traditional remote access is inflexible, inefficient, and inadequate for accommodating evolving broadband technologies. These technologies provide dedicated access to an Internet Service Provider (ISP), forcing the remote user to tie up his or her traditional phone line to access the private network of an organization. When the legacy phone network is used for remote access, the costs incurred per connection are based on the same rules that are used for voice communications. For mobile users, establishing a remote access connection may mean incurring long distance costs. In addition, evolving broadband communication technologies such as cable modem and Asymmetric Digital Subscriber Line (ADSL) cannot be supported by traditional remote access. By supporting traditional remote access, organizations also incur the ongoing costs involved in supporting the remote access devices, including the upgrade of these devices as technology changes. One good example of why this is a problem is the recent increase in analog connection speeds to 56K access. When the 56K connection speed was first introduced, there were two methods of signaling. Private organizations and Internet Service Providers (ISPs) could not be sure they were choosing the right signaling versions, and only later did equipment become available that could support both 56K signaling methods.

The Layer 2 Tunneling Protocol, or L2TP, is aimed squarely at lifting the physical connection burden from the organization. The traditional remote access system is split into two halves. One half is responsible for terminating the physical connections, and the other half provides access to the private network. Conceptually, a line is drawn down the middle of a traditional remote access device; half of the device provides physical call connections, and the other half provides access to the private network communicating over L2TP. With L2TP, analog modem, Integrated Services Digital Network (ISDN), and ADSL connections can be physically terminated by an ISP, and the user data can be carried to a device at the edge of an organization's private network. L2TP client software can also be used to make virtual connections all the way from the remote user device (that is, a PC) to the organization's private network in such a way that the remote user's physical connection is completely independent.

Although the outsourced remote access model is the starting point for deploying L2TP, other applications are possible. Essentially any time that running Point-to-Point Protocol (PPP) between two entities over a non–point-to-point connection would be advantageous, L2TP should be used to provide that functionality.

This book provides details of L2TP for the individual who will be implementing L2TP in a data communications device. A history of L2TP is also provided, along with comparisons to the protocol's two predecessors, L2F and PPTP. Implementation tips are provided to cover those areas of use that are not readily understandable solely from reading the L2TP technical specification.

Audience

There are two audiences for this book. The primary audience is those who will be writing L2TP code. The book attempts to provide tips, give history, and logically explain and lay out the architecture for L2TP and the crucial and sometimes subtle interaction between L2TP and the PPP software running over it. The other audience for this book is those considering L2TP for their Virtual Private Network (VPN) deployment. The early chapters on the basics of L2TP and the discussion of security and management will be of particular interest to this reader.

Organization

The first three chapters are geared to a somewhat general audience. L2TP implementers may simply ignore these chapters if they wish to focus only on the details of L2TP implementation. Chapters 4–10 provide the details of L2TP implementation. These chapters may be skimmed by the reader with only a general interest in the details of the protocol itself. Special attention to Chapter 10 ("Security") should be paid even by the general reader. Chapter 11 ("SNMP Management") may also be of some interest to the general reader, and undoubtedly of interest to the L2TP implementer or the implementer of network management applications for L2TP. Chapter 12 provides resources for learning more about L2TP and gives information on what future work in L2TP is currently under consideration.

Acknowledgments

When I first started writing this book I thought it was going to be much easier than it was. Writing a book on L2TP was particularly challenging because the protocol is a relatively young one. The L2TP specification was also in the Internet Draft stage throughout the writing of the book, providing a constant sense of tension that things may change again and require more rewrite. During the writing of the book, in fact, the Internet Draft for L2TP was significantly overhauled (compare revision 12 of the I-D with revision 13). The Internet Draft provided a much clearer technical specification of L2TP, but it necessitated my changing significant parts of this book.

I would like to thank my wife Denise and the rest of my family for their support and encouragement. My wife was particularly good about making sure I got up early enough before work to get significant parts of the book written.

I had not realized how much the character of a book could be shaped through the reviews of others. I had excellent reviewers throughout the process of writing this book. For their reviews I would like to thank Bernard Aboba, Dory Leifer, John Matias, William Palter, Tom Pincince, Paul E. Raison, Andrew Valencia of Cisco Systems, Rohit Verma of 3Com Corporation, and Glen Zorn. I would especially like to thank Jim Carlson of IronBridge Networks for his review. He stressed the ability of the LAC to inspect and translate PPP and significantly helped direct the character of the book through other very detailed critiques.

Thanks also to the editor Mary Hart and the staff at Addison Wesley Longman. Mary was always patient in adjusting the schedule as my needs and the underlying L2TP specification changed.

— Richard Shea

Background

The Layer 2 Tunneling Protocol (L2TP) was developed to carry Point-to-Point Protocol (PPP) traffic over non–point-to-point networks. PPP is the most commonly used protocol to provide remote access over dial-up lines such as traditional phone lines and ISDN. L2TP provides virtual remote access by tunneling PPP. Although this allows L2TP to provide other services, such as a virtual leased line, the initial target application for L2TP is to provide a mechanism for virtual remote access.

Figure 1-1 shows the traditional style of remote access using PPP over the switched telephone network. A PPP session is established between the remote user or remote network and a device at the edge of the data network called the Network Access Server (NAS). The role of the NAS is to terminate point-to-point connections to remote sites. Data can then be forwarded between the remote sites and the data network through the NAS.

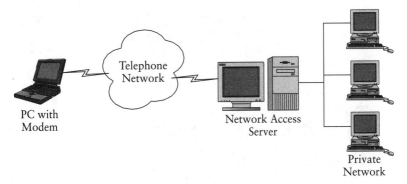

Figure 1-1 *Traditional remote access*

1

The L2TP protocol is used to explode out the work done by the NAS into two pieces and provide a communications mechanism between the two devices handling each piece of functionality. As a result, the device at the edge of the private network that the remote user is accessing does not need to support the particular physical connection type of the remote user. Figure 1-2 shows virtual remote access using L2TP.

Figure 1-2 shows two scenarios of L2TP being used to access a private network. All access to the private network is provided by the L2TP Network Server (LNS) at the edge of the private network. In the first scenario an L2TP Access Concentrator (LAC) is used to terminate point-to-point connections to remote users. The LAC then establishes an L2TP data session to the LNS for each point-to-point connection, and the PPP connection is carried between the remote user and the LNS. This method of tunneling a PPP session has come to be known as

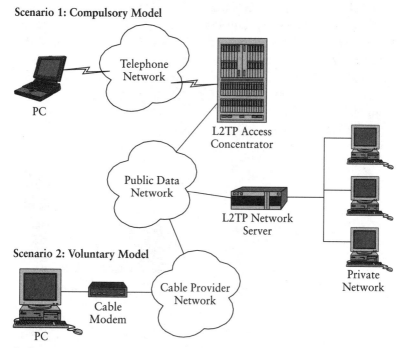

Figure 1-2 *Remote access with L2TP*

the *compulsory* (or *mandatory*) tunneling model because the remote user's computer does not control the tunnel. Another type of connection is shown under scenario 2 in Figure 1-2. The remote user connected through the network is a cable modem user. Generally the cable modem user has access to the public network through the cable data network. This type of user can connect to the private network through the LNS by using an L2TP client implementation. This can be done by establishing an L2TP connection directly between the remote user's computer and the LNS. To the remote user this looks like a "virtual dial-up" has occurred to the LNS, similar to dialing into an ISP with a modem. The PPP protocol is then run over the L2TP data session (the virtual dial-up connection) between the remote computer and the LNS. This method of tunneling a PPP session has come to be known as the *voluntary* (or *client*) tunneling model. The term *voluntary* is used because the remote user is aware of the connection made to the LNS through the action of having initiated a virtual dial-up connection, and the user can even decide which traffic will be sent into the tunnel (for example, based on routing information).

1.1 Remote Access

Remote access technology gets its name from its ability to enable users to have access to a network from remote locations. Remote access means that a computer user in another physical location can make a connection to a LAN and get the same services as if he or she were connected directly to the LAN via a LAN port.

When using remote access to a private network, the remote entity can be authenticated, assigned an IP address as defined by the IP address policy of the private network, and so forth. In remote access the remote caller connecting to the network generally has no need to authenticate the network access server answering the remote access call since it is generally accepted that if you dial a phone number a third party cannot intercept it. Since remote access connections are generally made via an organization's switched telephone network, which is perceived as being harder to snoop than the Internet, data security for remote access is generally an afterthought. Once a remote access connection has been authenticated, it is generally perceived to be unnecessary to further authenticate each packet received since the injection of packets into a modem connection is technologically difficult.

1.1.1 Telecommuters — Small Office/Home Office

With remote access, individuals can connect to the private network from another location, so they can work partly or completely at home. A telecommuter may also have a local network that has been referred to as a *small office/home office* (SOHO). The implication of the SOHO is that it is differentiated from a *remote office/branch office* (ROBO) only by scale (that is, a SOHO is considered to be appreciably smaller than a ROBO, and, therefore, the two have different traffic levels and IP address management demands).

Telecommuters are generally connected to the private network over traditional analog phone or ISDN networks, but in rare cases they may also be connected via Frame Relay or other dedicated direct links to the private network.

1.1.2 Remote Office/Branch Office

In the branch office connection, known as ROBO, there are two networks connected over a Wide Area Network (WAN) link, such as ISDN or Frame Relay. By providing a ROBO remote access connection to a corporate network, the corporation gives geographically separate networks (for example, corporate remote offices) access to corporate resources.

1.1.3 Partner

A partner connection is really the same as a ROBO connection except that there is usually some restriction placed on what resources can be accessed by the partner across the connection, whereas the branch office typically involves a looser trust model between the remote ends of the WAN connection.

1.2 Virtual Private Networks

One of the recent buzzwords related to the Internet has been the term *Virtual Private Network* (VPN). Attempts to define this broad category of technology have proven very difficult, mostly because different technologies have provided different services yet all manufacturers called these services VPN. L2TP is one of the protocols that can be used to provide a VPN service.

To understand the capabilities and limitations of the VPN services that L2TP can provide, one needs to know what is meant by a VPN. Let's start by looking at what each word in this term means. Though one may even take *network* to mean more than just a *data network*, we will in fact start with the assumption that *network* in this context refers to a *data* network. The term *private* attempts to qualify the type of network in some way. In general, a "private network" is one that serves a specific purpose. For example, a company may have a private network for the purpose of sending email between employees, running scheduling programs, and even for personnel management purposes such as keeping track of vacation time, expense reports, and so forth. One of the important aspects of a private network is that there is usually an assumed level of security for the network itself. For example, the network equipment may be wholly contained within the corporate offices, therefore inheriting some level of physical security. Corporations have generally considered their networks to be safe from competitors because their competitors can't physically enter the building where the network computers are housed. (*Note:* There is entire discourse possible on whether or not physical security is sufficient. Since this book is not about private network security policy, it should suffice to explain physical security as a property of private networks.) Another aspect of private networks is that the entity controlling the network can control who accesses the network (for example, access may be granted only to those who can physically access a LAN port). It is also possible for the entity controlling the network to manage such things as IP addressing and subnetting, and so forth.

The concept of a private network is only important when it is contrasted to a public network. The difference between a public network and a private network is similar to the difference between public and private property. Public property is for the use of everyone, as is the public network. Private property, on the other hand, is controlled by an organization and is often used for a specific purpose or set of purposes. Rules for who can access private property are generally established by the owners, as are the rules for who can use a private network and for what purposes they can use it.

Moving on, the *virtual* in *Virtual Private Network* refers to what the word generally refers to in technology—the simulation of some set of properties. For instance, *virtual reality* refers to a technology where some of the properties of reality (for example, a three-dimensional sensory environment) are provided by technology. In the term *Virtual Private Network*, then, *virtual* describes a network that simulates some of the properties of a private network. The implication is that a VPN exists over a public network yet provides some of the properties of a private network at the same time.

For example, a VPN may provide encryption services to "hide" data being carried over the public network. This encryption capability would provide the protection from eavesdropping by competitors that a private network generally relies on the physical security of the private network itself to provide. Table 1-1 lists some properties of private networks and what capabilities a VPN must provide in order to simulate the same properties when the network is running over a public network.

It should be noted that there are some properties of private networks that are particularly difficult to hide when one is running a private network over a public network. Some of these properties are

- The activity level of private traffic. It is difficult to disguise the amount of data transfer occurring over a VPN connection.
- The type of applications run on the private network. Some inference about the type of applications being run by the private network may be possible based on the timing and size of packets or other information that is obtainable by looking at traffic trends over the VPN connection.

Because it can provide a virtual remote access service, L2TP is well positioned to be a solution for providing Virtual Private Network ser-

Table 1-1   Properties of Private Networks

Private Network Property	VPN Service
Physical eavesdropping protection	Cryptographic encryption to "hide" data
Control over connectivity	Session and traffic authentication
IP address management	Separation of private IP realm from public IP realm

vices. L2TP benefits from tunneling the feature-rich PPP, and inherits from PPP its set of supported protocols, creating an impressive list of supported protocols, such as IP, Internetworking Packet Exchange (IPX), AppleTalk, and NetBIOS. Although this list of protocols supported by PPP is impressive, it is important to remember that in order for these protocols to be supported over L2TP, the L2TP remote endpoint known as the LNS must support each protocol explicitly in its PPP implementation. In contrast, in the compulsory model, the LAC does not need to support any of these protocols for them to be available to the remote user via L2TP.

1.3 Open System Interconnect Model

The Open System Interconnect (OSI) model is an idealized architecture for communication protocols. This is a layered model in which each layer has different responsibilities for communication. Figure 1-3 shows the layers of the OSI model. This book focuses primarily on the lowest three layers of the OSI model, because these are the layers that directly concern PPP and L2TP. Organizing protocols according to layers creates a logical structure wherein both protocols can be replaced, leveraged, and expanded while other protocols remain the same. This is accomplished by having protocols provide uniform interfaces to other protocols at adjacent layers. For example, User Datagram Protocol (UDP) and Transmission Control Protocol (TCP) belong to the *transport layer,* which operates over the *network layer.* Generally the network protocol used for both TCP and UDP is IP, but IP does not operate differently depending on whether a given packet is carrying TCP or UDP traffic. This illustrates how a single layer 3 (network layer) protocol, IP, can be used to support multiple layer 4 (transport layer) protocols, UDP and TCP.

Another important aspect of a layered protocol system is that a unit of data of a given protocol level can easily be transferred between networks of different lower layer types. For example, a given IP datagram can easily be transferred between PPP links, Asynchronous Transer Mode (ATM), Ethernet, and so forth.

As shown in Figure 1-3, the lowest layer of the OSI model, layer 1, is referred to as the *physical layer.* This layer serves to define a physical signaling of data for the communications medium. Generally this

Application Layer
Presentation Layer
Session Layer
Transport Layer
Network Layer
Datalink Layer
Physical Layer

Figure 1-3 *OSI layers*

means that at this layer a definition is supplied to indicate how bytes are signaled. Examples of well-known physical layer types are ISDN and T1. Sometimes physical layer types are not known independently of the datalink layer. Examples of this kind of mixed layer type are Ethernet 100BaseTx and 100BaseFx, where the 100 defines the speed of the physical layer used, the T and the F differentiate copper and fiber physical layer types, and the Ethernet standard also defines the datalink addressing.

The second layer is referred to as the *datalink layer*. This layer defines how frames of information are constructed. Generally this means defining how bytes are combined into units called *frames*. Datalink frames consist of data, in the form of layer 3 packets as well as information needed by the datalink layer itself. The datalink layer is responsible for multiplexing layer 3 protocols, and it is generally responsible for some simple means of network node addressing. The addressing provided by the datalink layer is typically used to define communication to other entities that are directly connected in some way. Examples of the datalink layer include PPP, Ethernet, and ATM.

The third layer is the *network layer*. This layer defines how packets of data are constructed. Network layer packets consist of layer 4 data, as well as information needed by the network layer itself. The network layer is responsible for multiplexing layer 4 protocols, and it is generally responsible for a more global means of addressing. Examples of the network layer include IP and IPX.

Layer 4 of the OSI model is referred to as the *transport layer*. For IP-based networks, the common layer 4 protocols are TCP and UDP. Normally in the OSI model a lower layer is said to *encapsulate* the layer above it. For example, Ethernet encapsulates IP, IP encapsulates TCP, and so forth. But a protocol can virtualize the services of a lower layer, and this process is referred to as *tunneling*. L2TP carries data like a layer 4 protocol, but the data that it encapsulates (PPP) is a layer 2 protocol, so L2TP is responsible for emulating any of the layer 1 behavior that the operation of PPP assumes. L2TP is therefore said to *tunnel* PPP.

It is often the case that a given protocol in the OSI model will be further layered within the OSI layer it occupies, becoming a sublayer. For example, a well-known layer related to Ethernet is the *Media Access Control* (MAC) layer, which refers to the sublayer of the Ethernet protocol operating within the Ethernet OSI layer 2. The MAC sublayer is responsible for the interaction of the Ethernet to the physical layer over which it is running. We use the concept of sublayering in describing how the PPP functionality is split between the L2TP tunnel endpoints.

1.4 Point-to-Point Protocol

Since L2TP tunnels PPP, having a grasp of the Point-to-Point Protocol (PPP) is crucial to a proper understanding of L2TP. Without a working knowledge of the operation and assumptions of PPP, it is impossible to understand how an L2TP implementation should work.

Early remote access technology consisted of establishing a simple connection between a private network and a remote machine. This connection was then used to send ASCII characters back and forth between the remote machine and the host machine. Such access was limited to whatever applications were available on the host machine connected to. This method of remote access was generally called "shell" access because the remote machine had a shell process run on the host machine. The early method of remote access also had the drawback of being a text-only method of connection, without the capability to display graphics. The Internet and the World Wide Web (WWW) with their graphical user interface are a major step forward from such systems.

The desire to connect to a network (for instance, the Internet) inexpensively, instead of connecting to a specific machine, drove the development of two new technologies: Serial Line IP (SLIP) and Point-to-Point Protocol (PPP). These technologies differed from shell access in that they defined a *framing* for data that traveled over the remote access connections, so that bytes of data could be delivered in forms other than the displayable ASCII characters available through shell access. With SLIP and PPP, data is sent over the remote access connections in larger units of data, called packets.

Although SLIP and PPP both define a framing protocol for serial lines, SLIP is somewhat specific to the Internet Protocol (IP), but PPP is structured to define the framing to be independent of the type of data carried. In addition, PPP includes Network Control Protocols (NCPs), which are responsible for the configuration of different network layer protocols to run over the PPP connection. Because of this flexibility, PPP can be used to carry multiple network layer protocols simultaneously (for example, IP, IPX, AppleTalk) over the same connection. PPP also allows the option to provide other services, such as compression and encryption, over the connection.

Because of its flexibility, PPP has become the primary remote access technology for non-permanent connections (for example, modem connections over analog telephone, ISDN). PPP is also used over some dedicated types of links such as Frame Relay or T1 interfaces.

1.5 Sublayers

Figure 1-4 shows a conceptual organization of sublayers for PPP within its layer 2 OSI layer. The figure shows PPP with a *media-dependent sublayer,* consisting of both a control-handling portion and a data-handling portion. The control portion, the Link Control Protocol (LCP), is a negotiation that occurs when PPP operation over a link starts. The LCP negotiates the behavior of the media-dependent sublayer as well as the operation of some of the features in the services sublayer (such as authentication and link loopback detection). Data handling in the media-dependent sublayer consists of PPP frame transformation dependent on the medium type over which PPP is running.

The second sublayer for PPP is the *services sublayer.* This sublayer also consists of a data-handling portion and a control-handling por-

| | Control |
Data Handling	Handling
Multiplex sublayer Multiplex network layer Demultiplex network layer	IPCP IPXCP Etc.
Services sublayer Compression Encryption	CCP ECP Auth
	LCP
Media-dependent sublayer HDLC addressing Escaping Frame Check Sequence (FCS) Framing	LCP

Figure 1-4 *Conceptual sublayering of PPP data and control handling*

tion. The data-handling portion consists of the operations of encryption and compression. The control-handling portion consists of the configuration of encryption and the compression on the link via the Encryption Control Protocol (ECP) and Compression Control Protocol (CCP) as well as authentication. The operation of LCP for loopback detection is also part of the PPP services sublayer.

The third sublayer, the *multiplex sublayer,* is responsible for PPP interaction with layer 3, and it also consists of a data-handling portion and a control-handling portion. The data-handling portion multiplexes layer 3 traffic on the PPP header protocol field. The control-portion is responsible for the configuration of layer 3 parameters for the various supported layer 3 protocols with a one-to-one mapping between control protocol and layer 3 protocol (for example, IP Control Protocol [IPCP] for IP, IPX Control Protocol [IPXCP] for IPX).

This breakdown of PPP into three sublayers should be taken only as a general guide. For example, Van Jacobson TCP/IP header compression is negotiated in IPCP, is aware of both layer 3 and layer 4 details, and would be seen to operate on packets in the PPP services sublayer.

1.6 The Layer 2 Role of PPP

A common responsibility of a layer 2 protocol is to provide some method of addressing. Because PPP runs over a point-to-point connection, there is no requirement of addressing in the general sense. In other words, if a PPP peer sends a packet over a link, there is no requirement to address the packet to one particular peer or the other. The peer on the other end of the link simply receives the packet. There are sometimes addressing requirements outside the scope of PPP itself that PPP must be aware of. The most common of these is the High-level Data Link Control (HDLC) addressing that pervades the definition of PPP operation. PPP makes use of HDLC framing, but it uses fixed address values. This means that the HDLC framing is used to identify the traffic as PPP but not to differentiate between PPP peers. Similarly, PPP over ATM AAL5 or FUNI brings requirements on the framing of PPP to identify the packets as PPP but not to differentiate between PPP peers (PPP peers would be identified by the Virtual Circuit [VC] defining the point-to-point connection). The basic PPP packet is therefore defined without any addressing fields and has a common header that consists solely of a 16-bit protocol field (which can be expressed as an 8-bit protocol field in some cases).

PPP also contains a mechanism for *escaping* data. This operation is a requirement when one is operating PPP over asynchronous HDLC (AHDLC). The escape character is 0x7d, and the special character 0x7e is used to delimit AHDLC frames. PPP allows the LCP negotiation of which characters must be escaped by each peer, although it is legal for a sender to escape any character. By default all characters between and including 0x00 and 0x1f are escaped as well as the escape character 0x7d and the framing character 0x7e. Today, typical negotiations are made to escape only 0x7d and 0x7e.

Also when running over HDLC, PPP must calculate a checksum (Frame Check Sequence or FCS) for the HDLC framing. The type of FCS used can be negotiated in LCP when the link is established.

It should be clear from what we've discussed so far that PPP has a media-dependent sublayer with the general responsibility of framing the PPP data for the physical layer. In the case of PPP running over AHDLC this includes character escaping, FCS calculation, and HDLC address header. Link Control Protocol (LCP) is used to configure the operation of the media-dependent sublayer options. For example, LCP can negotiate which characters (if any) should be escaped, what type of HDLC FCS should be used, and whether the HDLC address header needs to be present on all packets (an HDLC address header is present on all LCP frames regardless of this negotiation outcome).

PPP also defines services that are available for link management and data-handling options. Link management options such as loopback detection and error monitoring are part of LCP. Additional services are configured through other control protocols. The Compression Control Protocol (CCP) negotiates the operation of compression on data transferred between PPP peers.[1] The Encryption Control Protocol (ECP) negotiates the operation of encryption on data transferred between PPP peers. Session authentication is provided as a service of PPP and is achieved through the operation of the Password Authentication Protocol (PAP), Challenge Authentication Protocol (CHAP), or the Extensible Authentication Protocol (EAP). The services provided by PPP are optional and are not present on all links. It is possible (but not safe) to have a PPP link over which no authentication, compression, or encryption are done. The services sublayer is therefore comprised of the operation and configuration of optional services provided by PPP.

Finally PPP, because it is a layer 2 protocol, must provide multiplexing and demultiplexing of layer 3 protocol data. Figure 1-4 shows this as the third sublayer of PPP. The data-handling portion of this sublayer is simply responsible for identification of layer 3 protocols encapsulated by PPP between the PPP peers. This is simply accomplished via the protocol field of the PPP packet header. The control portion of this sublayer also spans layer 3 and is described in the next section.

1.7 The Layer 3 Role of PPP

Although PPP does not typically do any layer 3 processing of packets, PPP does have some exposure to layer 3 above and beyond just the multiplexing of layer 3 datagrams.

---

1. Oddly, the Microsoft Point-to-Point Encryption (MPPE) operation is negotiated as part of CCP instead of as part of ECP. Such is the legacy of proprietary protocol development.

The main responsibility of PPP with regard to layer 3 relates to the NCPs setting up layer 3 configuration (such as addressing). For each type of layer 3 protocol, there is a corresponding NCP. For example, when IP is set up on a PPP link, the IP Control Protocol (IPCP) is used; when IPX is set up, the IPX Control Protocol (IPXCP) is used. Prior to each type of layer 3 data being carried by the PPP link, the corresponding NCP must run through its state machine and reach the OPEN state.

PPP also has significant exposure to both layer 3 and layer 4, and it comes from the operation of Van Jacobson (VJ) TCP/IP header compression (RFC1144). Van Jacobson is negotiated on a PPP link as part of the IPCP operation. The observation that for a particular TCP/IP traffic flow the contents of the TCP/IP headers do not change much from one packet to the next is the basis for VJ Compression. VJ Compression replaces TCP/IP headers in a traffic flow with a VJ header that contains only the changes from the TCP/IP header in the last packet sent in the flow. On the receiving side, each VJ flow contains a copy of the last TCP/IP header reconstructed. When a VJ packet is received, the VJ header information is applied to the stored copy of the TCP/IP header, and this becomes the TCP/IP header for the current packet. As long as no packets are lost, this process works fine. But if a packet is lost, the VJ engine is informed, and it must drop all packets until a VJ packet containing a complete TCP/IP header for that flow is received. It may seem strange that a packet loss requires that the sending VJ engine send a complete TCP/IP header, since the receiver does not inform the sender that a packet loss has occurred. But the process works this way: the sender takes the retransmission of a TCP/IP packet as a signal that a packet may have been lost and in this case sends the entire TCP/IP header.

1.8 Physical Layer Assumptions

In order to tunnel PPP properly, L2TP must understand and conform to the assumptions the PPP has made about the characteristics of the layer 1 media over which it runs.

One assumption that is made in the case of VJ Compression is that the physical layer can detect a packet loss with a high degree of probability. The PPP layer can then be informed of the packet loss, and the VJ engine can drop received packets for each VJ TCP/IP flow until the next complete TCP/IP header is received for a flow. Because VJ headers contain no checksum and the receiver calculates the TCP and IP checksums for the reconstructed TCP/IP header in a VJ flow, a TCP/IP implementation receiving a packet with a reconstructed TCP/IP header cannot detect a problem with the headers. Undesirable behavior may then result if the TCP/IP header does not contain the same contents that the sending TCP/IP peer originally sent.

Another assumption made by various protocols within PPP is that packet reordering will not occur. Again, an example of VJ operation shows how this assumption can cause problems. Other protocols within PPP contain coherency counters (such as the compression and encryption protocols). It is important to note that these protocols lack the ability to reorder packets into their proper order. So if packets were received by these protocols in the order 1, 3, 2, when packet 3 is received, we can assume that packet 2 has been dropped. Then when packet 2 is received, it will either be dropped because it is outside of a receive window, or it could be processed as though it had wrapped the sequence number counters, and the result could be disastrous behavior if some sort of special operation by the protocol is supposed to happen when the sequence number wraps.[2]

A performance-related assumption made by compression protocols in PPP is that most of the delay in transmission between the two peers is owing to the transmission speed of the link. In other words, the physical medium is assumed to be low speed if there is a high delay. This fact can be used to the advantage of protocols that operate with history by allowing them to keep the number of packets processed through the history small without slowing down performance of the PPP link. This behavior is desirable when histories are involved because if a receiving peer detects a packet loss for a protocol with history, a reset-history indication is sent to the sending peer and the receiving peer must drop all packets using the history until an indication is received from the sender that the history has been reset. So the fewer packets the sender has processed through the history, the fewer packets will need to be dropped by a receiver before a reset indication can be put into effect.

---

2. For example, Microsoft Point-to-Point Encryption (MPPE) in non-historyless mode specifies that the encryption keys are recalculated every 256 packets. So artificially causing a wrap of the sequence number space can cause the keys of the two peers to be desynchronized and render the link inoperable.

Often L2TP operates over networks with both high delay and high throughput. The drawback to this mode of operation is that keeping the number of packets processed through the history at a small number results in bandwidth along the L2TP path being underutilized.

1.9 Control Protocol Operation

Each of the PPP control protocols is built on top of the same state machine. The purpose of this state machine is to provide for the configuration of options between PPP peers. The general behavior of a control protocol consists of a series of requests for configuration options and responses from the PPP peer. When each of the PPP peers agrees on the configuration options presented by the other peer, the control protocol reaches the OPEN state. Until the control protocol reaches the OPEN state, the behavior that it controls is not available. For example, compression cannot occur until CCP reaches the OPEN state, IP packets cannot be transferred between peers until IPCP reaches the OPEN state, and so forth.

An in-depth description of the control protocol operation can be found in *PPP Design and Debugging* by James Carlson.

1.10 Chronological Operation of PPP

So far we have described and broken down the operation of various portions of PPP with only an indirect mention of the chronological life of a PPP link. It is important to know when in the life of a PPP link all of the control protocols operate. The control of a PPP link happens in three distinct phases, starting with the configuration of the media-dependent sublayer, then (optionally) the authentication and then the configuration of the services and layer 3 protocols.

The first phase of PPP is LCP negotiation. The LCP has two main responsibilities: to negotiate options for the media-dependent sublayer processing, and to negotiate some of the service sublayer services. Some of the media-dependent sublayer options LCP controls are which characters must be escaped, what type of HDLC FCS will be used, whether the HDLC address framing must be present for all packets, and whether the protocol field of the PPP packet can be compressed to an 8-bit value in some cases. Some of the services sublayer options LCP controls are whether link loopback detection will be used, if a link keepalive will be operated, and what type of authentication is to be done between the peers. Until LCP reaches the OPEN state, no other PPP processing is done.

Once LCP negotiation is complete (that is, LCP reaches the OPEN state), an optional authentication phase is entered. This phase is optional only because LCP may not negotiate any authentication depending on the administrative configuration of the link. In the authentication phase, the authentication protocol negotiated by LCP in the first phase is used to authenticate the PPP peer. The specifics of how this is done vary among authentication protocols. The simplest is PAP, in which the authenticatee sends a request for authentication including a user ID and password. The CHAP authentication protocol does not send the password in the clear. In CHAP (including the Microsoft CHAP [MSCHAP] variant) the authenticator sends a randomly generated challenge. The authenticatee then sends a response that is the result of a mathematical transformation of both the challenge and the password (this is done with Message Digest version 5 [MD5]). With CHAP the user ID still appears unencrypted in the CHAP response message. A more recently developed authentication protocol called the Extensible Authentication Protocol (EAP) is another protocol that LCP may negotiate in the authentication phase. The EAP defines a framework within which future authentication methods can be used. The base EAP options include support for token card authentication and a CHAP-like authentication. There has also been work done on a method for providing advanced forms of authentication with EAP, such as with Digital Certificates and authentication and negotiation of encryption keys using ISAKMP/Oakley (see the Internet Engineering Task Force Web page for the PPPEXT working group for the current state of this work).

Once a PPP peer has been authenticated, the third and final phase of PPP is entered. In this phase all of the other services of PPP are configured and operated. In this phase the services sublayer and multiplex sublayer control protocols are run, and the PPP services and layer 3 protocols can operate once the corresponding control protocol has reached the OPEN state. Generally there is no connection between the different control protocols and the operations they configure. This means that services and layer 3 protocol operation can come and go on a PPP link without affecting the state or operation of the other PPP services or operationally supported layer 3 protocols. For example, IPCP may reach the OPEN state and PPP may start to send IP traffic between the PPP peers before the CCP has reached the OPEN state and the PPP peers are able to compress the traffic. Once CCP reaches the OPEN state, the compression service becomes available and the operation of compression can commence. One exception to this architecture is encryption. Since encryption is a security option, it may be undesirable to send data that is not encrypted between the PPP peers. For this reason, multiplex layer packets are not sent to the PPP peer until ECP has reached the OPEN state. Because the encryption service on a PPP link only encrypts data packets, the services and layer 3 protocol control protocols may reach the OPEN state before ECP, but no data is sent until ECP has reached the OPEN state. Conversely, if ECP leaves the OPEN state, data transmission between the PPP peers is halted.

1.11 Summary

The purpose of a VPN is to provide connectivity to a private network over the substrate of a public network. L2TP is a VPN technology because it provides the means to emulate private network connectivity by tunneling PPP, which is used for traditional remote access to private networks. Traditionally the substrate of the public telephone network, frame relay networks, and so forth, have been the communications medium over which VPN access was provided using remote access technology. The L2TP protocol entails using this same remote access technology to provide a VPN over packet-switched public networks (for example, the Internet).

The description of PPP provided by way of introduction in this chapter and the specific issues of PPP and L2TP given in later chapters by no means constitute an in-depth review of PPP protocol behavior. Providing a complete description of PPP design and operation would require a book dedicated to the subject. It is hoped that the level of PPP description found in this book is sufficient for the reader to understand how L2TP must conform to PPP. Further information on PPP implementation can be found in books dedicated to the subject such as *PPP Design and Debugging* by James Carlson.

1.12 The L2TP RFC

L2TP evolved from two similar protocols, the Point-to-Point Tunneling Protocol (PPTP) and the Layer 2 Forwarding (L2F) protocol. PPTP was developed outside of the IETF through a consortium of companies and is most commonly associated with Microsoft. L2F was developed by Cisco Systems. PPTP is available as Informational Request for Comments (RFC) 2637. L2F has become a Historic RFC, RFC2341. The PPTP protocol was developed solely to tunnel PPP, and from a high level L2TP is structured very similarly to PPTP. L2F specifies the tunneling of both PPP and SLIP.

L2TP actually got its name from the combination of the two names PPTP and L2F. The "L2" of L2F was simply combined with the "TP" of PPTP, yielding L2TP.

On June 15, 1999, L2TP was approved to become a Proposed Standard RFC. As this book was going to press, however, an RFC number was not yet assigned for L2TP. Throughout this book, the notation "RFC12tp" is in reference to the first RFC issued for L2TP.

2

L2TP Basics

The concept behind L2TP is really to provide a virtual remote access connection to a network. To achieve this, the protocol was designed to tunnel PPP, which is the primary remote access technology. The ability to tunnel PPP, in turn, provides a very convenient protocol for enabling a multiprotocol Virtual Private Network (VPN). One strength of the L2TP architecture is that it inherits all of the flexibility and breadth of protocol support present in PPP but it does not have to redefine or redesign this support. Authentication and accounting are two good examples of PPP functionality that are leveraged in an L2TP installation. L2TP need only correctly tunnel PPP data between the L2TP peers to enable the multiprotocol VPN. Such issues as, for example, how to communicate or "assign" an IP or IPX address inside the tunnel is beyond the scope of L2TP.

Figure 2-1 shows a traditional remote access model in a more basic form than that shown in Figure 1-1. A connection is made from the

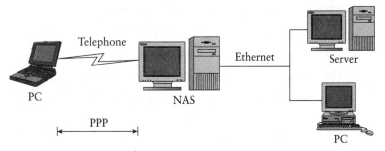

Figure 2-1 *Traditional remote access model*

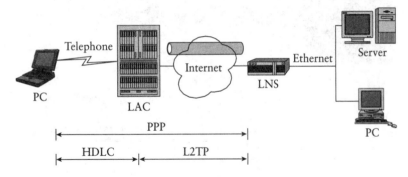

Figure 2-2 *L2TP compulsory tunneling model*

PPP client[1] machine (the remote computer) to the Network Access Server (NAS). The NAS PPP and client PPP can then negotiate LCP options that are appropriate for the physical connection type; the NAS PPP typically authenticates the client PPP, and PPP services and layer 3 protocols are negotiated. The life of the connection then consists of the NAS PPP transferring data back and forth between the PPP client and the rest of the network.

Figure 2-2 shows the L2TP compulsory tunneling model of virtual remote access[2] to a network. In this model the PPP roles played by the NAS in the traditional remote access case are split between the L2TP Access Concentrator (LAC) and the L2TP Network Server (LNS). In this model the PPP client has no control of the tunneling being done. For this reason, this model of tunneling has been labeled *compulsory tunneling*.

2.1 Layer 2 Role of LAC

The LAC PPP really just performs the role of the media-dependent sub-layer of layer 2 PPP, although in some cases it also performs a partial

---

1. The term *client* here should not be taken too literally. PPP does not specify a client-server framework; it is really a peer-peer framework. But in this model the PPP identified as the client is identified as such because it is accessing services provided by the NAS.

2. This type of access has been called dial-up outsourcing because it allows the entity owning the box that is the LNS not to have to terminate the actual dial-up connections.

authentication of the client PPP when the connection is first established. This role is illustrated in Figure 2-3.

There are two different ways in which the LAC handles PPP processing for a connection that ultimately gets tunneled using L2TP. In the first method there is no LCP negotiation and the LAC PPP does no authentication of the client PPP. In the second method the LAC PPP and client PPP do LCP negotiation and start the authentication process before the LAC tunnels the session to the LNS.

In the method in which no LCP processing or initiation of authentication of the client PPP is done by the LAC PPP, the client PPP session is tunneled based on some knowledge outside of PPP. One way to set up such a session would be to configure an NAS to tunnel all connections or all connections running over specific ports. Another approach is for the LAC to tunnel based on a Dialed Number Information String (DNIS), in which case the connection is tunneled to a given LNS based on the number dialed by the remote computer initiating the point-to-point connection. Another approach in which no LCP processing or authentication is done by the LAC PPP involves the LNS requesting the LAC to make an outgoing call. The outgoing call is made from the LAC to the PPP client, and the client PPP is tunneled to the LNS PPP right from the start.

In the method in which LCP processing and authentication are done by the LAC PPP prior to tunneling, the client PPP is generally tunneled based on the PPP authentication information received by the LAC PPP from the client PPP. In this case a true authentication isn't done by the LAC PPP, but the authentication information is parsed in some way so that the LAC can recognize where the client PPP should be tunneled. The canonical example of this is to use a PAP or CHAP

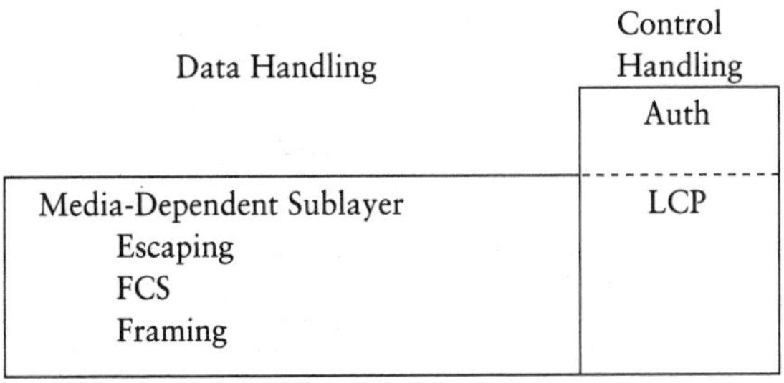

Data Handling	Control Handling
	Auth
Media-Dependent Sublayer Escaping FCS Framing	LCP

Figure 2-3 *LAC PPP processing*

username that includes domain qualifiers. For example, the client PPP may send *rshea@NortelNetworks.COM* as the PAP or CHAP user identity to the LAC PPP. The LAC PPP can then parse this user identity and perform a lookup for an entry that matches the NortelNetworks.COM domain to determine the LNS address. When the L2TP session is established the LNS PPP can complete the authentication.

Once the LNS to be tunneled to has been determined by the LAC and the L2TP connection for that PPP session has been established to the LNS, the LAC PPP continues to perform escaping/unescaping, framing/deframing, and FCS calculations, but the rest of the PPP protocol processing is performed by the LNS. This is true for both of the methods we have been describing, whether the LAC PPP did an initial LCP and partial authentication or the LAC did no PPP protocol processing initially.

Although it is outside the scope of the L2TP protocol definition to specify the criteria by which an LAC can decide to tunnel a PPP session to a given LNS, the DNIS and the PAP/CHAP username parsing are canonical examples. Likewise, it is also outside the scope of the L2TP protocol definition to specify how an LNS goes about picking an LAC when the LNS wants an LAC to make an outgoing call to a client PPP.

Figure 2-4 shows an alternate model of L2TP wherein there is no LAC that exists separate from the client PPP. In this model the client PPP and the LAC are coresident. This method of tunneling is called *voluntary tunneling* because the remote user initiates the virtual dial-up connection and can decide what traffic can be sent through the tunnel. Since there is no physical connection associated with the PPP traffic

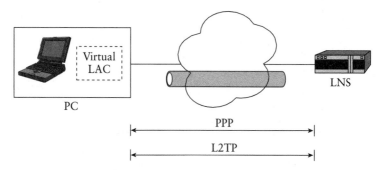

Figure 2-4 *L2TP voluntary tunneling model*

being tunneled by L2TP in this scenario, there is no actual Frame Check Sequence (FCS), escaping, or framing of the PPP traffic at any time. Also no LCP negotiation or authentication is done separately from the LCP, and authentication done with the LNS PPP. In fact, the LNS does not need to know that voluntary tunneling is being done. To the LNS, a voluntary tunnel connection looks the same as a mandatory tunnel connection with no proxy LCP or authentication information from the "LAC."

2.2 Layer 2 Role of LNS

LNS PPP is responsible for all the sublayers of layer 2 that are not handled by the LAC PPP. Since the LAC PPP really handles only the media-dependent sublayer, the LNS PPP is responsible for handling the other sublayers. Figure 2-5 shows the PPP sublayers for the LNS PPP.

LNS PPP is responsible for some of the media-dependent sublayer responsibilities. For the handling of PPP packets, the LNS PPP does the HDLC addressing. The PPP peers can negotiate during LCP that the HDLC addressing not be present (except in LCP packets), but if this is

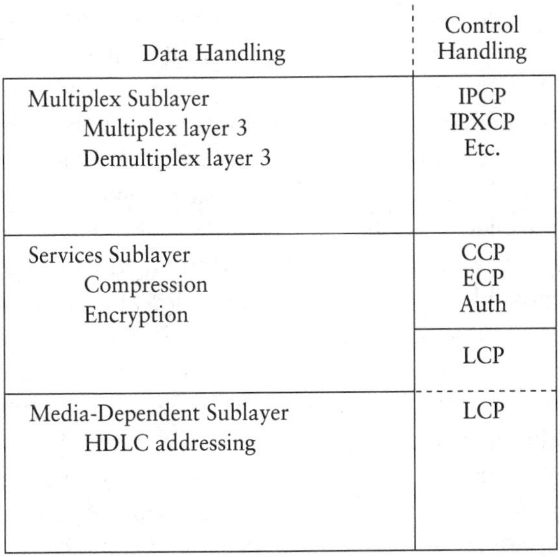

Data Handling	Control Handling
Multiplex Sublayer Multiplex layer 3 Demultiplex layer 3	IPCP IPXCP Etc.
Services Sublayer Compression Encryption	CCP ECP Auth
	LCP
Media-Dependent Sublayer HDLC addressing	LCP

Figure 2-5 *LNS PPP processing in layer 2*

done, then for PPP traffic moving from the LNS PPP to the LAC PPP, the LAC would have to inspect all PPP packets and make sure the HDLC addressing was added on all LCP packets. Likewise for PPP traffic originating from the client PPP, the LAC PPP would need to make sure that LCP packets received had the HDLC addressing present. Therefore, to minimize the work required of the LAC PPP after the session has been established to the LNS PPP, the LNS PPP has the responsibility of HDLC addressing. With regard to the LNS PPP implementation, the process of addressing is more straightforward when it is handled by the LNS PPP, since the LNS PPP implementation is likely to have been adapted from an existing PPP implementation, which will likely have checks already in the LCP portion of the code to ensure that the HDLC framing is present.

The LNS PPP also has the full LCP responsibility of the control portion of the media-dependent sublayer. But this role can be shortcut in the case where the LAC PPP has already negotiated LCP. For this reason L2TP allows for the LCP negotiation information between the client PPP and LAC PPP to be communicated to the LNS PPP. The LNS PPP can then optionally take this LCP information and store it as if LNS had been directly involved in the negotiation. In some cases this may not be possible because in doing the LCP negotiation the LAC PPP may have chosen some option that the LNS PPP does not recognize or does not want to use. If the LNS PPP decides that a renegotiation of LCP with the client PPP will be necessary, then the escaping, FCS, and maximum packet size option values negotiated by the LAC PPP should be renegotiated by the LNS PPP. This is because these options are truly dependent on the physical connection between the LAC and the client, and the LNS does not know better than the LAC the physical characteristics of the connection. Although it should be avoided if possible, the PPP protocol definition allows LCP to be renegotiated at any time on a PPP link, so there is technically no problem with the client PPP negotiating LCP with the LAC and then being forced to renegotiate LCP with the LNS. One word of caution: a very popular PPP implementation terminates a connection if LCP is restarted after authentication has been completed. In the case where the LAC performs LCP negotiations, this feature should not cause a problem if both the LAC and the LNS avoid completing the authentication phase if LCP is to be restarted.

The true authentication responsibility also rests at the LNS. As described earlier, the LAC may do enough of the authentication to obtain an identity from the client PPP in order to decide which LNS should handle the PPP session. Just as with LCP information, L2TP allows for the authentication information received from the client PPP by the LAC to be communicated to the LNS. The LNS can then complete the authentication, picking up where the LAC left off, or the LNS may ignore the information and restart the authentication (to the client PPP this activity will look as if its original response that was received by the LAC has been lost). If the LNS restarts the LCP negotiation with the client for some reason, then authentication will simply be redone after the LCP renegotiation is completed. In fact, one reason the LNS may decide to renegotiate LCP would be if LNS did not like the type of authentication that had been negotiated by the LAC in the original LCP negotiation between the LAC and the client PPP.[3]

The portion of the LCP that is part of the services sublayer is wholly the responsibility of the LNS PPP. These parts of LCP are not part of the LCP negotiation but perform ongoing services such as handling LCP keepalive messaging and error reporting.

Beyond the overlap with the LAC PPP with regard to LCP and the authentication and modifications to the initial state of the LNS PPP that are required because of this, the remainder of the LNS PPP sublayers behave no differently than they would if the LNS PPP were running over any other media. This means that no changes need to be made to the packet processing or state machines, although there may be favored configuration options for some of the protocols when they are running over an L2TP link. For example, it may be true that the connection between the LAC and LNS is more prone to packet loss than would normally be the case with a physical connection. Consequently, it is better to operate any protocols (such as compression) that operate with a history in a mode in which the history will be reset for every packet. When protocols are operating in a mode where history is kept across packets, if a packet is lost between PPP peers, generally even more packets will have to be dropped while an indication that a

---

3. For example, if the LAC and client negotiated CHAP but the LNS wants to do MPPE encryption, which requires that MSCHAP be done between the PPP peers.

packet was lost is sent to the transmitter and the transmitter communicates the fact that the history has been reset. Because it makes no sense to run VJ in a mode in which history is not kept between packets, it is also questionable whether VJ should be negotiated on a PPP connection over L2TP. The operation of VJ is even more sensitive to loss since the loss of any packet, and not just a VJ packet, causes VJ to enter a mode of dropping packets on each VJ-compressed flow until a full TCP/IP header is once again received for the flow (this is because VJ itself does not keep a coherency count).

2.2.1 Virtual Layer 1

With regard to the LNS PPP implementation, the L2TP protocol fulfills the role of being virtual layer 1. From the point of view of most of the LNS PPP, the L2TP connection between the LNS and the client simply appears as if it were a physical medium that required HDLC addressing but no escaping, framing, or FCS.

There are important differences between the traffic characteristics on a real point-to-point connection and the traffic characteristics on a network over which L2TP can form a tunnel. These differences require L2TP to have mechanisms that can provide the characteristics of a point-to-point connection where those characteristics are otherwise not present.

One instance of a point-to-point feature that L2TP must support in some cases is that packets not be reordered between PPP peers (between the client PPP and LNS PPP). Since L2TP may run over a network such as an IP network, which grants no such guarantee on the ordering of packets, L2TP provides the capability to reorder packets that are received out of order, so that the packets can then be sent up in order to the PPP layer.[4] To this end, L2TP can run in a mode that involves the use of sequence numbers so that PPP packets can be sent up the PPP layer in the same order as they were sent by the L2TP peer.

Another instance of a point-to-point feature that L2TP must provide in some cases is the ability to detect lost packets sent between the PPP peers. On a real point-to-point network it is highly improbable

---

4. More in Chapter 9 on the performance impact of providing this service in the case where there is packet loss but no packet disordering occurring between the LAC and LNS.

that a packet on the connection will be silently dropped. If a packet must be dropped, it is generally owing to a line error during transmission of the packet, an error that will result in the receiving peer detecting a framing error or FCS mismatch. In the real point-to-point network the media-dependent sublayer signals the rest of the PPP software stack that a packet has been lost (as is a requirement for proper VJ handling). Again, L2TP may operate over networks such as IP networks where packets can be silently dropped on their way between two peers. The L2TP mode in which sequence numbers are present enables L2TP to react as the real point-to-point system would, so L2TP detects when a packet that was sent by the L2TP peer was not received. And then the L2TP layer can send a signal to the PPP software that a packet has been lost. When the L2TP and PPP software are coresident, this is not a problem. But in the case we have been considering in which the LAC and the client PPP are on opposite ends of a point-to-point connection, as in the compulsory model, there is no direct mechanism to inform the client PPP that a packet sent by the LNS was not received by the LAC. But this shortcoming can be worked around if the LAC can cause a framing error or FCS error on the connection between the LAC and the client in the hopes that the client will infer from this that there has been a packet loss on the point-to-point connection, thereby signaling the client PPP stack to take appropriate actions. In the opposite direction, when the LAC detects an FCS error on the connection to the remote client, it can increment its L2TP session sequence number so that the LNS can detect a lost packet.

A final example is the point-to-point pacing of packets in transit between peers. When protocols that keep an inter-packet history, such as the compression protocol, are in operation and even a single packet is lost, the effects are magnified. The history protocol is forced to drop all packets in transit until the histories between the two peers can be resynchronized. Since typical traditional dial-up connections have only a fairly small number of packets in transit between the point-to-point peers at any one time, the effects of packet loss to protocols with history can be minimized by keeping to a minimum the number of packets that have been processed (for example, compressed) and need to be transmitted (but keeping the flow of packets substantial enough so that the link does not become underutilized). In contrast, it is common for L2TP to run over networks in which many packets are in transit between two peers at any one time. Without some sort of rate pacing of the packets moving between L2TP peers, it is possible for many compressed packets with inter-packet history to be in transit between L2TP peers at a given time, therefore increasing the risk that packet loss could cause serious problems.

2.2.2 History

The L2TP protocol was created from the combination of two other protocols: the Point-to-Point Tunneling Protocol (PPTP), which specifies the tunneling of PPP; and the Layer 2 Forwarding protocol (L2F), which specifies the tunneling of PPP and SLIP. Both PPTP and L2F were designed on the model of operation that has since become known as *mandatory tunneling,* and both protocols are still used today. The goal of both protocols was to allow for the separation of the physical connection hardware (modems) from the software controlling communication over the physical connections (that is, PPP or SLIP).

Many of the architectural aspects of PPTP and L2F are similar because both protocols start with the mandatory tunneling model. The overall operation of PPTP, L2F, and L2TP are therefore very similar, although the details of their mechanisms may differ. For example, all three specify the use of a control channel. In PPTP, the control channel is over a TCP connection, and the data processing is over a GRE connection.[5] In L2F the control channel is differentiated from data traffic within the L2F-specific header, and no particular communication method is presupposed, although for IP networks L2F operates over UDP. L2TP inherits the design of its control channel more from L2F than from PPTP; over IP networks L2TP operates over UDP. All three protocols specify mechanisms for receiving incoming calls and making outgoing calls. Although L2F and PPTP were both developed on the mandatory tunneling model, PPTP is also deployed as client software enabling the voluntary tunneling mode of operation.

Providing a list of the similarities and differences between L2F, PPTP, and L2TP without first establishing the context for what each of the features are would be premature. Throughout the rest of the book, therefore, the similarities and differences between L2TP and its predecessors L2F

---

5. Since the PPTP control channel is over TCP, the use of PPTP is tied to networks over which a TCP connection can be made.

and PPTP will be highlighted as features of the newer protocol are introduced, in order to underscore the decisions made in the design of L2TP.

There is generally some confusion among those who are not familiar with the Internet Engineering Task Force (IETF) procedures as to the degree to which the IETF recognizes and supports the L2TP, PPTP, and L2F protocols. L2TP is the only protocol of these three that is a part of the IETF standards process. This means that it is the only protocol of these three that is being developed, tested, and sanctioned within a working group of the IETF. Both PPTP and L2F specifications are available through the IETF, though not as Standards Track documents. The L2F specification is available as a Historic RFC (RFC2341). PPTP is available in the form of an Internet Draft, and this protocol is expected to become an Informational RFC. Informational RFCs are submissions audited by the IETF for editorial content only and can be submitted to the task force by any individual or organization that wants to make public some Internet-related work. In contrast, L2TP is available as a Proposed Standard RFC (RFCl2tp), which means that the protocol has been subject to the IETF process wherein engineers from many companies have had a hand in designing the protocol, and many individually developed implementations have gone through interoperability testing. Because the IETF supports L2TP and has published the L2TP specification as a Proposed Standard RFC, the competing PPTP and L2F protocols will never be IETF standards-track material.

Once we have highlighted some of the differences between L2TP, L2F, and PPTP, the reader will see how L2TP is operationally superior to both L2F and PPTP as they are currently specified. Anyway, there is no recognized and controlled process in place to improve L2F and PPTP, so they are likely to remain inferior to L2TP in interoperability and reliability.

2.3 L2TP Patent Issues

Developers of L2TP should be aware of possible patent issues regarding the implementation of L2TP. Before L2TP was approved as an RFC, the IETF was notified by Cisco that patents relevant to L2F and L2TP are pending, but the content and scope of these patent claims and their effects on the implementation of L2TP were not available. Following is the email sent to the L2TP mailing list regarding this matter.

```
To: l2tp@ipsec.org
Subject: FYI: L2TP and IPR
Date: Wed, 03 Mar 1999 12:29:59 -0500
From: Thomas Narten <narten@raleigh.ibm.com>
Sender: owner-l2tp@sailpix.com
```

FYI, the following was just posted to the IETF Page
of Intellectual Property Rights Notices page
(http://www.ietf.cnri.reston.va.us/ietf/IPR/). I've
included the text for your convenience.

The following was received on March 2, 1999 from
Andy Valencia (vandys@cisco.com)

Cisco has a patent pending that may relate to this
proposed standard. If this proposed standard is
adopted by IETF and any patents issue to Cisco or
its subsidiaries with claims that are necessary for
practicing this standard, any party will be able to
obtain the right to implement, use and distribute
the technology or works when implementing, using or
distributing technology based upon the specific
specification(s) under openly specified, reasonable,
non-discriminatory terms.

Requests may be sent to:

```
Robert Barr
Suite 280
2882 Sand Hill Road
Menlo Park Ca 94025
```

Phone: 650-926-6205

On June 15, 1999, L2TP was approved as a Proposed Standard
RFC. On July 29, 1999, patent number 5,918,019 was issued to
Andrew Valencia of Cisco. The contents of the patent are available on
the Web directly from the U.S. Patent and Trademark Office by searching on the patent number at *http://www.uspto.gov/patft/*. The patent
covers most aspects of L2F, which were inherited by L2TP.

3

L2TP Deployment Models

In this chapter we look at the ways that L2TP is being deployed, primarily to provide VPN services. Because L2TP can be deployed in both voluntary and compulsory tunneling models, VPN services can be managed completely by the entity requiring a VPN, or these services can be sold through a service provider to a VPN consumer. As the Internet Service Provider (ISP) market becomes more competitive, ISPs are searching for additional services to provide to customers. L2TP enables ISPs to provide all or part of a customer's VPN solution. By selling VPN solutions, ISPs can differentiate themselves from their peers. By tunneling PPP, L2TP also provides a solution to the multibox multilink PPP problem. At the end of this chapter we describe some other VPN technologies and compare and contrast them to L2TP.

3.1 VPN Deployment Models

3.1.1 LAC Deployment, Distribution, and Support

LAC Compulsory Tunneling: An Internet Service Provider can be part of a VPN solution by providing L2TP LAC functionality at its Point of Presence (POP) locations and thus providing the customer VPN with compulsory tunneling. This functionality can be provided regardless of how the L2TP LNS portion of the VPN is managed. For the ISP to provide this half of the VPN picture, all that is necessary is an agreement between the ISP and the customer on how calls are to be recognized by the ISP as belonging to the customer VPN (for example, through the use of DNIS or by parsing user authentication).

LAC Voluntary Tunneling: If a VPN solution involves the voluntary tunneling model, the L2TP LAC client software can be distributed to users' computers and supported directly by the organization using the VPN or it can be sold as a service by an ISP. The benefit to the VPN customer of using an ISP VPN solution is that the responsibilities of distribution, support, and updating the client applications, which need to be synchronized with server software versions, are outsourced to the ISP.

3.1.2 LNS Deployment, Distribution, and Support

The most common place for the LNS to reside is at the edge of the private network. In this instance, the VPN user may purchase and individually manage the LNS, or the LNS may be provided as a service and partially managed by an ISP as part of its VPN service offerings.

When the ISP provides the LNS, the VPN customer is able to outsource some of the LNS configuration work, such as configuring the set of LACs that the LNS is allowed to communicate with. The VPN customer is then free to focus on establishing policy for its VPN users.

On the other hand, the organization using the VPN retains more control of the VPN configuration if the organization purchases and manages the LNS equipment in-house instead of outsourcing this responsibility. With this level of control comes the burden of configuration. It should be noted, however, that this level of burden is basically the same as the management burden associated with owning traditional remote access equipment.

LNS at the Edge of the Private Network: The LNS is most naturally found at the edge of an organization's private network. Connections to the LNS are made through a point-to-point connection between the edge of the private network and the edge of the service provider network. The LNS can then control access to the private network through tunnels established to the LNS over the public network. It is also common for a device known as a firewall to exist at the edge of the private network, controlling access to private network resources from the public network. Firewalls perform functions such as filtering and Network Address Translation (NAT). A common scenario is to have the firewall and LNS existing in parallel, as shown in Figure 3-1.

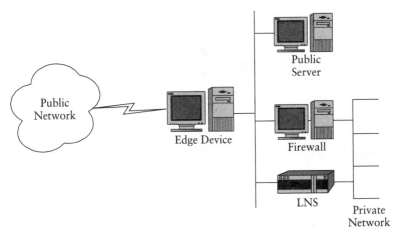

Figure 3-1 *Firewall and LNS operating in parallel, providing access to the private network*

Notice in Figure 3-1 the use of the physical connection between the service provider, or public network, and the customer premises. Three different types of access to the customer premises network are provided over this same connection. The first type is uncontrolled access to public servers. The second type is controlled access to the private network from the public network through the firewall. The third type of access is through L2TP tunnels established to the LNS.

3.1.3 LNS "in the Cloud"
VPN users should understand LNS in the cloud before they consider installing this kind of system. Today's model of public network access is generally that depicted in Figure 3-1. Figure 3-2 shows the model of the LNS existing at the edge of the service provider cloud instead of at the edge of the private network.

The major difference between Figures 3-1 and 3-2 from the point of view of the organization using the VPN is that for the scenario where the LNS resides at the public network edge, the traffic coming from the connection through the LNS has been received through an authenticated tunnel. If the customer also wants to receive traffic directly from the public network, traffic that will subsequently be controlled by a firewall, then that traffic would come over a separate connection.

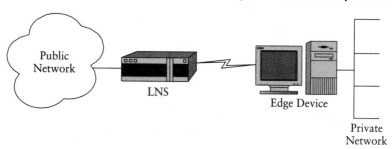

Figure 3-2 *LNS at the public network (service provider) edge*

Of course, one can imagine that someday three different types of connections will be ordered from a service provider: one connection providing unprotected public network traffic, one connection providing VPN access (with LNS at the service provider edge), and one connection providing protected direct access to the private network from the public network (that is, with a firewall at the service provider network edge).

3.2 Compulsory versus Voluntary Tunneling

A VPN solution built on L2TP does not need to be modeled completely on compulsory tunneling or completely on voluntary tunneling. An LNS should be able to accept both types of tunnels simultaneously, giving the VPN user the flexibility to employ a mixed solution.

If the organization using the VPN wishes to build its VPN with L2TP completely on the voluntary tunneling model, the organization can provide its own VPN independent of the ISP. The LNS can be positioned at the edge of the company's network and provide VPN users with the LAC Client software.

When a company chooses compulsory tunneling, it cannot avoid at least an agreement between the ISP providing the LAC support. A VPN customer may also decide to use more than one ISP for its LAC support.

3.3 VPN Performance Considerations

In traditional remote access, the remote users' traffic comes over physical connections such as analog phone lines or ISDN and is terminated by an edge device located next to the private network. The performance of the network being accessed and the speed of the remote access connection therefore govern the performance of a particular remote access service.

With the virtual network the traversal of the tunneled traffic over the public network is a factor in the performance of the remote access service. The performance of a VPN connection is therefore dependent on the performance of the private network being accessed through the VPN, the speed of the remote access to the public network, and the performance of the public network on the path that the VPN traffic is being tunneled over. The efficiency of the VPN implementation also affects performance, because VPN traffic generally requires some sort of processing such as encryption processing or authentication.

In traditional remote access, generally the physical connection is the performance bottleneck. As long as the physical connection remains the bottleneck and the bottleneck does not become the operation of the VPN tunnel over the public network, VPN users will achieve the same level of service with a VPN that they receive with traditional remote access.

Because VPN service is sensitive to the performance of the public network being tunneled over, the organization using the VPN needs to investigate the best ISP to carry its VPN traffic, and it should consider the performance characteristics it desires in the public network being tunneled over. The Internet is currently formed by the interconnection of multiple ISP backbones. Although each ISP is responsible for managing the performance of its own backbone network, when traffic leaves the ISP network and is transferred to a different network, control over the handling of the traffic is lost (but in some cases agreements exist between ISPs). Nonetheless, ISPs are beginning to be able to offer customers Service Level Agreements (SLAs)—contractual guarantees on performance to the ISP customer. An ISP providing SLAs does not simply provide access to the Internet to its customers; it also assures the customer a given level of performance when connecting through the ISP. By keeping a VPN solution operating over a single ISP with an SLA for the VPN traffic, the organization using the VPN can be more secure about the performance of its VPN.

The performance of the LNS should also be monitored, because it can quickly become the VPN access bottleneck. Each LAC has to support the physical connections it supports already, so it will likely support as many tunneled data sessions as it does physical connections. But the LNS, on the other hand, is not bound by physical connections, so it is easier for it to oversubscribe its resources to the point where overall performance may degrade. As more and more LAC devices are added to a VPN model, the number of LNS devices required to meet the new combined demands should be examined as well.

3.4 Multibox Multilink PPP

By tunneling PPP traffic, L2TP provides a natural solution to the "multibox multilink PPP" problem. Before we get into the problem, we will first take a look at how the protocol operates. Multilink PPP (MP) is a protocol that takes PPP running over multiple connections and combines these connections into one larger connection. The MP protocol creates a PPP entity that runs on a virtual link called a *bundle* that conceptually runs on an aggregation of multiple physical links. The purpose of the MP protocol is to aggregate the bandwidth available to all of the PPP links between two systems and to make that bandwidth available as one higher-speed PPP connection. For transmitting packets, the PPP instance acting as the bundle fragments packets and sends these fragments to the physical link PPP instances. On reception, fragments are received by the physical link PPP instances and are sent up to the bundle, which then reassembles these fragments and processes them. The MP protocol handles fragmentation and reassembly, and it detects packet loss. The details on MP operation can be found in [James Carlson, *PPP Design and Debugging*, p. 114]; the pure technical specification of MP operation can be accessed at RFC1990.

Figure 3-3 shows the conceptual framework for MP operation, with the MP fragments inbound to the PPP links. These fragments are sent up to the bundle, which reassembles the fragments back to the original PPP packet (this conceptually happens in the media-dependent sublayer of the bundle PPP) and processes the reassembled PPP packet.

The multibox multilink PPP problem arises from the fact that the same device may not terminate the individual physical connections for the PPP links, for instance, in an ISP POP that has multiple Network

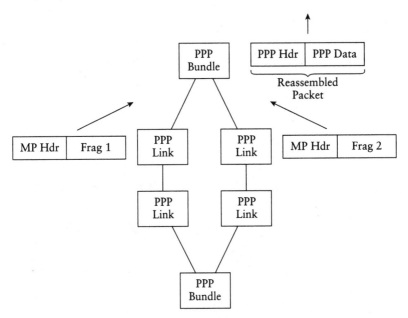

Figure 3-3 *Conceptual framework for Multilink PPP (MP) operation*

Access Server (NAS) devices but a single phone number. As calls come in to the POP, they are routed to the NAS devices. Since ISDN B channels are brought up as separate calls, there is no guarantee that two B channels belonging to the same end system will be terminated by the same Network Access Server, as is shown in the scenario of Figure 3-4. In the top part of the illustration, two ISDN B channels have been brought up from the ISDN device on one end to two separate NAS devices on the other end. Without introducing new concepts, there is no method for the two links on separate boxes to share a single bundle, so MP is broken in this case.

3.4.1 Compulsory Tunneling Solution

But in the bottom part of the figure we can see how L2TP may solve this problem of sharing a bundle if the individual link connections were to be tunneled to the same LNS. In fact, L2TP naturally tunnels the two links independently even if they are terminated by the same NAS, as is shown in Figure 3-4.

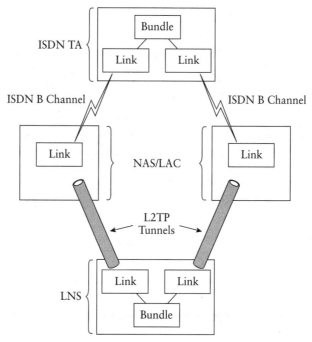

Figure 3-4 *Compulsory tunneling multibox multilink PPP solution*

3.4.2 NAS Pool Solution

L2TP, as opposed to a VPN service, has also been specified as a tool for locally solving the multibox multilink PPP problem using a pool of NAS devices. This solution is specified in [draft-ietf-mmp-discovery-01.txt]. Figure 3-5 shows the resulting communication flow. One of the NAS devices terminating a link for the remote user also contains the bundle (basically this is the NAS that brought up the first chronological PPP link). As new links belonging to the same bundle are established on separate NAS boxes, they discover which NAS contains the bundle and tunnel the new PPP links to the NAS containing the bundle.

In order for this solution to work reasonably well, the two NAS devices shown in Figure 3-5 should run the L2TP tunnel over a segregated high-performance network. That way the act of tunneling the link fragments from one NAS to the other would not affect the performance of MP.

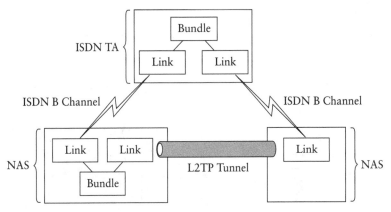

Figure 3-5 *NAS pool multibox multilink PPP solution using L2TP*

3.4.3 Combined VPN Service and LNS Pool Solution

Another multilink PPP situation that can arise when a network is tunneling with L2TP is the mixed case of having multiple links for an end system tunneled to more than one LNS. The LNS devices can then use L2TP as a tool to terminate the multiple links to a single LNS that contains the bundle. This communication flow is shown in Figure 3-6. In the illustration the PPP sessions for two separate physical links are being tunneled to more than one LNS as part of a VPN service (the physical connections could be terminated by the same or different NAS devices; it is not important which). The two LNS devices then use L2TP as a tool to tunnel one of the PPP sessions to the LNS device that contains the multilink bundle.

3.4.4 Performance Implications

Although this topic is covered in detail later in the book, an introduction to the performance implications of tunneling the multilink PPP protocol is useful here. When tunneling multiple PPP sessions that belong to the same MP bundle over a network, the traffic's exposure to the underlying characteristics of that network is increased over the case of tunneling a single PPP session. The two factors that come into play are the statistical packet loss rate of the underlying network and the delay values along the network path(s) between the LAC and LNS devices.

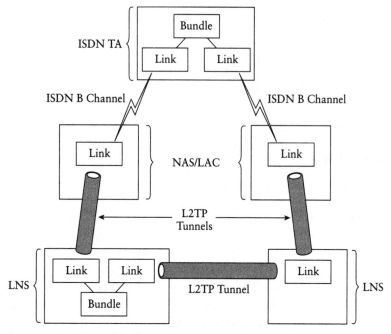

Figure 3-6 *L2TP used both as a VPN service and as a multi-LNS MP solution*

In MP the loss of a fragment results in the loss of the entire original packet of which the fragment was a part. Given a nonzero packet loss rate along the path between the LAC and LNS devices, the probability of losing the original packet increases as the original packet is broken down into more and more fragments. The more "bursty" the packet loss rate is, the less this will be a factor because the probability is good that multiple fragments getting dropped will belong to the same original packet. In general, this increased sensitivity to packet loss will result in lowering the performance of the bundle session.

The tunneling of MP also increases the delay of getting each original packet processed through the receiving bundle. The delay in processing the original packet is equal to the path delay between the L2TP endpoints as well as the time required to receive all of the fragments. Increasing the delay along a communications path generally has the effect of lowering the performance along the path, so overall performance is affected by the increase in MP delay.

The goal of using MP is to aggregate the bandwidth of multiple physical links (for example, multiple ISDN B channels) to create one high-speed connection, but MP becomes a liability if the performance of the session pays a high penalty because of the characteristics of the underlying network.

3.5 Comparing L2TP to L2F and PPTP

Although the overall structure of L2TP is inherited from both L2F and PPTP, there is one area in which L2F and L2TP both differ from PPTP. L2TP inherits from L2F the mechanism for sending LCP and authentication information from the LAC to the LNS when a data session is being established in the tunnel. PPTP does not include this capability. As a result, the PPTP equivalent to the LNS—the PPTP Network Server (PNS)—is not aware of any prior PPP activity of the PPP session before the tunnel session is established. At a minimum, this has the effect of requiring a renegotiation of LCP if any LCP negotiation between the remote computer and the PPTP equivalent to the LAC— the PPTP Access Concentrator (PAC)—has occurred.

Because L2TP can communicate proxy LCP information it is a more robust protocol than PPTP. One practical implication of PPTP's not performing proxy LCP is that in the case of tunneling MP, the PNS does not learn the endpoint discriminator that the PAC might have advertised to the remote computer. The PNS is also just as ignorant of information about the point-to-point connection such as the Asynchronous Control Character Map (ACCM) and the maximum receive unit (MRU) that the PAC would prefer to have negotiated. In the case of a client implementation of PPTP, this difference in functionality between PPTP and L2TP does not matter since it does not come into play.

3.6 Asymmetric Digital Subscriber Line Forum Model

The Asymmetric Digital Subscriber Line (ADSL) defines a physical layer signaling over standard telephone lines that can achieve speeds of 6 Megabits per second (Mbps) or more. The term *Digital Subscriber Line* (DSL) refers to the copper connection between the customer premises and the telecommunications provider's central office (this is also referred to as the *local loop,* and sometimes as the *last mile*). The transmission rates for signaling headed downstream (toward the customer premises) are different from those for signaling headed upstream (away from the customer premises), hence the use of the term *asymmetric*. The difference in speeds between downstream and upstream is generally 10 to 1. For distances below 9,000 feet for the local loop, ADSL achieves 6+ Mbps downstream speeds and has a maximum range of 18,000 feet for the local loop with a downstream rate of about 2 Mbps.

The ADSL Forum (*www.adsl.com*) is a multi-vendor organization concerned with defining the architectural specifications of how ADSL can be deployed as a service to the home and to the corporate customer. The physical layer signaling standard for ADSL is contained in the American National Standards Institute (ANSI) standard T1.413.

The ADSL Forum model for networking over ADSL specifies that PPP running over ATM be used to provide the balance of the physical layer and datalink layers in the ADSL model. The ADSL Forum technical reports also describe a couple of different ways in which L2TP can be used as part of ADSL deployment.

Figure 3-7 shows the first way in which L2TP can be used in the ADSL model. In this scenario there is an ADSL modem at the PC end of the ADSL connection, which has a special PPP over an ATM dial-up-like driver. The DSL Access Multiplexer (DSLAM) is a device that terminates the many ADSL physical connections and switches the ATM layer between the DSL and the traditional ATM network. An

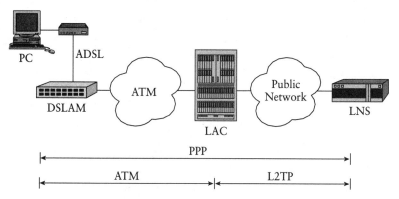

Figure 3-7 *Compulsory L2TP tunneling using ADSL*

ATM-connected router can then act the same as an NAS with LAC functionality in the traditional remote access model. The portion of the ADSL model extending from the PC to the ATM switch with LAC functionality is an alternative to the PSTN picture from the PC modem to the NAS device. The rest of the scenario is the same as the compulsory tunneling scenario we have already described. The PC application running the PPP over the ATM dialer specifies the network it wants to contact by giving PPP authentication information in the PPP negotiation, and the LAC, in turn, can use this information to identify the correct LNS to tunnel to.

Figure 3-8 gives another scenario in which L2TP has been suggested as part of the ADSL deployment picture. In this model there is an ADSL network termination (ADSL-NT) device at the customer premises acting as a front end for multiple devices on a private network (in this example Ethernet). The PCs on the Ethernet network behind the ADSL-NT tunnel PPP over L2TP to the ADSL-NT, which then maps the PPP to an ATM virtual circuit for an ATM path to one of two ATM-connected IP routers. The ADSL-NT in this picture acts as the LNS and can map each tunneled PPP to a different ATM VCC so that each device on the private network can connect to remote networks independently.

Of course, it is not necessary to operate L2TP in order to deploy ADSL, but L2TP can be used to add flexibility to the ADSL model and to enable ADSL customers to dynamically connect to different service providers.

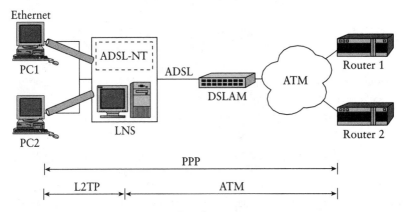

Figure 3-8 *Voluntary L2TP tunneling for ADSL service provisioning*

3.7 Other VPN Technologies

Several technologies other than L2TP can be used to provide a VPN solution. Several vendors have created their own proprietary tunneling protocols for use as VPN solutions, and there are several other protocols that have been developed in a more public forum.

In this section we describe some of the protocols that have been developed in a public forum, but not any proprietary VPN protocols. It is generally believed that protocols developed in a public forum will be the more robust protocols. In the public forum, numerous individuals can consider a protocol from multiple angles, so there is a higher probability that the protocol will receive a broad and in-depth review. Nonproprietary solutions also typically are deployed more rapidly and in a more widespread manner. History bears out the advantages of these factors. For example, one can consider the current ubiquity of IP deployment and compare it to the past when IPX, DECNet, AppleTalk, and other protocols were all competing with IP to provide network services. Another example is the development of security over time. In the past, part of a security solution was "security through obscurity." This meant that part of being secure was simply having some procedure that no one "knew" about. History has shown and continues to show that when this approach is taken, a motivated individual or group of individuals with enough time will find the weaknesses in the existing security scheme. A look at high-tech headlines bears this out as we are constantly alerted of security holes in particular Web browsers or operating systems that need to be "patched" by the vendors as they discover flaws in their privately developed products. The advantages of developing a security protocol or procedure in the public forum have now been widely accepted. By opening security up to the scrutiny of a vast audience, a stronger theoretical basis can be developed for why the protocol or feature is secure or is not secure, as opposed to relying on developing an arcane procedure for security and hoping nobody "figures it out."

One feature of some proprietary tunneling protocols is the ability to retransmit lost tunneled packets. Although this feature can be useful, it can also cause unnecessary traffic without bringing better performance. This is because retransmission facilities are generally provided by upper-layer protocols, the most prominent being TCP. In

TCP, if packets need to be retransmitted, then the congestion control features of TCP kick in and TCP slows itself down. If TCP is running over a protocol that will also retransmit, it is not likely that the lower layer will retransmit the packet before TCP detects that the packet is lost. As a consequence, the lower layer may retransmit the packet, but the packet will also be retransmitted by the upper layer (TCP). As a result, every packet sent by TCP (including retransmissions) eventually gets across due to the retransmissions of the lower layer, but TCP's congestion control mechanisms will still slow the connection down.

From a global network perspective, VPN protocols that retransmit lost tunneled packets are also bad for congestion control. The purpose of TCP's congestion control mechanisms is to adjust for network congestion and to slow TCP connections down until the congestion in the network is alleviated. If a protocol tunneling TCP is also doing retransmissions (even if it also does congestion control with its retransmissions), the load on the network is greater than if only TCP were retransmitting, since the tunneling protocol will retransmit the retransmissions. This reduces the efficacy of congestion control in the network, and therefore protocols that retransmit should be avoided.

Following are some descriptions of other nonproprietary technologies that are used or can be used to provide VPN services in one way or another.

3.7.1 IP Security Protocol

The IP Security (IPSEC) protocol has been developed to provide security services on IP networks. The two main services that IPSEC provides are encryption and authentication on a per packet basis. IPSEC also provides other services such as protection against replay attacks.

To provide security services, IPSEC relies on the existence of secret data, called a *key,* shared between two endpoints. The strength of the protection provided depends on both the size of the key and the authentication and encryption protocols being used. The standard encryption methods are the Data Encryption Standard (DES) and Triple DES (3DES). It is generally accepted that a key length of 128 bits is required to adequately provide encryption and authentication, although methods for operating DES or 3DES with 56-bit and 40-bit keys have also been specified because of the international security import and export laws of various nations.

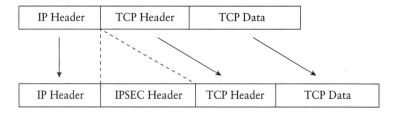

Figure 3-9 *IPSEC transport mode packet*

IPSEC on its own specifies how these security services are provided once a Security Association (SA) has been established between two IP systems and some key is shared between the two systems. To establish IPSEC SAs between IP systems with dynamic keys, the use of the Internet Key Exchange (IKE)[1] protocol is specified. IKE is used to authenticate the IP systems with each other and to negotiate dynamic keys between the IP systems. IKE is also used for such purposes as to tear down the IPSEC SA when it is no longer needed or to rekey an IPSEC session (another replacement SA is established with a new key, and the old SA is removed).

For the protection of data, IPSEC has two major modes. The first mode, called *transport mode*, is used to add security directly to packet flows between the two IP systems. Figure 3-9 shows the difference between a packet sent between the two IP systems without an IPSEC SA present and a packet sent between two IP systems with a transport mode IPSEC SA in place between the two systems. In transport mode an IPSEC header is wedged between the original IP header and the IP data in order to provide security to the traffic. Note that in the figure if encryption is specified for the SA used for this traffic, then the TCP header and TCP data will be encrypted, as will some of the IPSEC header, whereas the IP header preceding the IPSEC header will remain unencrypted so that the packet may cross the network between the two systems. When the packet is received by the peer at the IP layer, the IPSEC header is used for security purposes, and the original packet is recovered. Processing can then continue as normal with the packet looking as it originally did in the upper portion of Figure 3-9. As we will see, IPSEC transport mode can be used to secure tunnels between LAC and LNS devices to provide truly secure multi-protocol VPN services.

---

1. Formerly ISAKMP/Oakley.

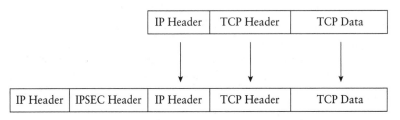

Figure 3-10 *IPSEC tunnel mode packet*

The second mode of IPSEC is called *tunnel mode*. This mode was developed to provide security services between two IP systems acting as *Security Gateways* (SGs). An SG is essentially a router that can tunnel IP traffic to another SG. Figure 3-10 shows an IP packet that is to be tunneled between two SGs, and it also outlines what the packet looks like while it is being sent between two SGs. The original IP packet is encapsulated completely by the IPSEC header and then sent from one SG to the other. When the packet is received, the peer SG at the IP layer uses the IPSEC header for security purposes, the original IP packet is recovered, and the SG can perform routing of the packet to its final destination.

Figure 3-11 shows the traversal of a packet between two IP hosts through a pair of Security Gateways with a tunnel mode IPSEC SA defined between them. From this picture it is clear why IPSEC running in tunnel mode can be used to provide a VPN service: to the end systems in Figure 3-11, the Security Gateways seem like ordinary routers, but the Security Gateway pair tunnels IP traffic between each other over a tunnel mode IPSEC SA. Figure 3-11 also shows why IPSEC is

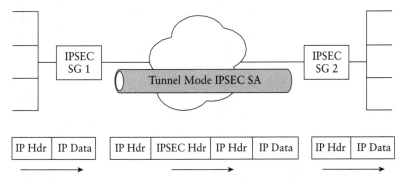

Figure 3-11 *IPSEC tunnel mode packet traversal*

said to provide layer 3 tunneling: because the traffic tunneled by an IPSEC SA is IP traffic, and IP is a layer 3 protocol.

The key difference between IPSEC tunneling IP directly and L2TP tunneling IP by way of PPP is that with IPSEC the protocol used to do the tunneling is directly aware of the IP processing. Since IPSEC provides security services to the IP traffic, it also controls the policy for the IP traffic being tunneled. For example, in a tunnel mode IPSEC SA the range of addresses that is seen "behind" each of the Security Gateways from the point of view of the other is fixed when the IPSEC SA is established. In contrast, with IP traffic running over PPP over L2TP, L2TP is providing the service of a "virtual wire" between two systems. In the L2TP scenario it is straightforward for a routing protocol to run over an L2TP connection. In IPSEC there are no provisions for dynamic routing over tunnel mode IPSEC SAs. It should be noted that dynamic routing over a VPN connection is not necessarily desirable from a security standpoint, depending on the relationship of the two Security Gateways and the networks from which they tunnel to each other. From a security standpoint it is better to err on the side of static routing. The IETF IPSEC group is currently looking into how dynamic routing is to be accommodated into security policy.

3.7.2 Generic Routing Encapsulation

Generic Routing Encapsulation (GRE) [RFC1701] was developed to provide a method for encapsulating layer 3 protocols such as IPX, AppleTalk, DECnet, and others over IP networks, providing a layer 3 tunneling mechanism. GRE is an informational RFC; it is not the product of group development in the IETF. Essentially GRE provides tunneling of layer 3 protocols, but it lacks the concept of setting up a session or providing security. The purpose behind the creation of this method was to provide an insulating layer between IP and the other layer 3 protocols so that specifications would not have to be developed for running each of the other layer 3 protocols over IP directly.[2]

---

2. Since IPv4 has only an 8-bit protocol field, the use of GRE also helps conserve the allocation of these protocol numbers by using a single number for GRE and then specifying the layer 3 protocol by a field in the GRE header. Some protocols have also been defined to be run directly over IP, as is the case with IPX and IP itself.

GRE provides a flexible header structure that is composed of a set of fixed fields, a set of bits that specify which optional fields are present, and the optional fields as appropriate. The protocol encapsulated by GRE is specified with a 16-bit number that generally contains the Ethernet protocol type of the encapsulated protocol.

L2F, PPTP, and L2TP all base their packet headers on the GRE header structure. PPTP uses GRE most directly, however. The data portion of a PPTP tunnel is carried over a modified GRE header. This is a convenient choice because the GRE header already provides an encapsulation method and the concept of optional fields. By using GRE as the data encapsulation method and by specifying TCP as the mechanism for the PPTP control channel, the use of PPTP is effectively restricted to operation over IP networks. Although it is not specified in any other document except the PPTP Internet Draft, PPTP specifies that an "enhanced GRE" header is used. The PPTP GRE header is distinguished from the published GRE header via the GRE version field, which is specified to be 0 in RFC1701, but 1 in the PPTP Internet Draft. The protocol field of the GRE header used by PPTP contains the value 0x880B, which has been reserved with Xerox Corporation as an Ethernet protocol number.

3.7.3 Mobile IP Protocol

The Mobile IP protocol [RFC2002] was developed as a way for a host to change its point of attachment to the Internet without changing its IP address on the private network. The encapsulation done by Mobile IP can be IP-in-IP or IP-in-GRE encapsulation with security provided by IPSEC if desired. When one uses IP-in-IP encapsulation there is no direct support for tunneling other types of traffic to the home network, such as IPX. The serious drawback with Mobile IP is that the mobile node being tunneled to the home network must have a fixed address on the home network.

Figures 3-12 and 3-13 show how Mobile IP achieves connectivity to the private (home) network. The three major architectural pieces are the mobile node, which wants connectivity to the private (home) network; the foreign agent, which tunnels traffic to the home network on behalf of the mobile node; and the home agent, which terminates Mobile IP tunnels at the edge of the home network.

As with L2TP where the LAC either can be a separate machine or can be virtualized within the dial-up host, in Mobile IP the foreign

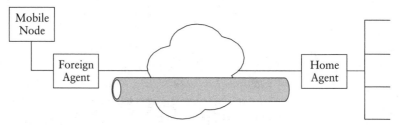

Figure 3-12 *Mobile IP architecture*

agent also can be a separate machine or can be virtualized within the dial-up host.

Mobile IP was envisioned to operate in an environment where the mobile node would literally be changing its point of attachment to the Internet in the middle of data sessions. Examples given in RFC2002 include the connection of a mobile node to the Internet from an airplane so that as the airplane leaves one geographical area and enters another the session can be switched from one point of attachment to the Internet to another. The only limitation given in RFC2002 is that these changeovers not happen more often than once per second.

3.7.4 Multiprotocol Label Switching Protocol

The Multiprotocol Label Switching (MPLS) protocol has been developed as a way to optimize routing. The general principle of this protocol is to replace the forwarding of IP packets through the network based on route lookups performed at each hop by switching on a flow label value at each hop.

MPLS has been investigated as a method of providing a level of VPN service because by disassociating the act of forwarding IP pack-

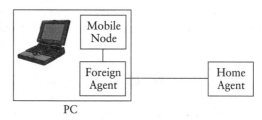

PC

Figure 3-13 *Mobile IP with mobile node and foreign agent*

ets from the contents of the IP header, MPLS can carry private address space traffic over a public network. MPLS is a method of encapsulation of IP packets with minimal authentication of VPN sessions or other security features.

A drawback of MPLS is that it can be effectively used only if every hop along the path supports the MPLS protocol. The extent of an MPLS VPN therefore depends on the breadth of available MPLS-capable devices. Despite the limitations of MPLS, ISPs that want to carry private customer traffic over the ISP backbone between the customer's private network locations can conceivably offer MPLS as a VPN service. As long as the private network customer trusts the integrity of the ISP's backbone, using MPLS can be a satisfactory solution. If the customer believes the security of the ISP's network may be compromised, then using MPLS as a VPN technology is probably inadequate.

3.7.5 Secure Shell Protocol

The Secure Shell (SSH) protocol is a UNIX-style protocol that can be used to provide VPN access. SSH provides a replacement for the UNIX `rlogin`, `rsh`, and `rcp` utilities. SSH can therefore provide the following capabilities: secure logging into a remote machine, secure executing of commands on a remote machine, and secure copying of files to and from a remote machine.

Unlike the other VPN technologies that have been discussed thus far, SSH does not specify a general mechanism for forwarding packets from client applications onto the private network. There are two ways that SSH can be used. The first is to run X Window System and use remote shell connections to run applications on the SSH server with the client viewing the user interface. The second is for the server to act as a TCP proxy for the client, allowing the client to effectively make TCP connections to hosts on the private network behind the SSH server. The SSH connection itself is a TCP connection between the SSH client and the SSH server. The client and server can negotiate in such a way that the server will listen on a specific port on the private network and proxy connections between the port and the client via the SSH connection. The client can also initiate connections to hosts on the private network by prompting the SSH server dynamically to proxy a client-initiated TCP connection to a specified TCP host on the private network.

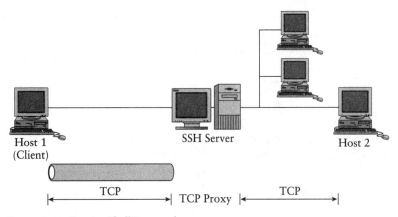

Figure 3-14 *Service Shell Protocol*

Figure 3-14 shows the architecture of SSH operation. An SSH connection is established between the SSH client and the SSH server, and the UNIX utilities such as with `rcp` and `rlogin` are made available as well as the TCP proxy mechanism.

The session can be authenticated against a UNIX .rhosts file together with RSA-based host authentication or via pure RSA authentication. Encryption of the SSH session can be provided by International Digital Encryption Algorithm (IDEA), DES, or 3DES, and compression can be provided through GZIP (Gnu Zip).

It is important to note that SSH is available on almost all major operating systems. The TCP port forwarding mechanism of SSH makes simple such applications as email and Web access.

4

L2TP Protocol Overview

In this chapter we offer an overview of how the L2TP protocol is designed and how it operates. We also outline and explain some important assumptions of the protocol. Subsequent chapters will go into the details of operation for different portions of the protocol. After absorbing this chapter, the reader should have an understanding of the terminology used in RFCl2tp, the assumptions that the protocol is based on, and the overall structure of the protocol itself.

4.1 Tunnel Structure and Terminology

So far we have introduced the endpoints of an L2TP tunnel, the LAC and the LNS, but we have not really gone into detail about what defines a tunnel between the two peers.

A tunnel is composed of two components. The first component is a single *control connection*. The second component is a set of zero or more *L2TP data sessions*, each carrying one and only one tunneled *PPP session*. The existence of a tunnel between two peers is tightly linked to the existence of a control connection between two peers. Therefore the terms *tunnel* and *control connection* are sometimes used interchangeably. For example, a tunnel is considered to be established as soon as the control connection is established. Figure 4-1 shows the components of a tunnel.

An L2TP data session (also referred to as simply an L2TP session) is the state associated with tunneling a single PPP session between the LNS and a remote system connected through an LAC. PPP packets are encapsulated in L2TP data messages between the LAC and the LNS. Where the context is clear, the term *session* will simply be used for the L2TP data session. Where necessary, the terms *L2TP session* or *PPP*

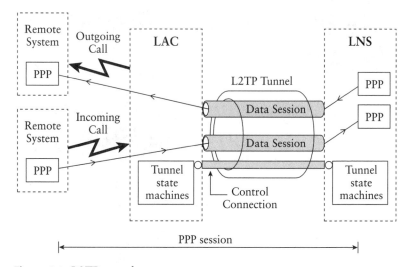

Figure 4-1 *L2TP tunnel components*

session will be used. The state machines for setting up L2TP sessions are discussed in Chapter 8.

The control connection for the tunnel is that part of the tunnel that is responsible for establishing, maintaining, and releasing data sessions as well as the tunnel itself. The bulk of the control connection's responsibility involves establishing, maintaining, and releasing the tunnel. The *control channel* is sometimes considered part of the control connection. It is responsible for the reliable delivery of control messages between L2TP peers. We explore the state machine for the control connection in Chapter 5. Chapter 7 describes the operation of the control channel and how the reliable delivery of control messages can be established.

RFCl2tp uses the term *call* when describing L2TP data sessions. Figure 4-1 shows what is meant by this term; a call refers to the physical connection between the LAC and the remote system. There are *incoming calls* and *outgoing calls*. Note that the calls are named relative to the LAC, so that an incoming call is a call initiated by the remote system, and an outgoing call is a call initiated by the LAC.

Figure 4-2 gives a view of the communication stacks involved in carrying the PPP session between the LNS and the remote system using the example of an ATM call. PPP frames encapsulated in L2TP are received by the LAC, and the HDLC encapsulation has to be replaced with ATM encapsulation before the PPP frame is forwarded to the remote system.

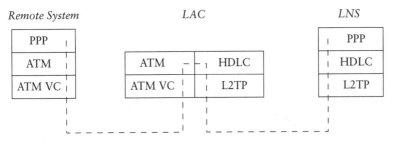

Figure 4-2 *L2TP protocol layering with an example using an ATM call*

4.2 Protocol State Machines

There are five state machines given in RFCl2tp. These state machines define the steps required to establish and tear down a control connection and to establish and tear down sessions. None of the state machines contains details of the progression of sequence numbers for reliable delivery, since this is the responsibility of the control channel.

The first of these state machines is the state machine for the control connection (discussed in more detail in Chapter 5). The control connection state machine defines the necessary steps for establishing and tearing down an L2TP control connection (and therefore the steps for establishing and tearing down an L2TP tunnel).

The other four state machines describe the steps necessary in establishing a session. There is one state machine for each combination of LAC or LNS and incoming call or outgoing call. These state machines are discussed in Chapter 8, "Session Setup."

The control channel provides a transport mechanism for L2TP control messages. Providing reliable delivery of control messages is the main feature of the control channel. Because the details of reliable delivery are handled by the control channel, the L2TP state machines do not have to contain timeout events that may result from the retransmission of messages, handle duplicate messages received, or receive out of order control messages. When we refer to the L2TP state machines receiving a control message, it should be taken to mean that the message is passed to the L2TP state machine from the control channel. Likewise, when we refer to the L2TP state machines sending a control message, it should be taken to mean that the state machines hand the control message to the control channel, which then ensures the proper delivery of the control message to the peer.

4.3 The Typical Life of a Tunnel

It is often easier to understand the composition of something once we have a mental picture of how it operates over time. To that end, we will take a good look at the life of an L2TP tunnel.

In general, a single L2TP tunnel will exist between a given LAC-LNS pair, and multiple sessions can be operating over that tunnel simultaneously. Of course, there are circumstances in which this is not the case. For instance, there may be some policy on differential treatment of PPP sessions such as different levels of quality of service (QoS) or security. This policy could be accomplished by establishing multiple tunnels between an LAC and an LNS, one for each type of differentiated treatment. Another deviation is in the case of a client implementation where the LAC exists in the same software stack as the remote system PPP. In this circumstance there will probably be only one connection to a given LNS, and there will probably be only one session going on at one time within the tunnel as well.

The life of a tunnel begins with the establishment of a control connection for the tunnel. Either an LAC or an LNS can initiate a control connection. Once the control connection is established, the tunnel is said to be established (because there is a control connection and zero or more sessions).

Once the control connection is established, sessions can be brought up within the tunnel (again, initiated by either side). For an incoming call, the LAC will initiate a session to the LNS. For an outgoing call, the LNS will initiate a session to the LAC.

Once a session between the LAC and LNS is established, a PPP session is tunneled within the L2TP data session. The details of what stage the PPP session is in at the beginning of the L2TP data session vary depending on what PPP processing has already occurred between the LAC and the remote system. When a PPP session is completed between an LNS and a remote system, the associated session between the LAC and the LNS is brought down. Either the LAC or the LNS can decide that the tunnel between the two is no longer needed. In this case either entity will initiate teardown of the tunnel, as defined in the control connection state machine. Any data sessions that are within the tunnel are brought down before the control connection is broken. Once the data sessions are gone the control channel is brought down (and, by definition, the tunnel is now considered down).

Note that the life of a tunnel is basically just a symmetric cycle of establishing the control channel, initiating the data session, processing PPP, tearing down the data session, and tearing down the control channel.

Of course, what we have been discussing is the typical life of a tunnel. Teardown may not happen so symmetrically, because failure conditions may ensue, resulting in the premature teardown of the tunnel. For example, connectivity between the LAC and the LNS may be lost while there are active data sessions within the tunnel between the two. In this case, the state machines for call and tunnel teardown cannot run gracefully and the sessions and tunnel are brought down abruptly.

4.4 Protocol Assumptions

The L2TP protocol involves a few important assumptions that are important to understand. These assumptions guided the design of the protocol as well as the way the protocol is presented in RFCl2tp. Some of these assumptions are that non-IP operation is possible, the LAC and remote system are separate entities, and LAC participation is passive.

4.4.1 Non-IP Operation

The requirement that L2TP should be able to operate over non-IP networks guided a few of the decisions in the design of the protocol. One such decision was that the L2TP be self-describing and that the control channel be handled "in-band"; that is, all that is required of the layer below L2TP is to identify that the protocol encapsulated is L2TP. The L2TP header contains the necessary information to differentiate control and data messages, and so forth.[1]

---

1. This creates a problem in the case where an agent external to L2TP needs to differentiate L2TP control traffic from L2TP data traffic. One instance of this would be where IPSEC protection of L2TP is desired, but there are different security policies between the control and data traffic. Another instance would be in affecting different levels of QoS for the control and data traffic.

Another consequence of specifying L2TP to run in non-IP environments is that the control channel has to define its own reliability operation. This is in contrast to PPTP, which simply defined the PPTP control channel to operate over TCP. Unfortunately, this means that L2TP control channel operation has to reinvent the mechanisms of TCP while not evolving with TCP as it is improved. We will explore how L2TP control channel operation is similar or dissimilar to TCP in more detail in Chapter 7.

4.4.2 Separate LAC and Remote System

The L2TP specification is mostly written in such a way that the LAC and remote system are taken to be separate devices connected via some type of call.

Client implementations are also supported by L2TP, because some of the call-specific parameters are optional in the session setup messages and can simply be omitted in the case of a client implementation. A client implementation need only include the LAC functionality required to establish a control connection (tunnel), and a data session to an LNS where no PPP communication between the LAC and remote system is presupposed.

4.4.3 Passive LAC Participation

A nonexplicit but pervasive assumption made in RFCl2tp is that once a PPP session is being tunneled in an L2TP data session, the LAC simply passes packets back and forth between the remote system and the LNS. This process has the unfortunate consequence of exposing the details of the type of connection between the LAC and the remote system to the LNS. The protocol is written from the perspective of making the LAC devices have less intelligence at the expense of complicating the protocol and the implementations in the LNS devices.

It is perhaps not all bad that L2TP has made this assumption, as long as it is recognized what shortcomings are created as a result. In the case of a simple LAC implementation that can live with the consequences, the LAC can operate as specified in RFCl2tp. In a more complex situation an LAC could operate in a nonpassive mode, without the LNS being aware of it.

The next section describes some of the difficulties associated with L2TP because of the assumption of passive LAC participation. In Chapters 8 and 9 we will revisit these problems, placing more emphasis on how a nonpassive LAC could operate in order to solve these problems.

4.5 Protocol Difficulties

Mainly owing to the assumption that the LAC is passive, the L2TP protocol on its own currently has difficulty addressing some of the features of PPP operation, or it performs these operations in a suboptimal way.

4.5.1 Multilink PPP

The interaction between MP and L2TP is an interesting one. On the one hand, L2TP provides a mechanism for solving the splitting of multilink links across multiple devices. The two ways in which L2TP solves this problem were given in Chapter 3 in the "Multibox Multilink PPP" section.

At the same time that L2TP provides a solution for multibox MP, it also creates problems for it. To optimize the performance of MP fragmentation and reassembly, you want to minimize the variance in delay in receiving fragments so that reassembly can take place as soon as possible. Unfortunately, L2TP pushes the MP bundles as far away from each other as possible. As a result the variance between fragment delivery is usually greatly increased because in order to reassemble, the fragments must traverse the public network over which the tunnel is being carried.

In some cases the operation of MP over L2TP may require some coordinated configuration between the LNS and the LAC, because the MP specifies the communication of an identity for the MP endpoints so that links will be properly aggregated. Chapter 9 investigates in more detail the interaction of L2TP and MP, providing some suggestions on what could be done to make the operation of MP over L2TP smoother.

4.5.2 Link Awareness in LNS

Specifying LAC as passive in L2TP means that the LNS must have awareness of link options for the connection between the remote system and the LAC. In at least one case, the operation of FCS Alternative, this mode does not work.[2] Chapter 9 will outline the FCS

---

2. It has been suggested that the FCS Alternative be deprecated, because there is some question of how common its use is. So the point is more one of illustration than of practicality.

Alternative, as well as suggest ways in which a nonpassive LAC could isolate the details of the physical connection configuration from the LNS.

Ideally, a protocol such as L2TP should isolate the details of the physical connection from the LNS as much as possible. This would keep the split of responsibilities between the LAC and the LNS clear. In turn, new physical connection types with new PPP connection options could be made available without requiring upgrades to LNS devices. In this regard, L2TP as specified in RFCl2tp can be said to have fallen one step short of enforcing the proper split between physical connection options between the LAC and the LNS.

4.5.3 A Look Ahead

The next five chapters (Chapters 5 through 9) cover the details of L2TP operation. Chapter 5 covers the specification of the control connection state machine. Chapter 6 goes into depth on the formats for L2TP control and data messages. The detail for how the reliable delivery mechanism of the L2TP control channel runs is provided in Chapter 7. The state machines associated with L2TP data sessions are given in Chapter 8. Chapter 9 goes into the detail for PPP frame handling in L2TP sessions by the LAC and LNS.

5

Control Connection
State Machine

As we learned in the previous chapter, L2TP tunnels are architecturally split into two pieces. The first is the control connection, and the second is the collection of L2TP data sessions that are active within the tunnel.

In this chapter we focus on the L2TP control connection state machine, which describes the establishment, maintenance, and teardown of the L2TP tunnel control connection. The state machines for establishing data sessions are discussed in Chapter 8.

5.1 State Machine

When a tunnel is being established, both sides start in the IDLE state and both sides transition to the ESTABLISHED state (at which time the control connection is considered to be established). Tunnel establishment is achieved via three messages exchanged in a three-way handshake. The initiator of the tunnel sends a Start-Control-Connection-Request (SCCRQ) message to the receiver. If the receiver of the SCCRQ is willing to bring up the tunnel to the initiator, the receiver responds with a Start-Control-Connection-Reply (SCCRP) message. The tunnel establishment is completed when the SCCRQ sender responds to the SCCRP with a Start-Control-Connection-Connected (SCCCN) message. To bring the tunnel down, both sides transition the state machine back into the IDLE state. The overall state machine for L2TP control connections is shown in Figure 5-1. In RFCl2tp, this state machine is given in table form in section 7.2.1.

Figure 5-1 also depicts some events and transitions that are not present in the state machine in the underlying specification. These added states and transitions represent three requirements given in RFCl2tp that are not reflected in the state machine. The first is the requirement to wait before cleaning up tunnel resources. The second is the event of a control channel reliable delivery timeout. The third is the addition of sending HELLO messages as a keepalive mechanism. The portions of the state machine not present in the table form from RFCl2tp are indicated with dotted lines.

The events that are present in this state machine are

- *LocalOpen.* This event indicates that the local system containing the L2TP implementation desires the tunnel to be brought up. One cause for this event is the detection that a new PPP session is available to be tunneled.
- *GoodSCCRQ.* This event indicates that an SCCRQ has been received and that it is acceptable. GoodSCCRQ occurs when the SCCRQ has been parsed to the satisfaction of the receiver and none of the information present in the SCCRQ is contrary to local policy.
- *BadSCCRQ.* A BadSCCRQ is an indication that an SCCRQ has been received but it is not acceptable. This can occur if some local policy disagrees with information presented by the SCCRQ. For example, if the peer sent a challenge in the SCCRQ but the receiver was unable to determine a secret to be used for the tunnel.
- *GoodSCCRP.* This event occurs when an SCCRP has been received and is acceptable. For example, if tunnel authentication is being done, a GoodSCCRP indicates that the response in the SCCRP to the challenge sent in the SCCRQ is acceptable.
- *BadSCCRP.* This event indicates that an SCCRP has been received and is not acceptable. Again, using the tunnel authentication example, a BadSCCRP could indicate that the response found in the SCCRP to the challenge sent in the SCCRQ did not match the expected response.
- *GoodSCCCN.* A GoodSCCCN indicates that an SCCCN has been received and is acceptable. The only information optionally accompanying an SCCCN message is a response to a challenge found in the SCCRP. If no tunnel authentication is

being performed, a GoodSCCCN should always occur upon
reception of an SCCCN.

- *BadSCCCN.* The occurrence of this event indicates that an
  SCCCN has been received but it is not acceptable. Since only a
  response to a challenge found in the SCCRP can optionally be
  contained in an SCCCN, this event should happen only if a
  challenge was present in the SCCRP but there is no response in
  the SCCCN or the response in the SCCCN is incorrect.

- *LoseTie.* This event indicates that both endpoints tried to bring
  the tunnel up as the initiator at the same time and that the local
  implementation determined that it lost the tiebreaker. The
  details of tiebreaking are found later in this chapter in the
  section entitled "Tunnel Initiation Tie Breaker." The tiebreaker
  mechanism is used when either L2TP endpoint determines that
  only a single tunnel to the peer is desired.

- *StopCCN.* The StopCCN event indicates that a StopCCN, Stop-
  Control-Connection, has been received. This message is used to
  indicate that the sender of the StopCCN is tearing down the
  tunnel.

- *Control Channel Timeout (CCTO).* The CCTO event indicates
  that the reliable delivery mechanism of the control channel has
  timed out trying to send a message to the peer. In this case the
  connection to the peer is considered to be lost, and the state
  machine must transition back into the IDLE state.

- *CleanupTO.* This event indicates that the state machine has
  timed out, giving the tunnel control channel time to run through
  the reliable delivery of any outstanding messages that need to be
  sent to the peer.

- *AdminClose.* The AdminClose event indicates that some entity
  outside of L2TP is initiating a teardown of the L2TP tunnel.

- *NeedHELLO.* The criteria for receiving the NeedHELLO event
  depend on the implementation. The event indicates that a
  HELLO message needs to be sent to the peer to check on whether
  the peer tunnel endpoint is still reachable. An implementation
  may simply trigger this event based on a simple timer, in effect
  sending a HELLO message at regular intervals. A better approach
  is to keep track of whether control or data messages have been
  successfully received from the peer within some period of time
  (not including repeat or out-of-order messages).

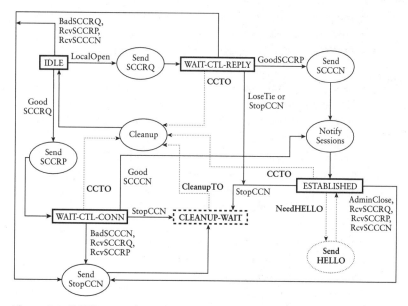

Figure 5-1 *L2TP control connection state machine*

5.1.1 IDLE State

The IDLE state is used to represent the state of a tunnel endpoint that has not yet attempted to connect with its peer. When a tunnel endpoint is first created, it should start in the IDLE state, and then the appropriate event should be passed to the state machine to start the protocol.

Entering the IDLE state after "Cleanup" actions signifies that the tunnel endpoint is completely disassociated from its peer. Depending on the implementation requirements, this may mean that the tunnel endpoint resources are deallocated or simply that the instance remains with the state set to IDLE.

For a tunnel in the IDLE state, the valid events are to receive a Start-Control-Connection-Request (SCCRQ) from the peer or to receive an indication locally that a tunnel should be established. In the case of receiving an SCCRQ from the peer, the determination of whether the SCCRQ is acceptable or not is also made when the tunnel endpoint is in the IDLE state. These events are represented as LocalOpen, GoodSCCRQ, and BadSCCRQ.

The LocalOpen event occurs when the local system determines that the tunnel should be brought up. It is assumed that while in the IDLE state the tunnel endpoint was configured with all of the necessary information needed to bring up the tunnel. Such information includes whether or not to do tunnel authentication and the transport information necessary to communicate with the tunnel endpoint (for example, the remote peer IP address). The LocalOpen event transitions the tunnel into the WAIT-CTL-REPLY state. The tunnel endpoint that initiates the tunnel establishment in this way is said to be the *tunnel originator.*

If an SCCRQ is received when the tunnel endpoint is in the IDLE state, the SCCRQ is parsed, and the information along with local configuration is used to determine if a tunnel to the requesting peer will be brought up. If the SCCRQ contains a challenge from the peer indicating that tunnel authentication is necessary, then the authentication information must be set up while in this state. This allows a proper Start-Control-Connection-Reply (SCCRP) to be sent while transitioning to the WAIT-CTL-CONN state.

To determine if an SCCRQ is acceptable, an implementation may take actions such as looking up information in a database required to continue tunnel establishment based on parameters found in the received SCCRQ. One typical key into a database would be the host identity that is included in the SCCRQ.

When a GoodSCCRQ event occurs, the tunnel transitions into the WAIT-CTL-CONN state through the Send SCCRP actions. When a BadSCCRQ event occurs the tunnel transitions into the CLEANUP-WAIT state after passing through the Send StopCCN actions.

5.1.2 Send SCCRQ Actions

Send SCCRQ actions are taken while transitioning from the IDLE state to the WAIT-CTL-REPLY state. An SCCRQ is created based on the local policy for the tunnel and is sent down to the control channel to be sent to the peer. The section "Tunnel Authentication" later in this chapter describes what happens to the SCCRQ message based on whether or not tunnel authentication is being performed. The "Tunnel Initiation Tie Breaker" section describes the impact on the SCCRQ contents of requiring only a single tunnel between two L2TP devices.

The SCCRQ is the first message of the three-way handshake for tunnel establishment.

5.1.3 WAIT-CTL-REPLY State

While in the WAIT-CTL-REPLY state, valid events are the reception of an SCCRP (there are two possible events, good SCCRP and bad SCCRP), reception of a StopCCN, a control channel timeout, or the loss of a tiebreaker when both the local and the peer tunnel endpoints are simultaneously attempting to be the originator of a tunnel. These events are labeled as GoodSCCRP, BadSCCRP, StopCCN, CCTO, and LoseTie respectively.

A GoodSCCRP event occurs when an acceptable SCCRP has been received. The most obvious criterion for this event is in the case where tunnel authentication is being done as part of the tunnel establishment and the response in the SCCRP to the challenge sent in the SCCRQ matches the expected value. This event causes the tunnel to transition to the ESTABLISHED state via the Send SCCCN actions.

The BadSCCRP event is indicative of a disagreeable parameter found in the SCCRP message. For example, when performing tunnel authentication, a response must be found in the SCCRP with a value equal to an expected value based on the challenge sent in the SCCRQ. If the proper value is not found or if the challenge-response is not present in the SCCRP then it is deemed unacceptable (that is, bad) in this case. This event transitions the tunnel into the CLEANUP-WAIT state through the "Send StopCCN" actions so that a StopCCN will be sent to the peer and the tunnel can be gracefully terminated.

The occurrence of the StopCCN event while in the WAIT-CTL-REPLY state indicates that the peer found the SCCRQ it received was unacceptable. The StopCCN message contains parameters to indicate why the message was sent. This event transitions the tunnel into the CLEANUP-WAIT state so that the tunnel can be terminated gracefully.

An occurrence of the LoseTie event indicates that only a single tunnel between two endpoints is desired, that an SCCRQ was received by the peer to which the tunnel endpoint has sent its own SCCRQ, and that this tunnel endpoint has lost its bid to be the originator. As we will find out in more detail later, each tunnel endpoint can indicate whether or not it desires only one tunnel to exist between itself and a peer by including a tiebreaker value in the SCCRQ message. If the two endpoints simultaneously attempt to bring up the tunnel by sending SCCRQ messages to each other, there will be a tiebreaker and one of the endpoints will lose the tiebreaker. Then its tunnel instance will be signaled with the LoseTie event. This event transitions the tunnel into the CLEANUP-WAIT state so that the tunnel can be gracefully terminated. The SCCRQ message should then be handed to a tunnel in the IDLE state, so that a tunnel to the peer with the peer as the initiator can continue.

5.1.4 Send SCCCN Actions

The "Send SCCCN" actions are taken while the state machine transitions from the WAIT-CTL-REPLY state to the ESTABLISHED state. This sending of the SCCCN completes the three-way handshake for establishing a tunnel. Provided that the peer accepts the SCCCN once it is received, the peer will also enter the ESTABLISHED state and the tunnel is then considered fully established.

As of RFCl2tp, the only defined content of the SCCCN message is the presence of a challenge response if a challenge was present in the received SCCRP. In Chapter 6 we show how L2TP control messages are extensible. In the future, extensions to L2TP may specify that more information be present in the SCCCN.

5.1.5 Notify Sessions Actions

These actions notify any waiting PPP sessions that the tunnel has been established. This is most commonly necessary for the tunnel initiator, since the tunnel was probably initiated based on the presence of a PPP session to be tunneled. There is no reason that this notification cannot also occur in the case of a tunnel responder, however, since a new PPP session may come along on the responder side while the tunnel is being established.

5.1.6 ESTABLISHED State

The steady state for the tunnel state machine is the ESTABLISHED state. While in the ESTABLISHED state the L2TP call state machines can establish calls within the tunnel (this topic is covered in more detail in Chapter 7).

The events leading out of the ESTABLISHED state are the StopCCN, CCTO, and AdminClose events. These events cover, respectively, the case of the peer requesting that the tunnel be torn down, the local control channel reliable delivery mechanism timing out, and some L2TP-external entity requesting that the tunnel be torn down.

While in the ESTABLISHED state the NeedHELLO event may be generated, indicating that a HELLO message should be sent to the peer. In this case the state machine goes through the "Send HELLO" actions but never leaves the ESTABLISHED state, and other L2TP functions are not interrupted.

5.1.7 Send SCCRP Actions

The "Send SCCRP" actions are taken between the IDLE and WAIT-CTL-CONN states for a tunnel responder. The SCCRP contents are established based on local policy and the contents of the received SCCRQ message.

5.1.8 WAIT-CTL-CONN State

The purpose of the WAIT-CTL-CONN state is for the initiator to wait for a Start-Control-Connection-Connect (SCCCN) message from the peer. The state machine leaves this state when it receives a good or a bad SCCCN (GoodSCCCN and BadSCCCN events), a StopCCN message (StopCCN event), or when the control channel reliable delivery mechanism times out (CCTO).

Subject to future extensions made to the contents of the SCCCN message, the determination between a "good" and a "bad" SCCCN is made based solely on tunnel authentication considerations. If a challenge was present in the SCCRP that was sent to the peer, then a Good-SCCCN is indicated if and only if a challenge response is present in the SCCCN and the response matches the expected response. Notice also that the opposite circumstance is considered a failure. If a challenge was sent in the SCCRP, then a response is expected in the SCCCN; if a response is not received then this is a BadSCCCN.

If no challenge was present in the SCCRP sent to the peer, then a GoodSCCCN should only be indicated if no challenge response is present in the SCCCN. This tunnel responder logic is represented through the following pseudocode:

```
If ( challenge sent in SCCRP )
{
    if ( response in SCCCN )
```

```
    {
            if ( response same as expected response )
                    GoodSCCCN
            else
                    BadSCCCN
    }
    else
            BadSCCCN
}
else
{
    if ( response in SCCCN )
            OK to ignore, GoodSCCCN
    else
            GoodSCCCN
}
```

Notice in this pseudocode that the case of not having sent a challenge in the SCCRP but receiving a response in the SCCCN is handled. A robust implementation will log a message that this unexpected condition has occurred but will continue generating a GoodSCCCN event anyway. This occurrence is indicative of a bug in the L2TP peer, but the tunnel may be brought up anyway.

5.1.9 Send HELLO Actions

These actions are taken as a mechanism for determining if the tunnel peer is still reachable. A HELLO message is sent to the peer. If the peer is still reachable, it will acknowledge reception of the HELLO message. If the peer is not still reachable, then the local control channel reliable delivery mechanism will fail for the HELLO message and the state machine will receive a CCTO event.

5.1.10 Send StopCCN Actions

The "Send StopCCN" actions are taken while transitioning into the CLEANUP-WAIT state when a local decision has been made to tear down the tunnel. A StopCCN message is sent to the peer. The contents of the StopCCN message are set to indicate why the local side decided to tear down the tunnel.

5.1.11 CLEANUP-WAIT State

The purpose of the CLEANUP-WAIT state is to ensure that the control channel's reliable delivery mechanism is able to run when the tunnel teardown is indicated.

Because L2TP does not have a mechanism like a TCP FIN that is sent in both directions, there is no mechanism for the receiver of the StopCCN to know that its acknowledgment of the StopCCN was received by the peer. In order to guarantee that the control channel's reliable delivery mechanism runs, it is necessary to keep the control channel around until it is reasonable to assume that the peer's control channel is no longer retransmitting messages.

The CLEANUP-WAIT state depicted in Figure 5-1 is not part of the state machine given in RFCl2tp. This state is suggested as a mechanism so that implementations can conform to the requirement that "regardless of the initiator of the tunnel destruction, the reliable delivery mechanism must be allowed to run . . . before destroying the tunnel," as stated in section 7.1 of RFCl2tp. If a StopCCN message is received while the state machine is in this state, such a message should be ignored.

5.1.12 Cleanup Actions

The actual "Cleanup" actions depend on the requirements of the implementation. If the implementation creates tunnel instances on demand as requests for tunnels are received (typical LNS behavior), then the resources used for building the tunnel data structures can be deallocated and all references to the active tunnel can be removed. Some implementations may also keep tunnels allocated with state variables set to IDLE after whatever implementation-specific cleanup may be desired (for example, the local and peer tunnel IDs are no longer valid once a tunnel leaves the Cleanup state).

5.2 Tunnel Authentication

During the three-way handshake used to establish the tunnel, mutual authentication of the L2TP endpoints can be performed. This process is carried out in a manner similar to CHAP in PPP, although with L2TP there is a single shared secret. When CHAP is used in PPP with mutual authentication, a single shared secret should not be used since it is prone to a reflection attack (this topic is covered in Chapter 10), but since L2TP requires that the peer response and challenge be sent together, this limitation does not apply. But L2TP security can be compromised by a dictionary attack owing to the use of a single shared secret versus a shared secret for each direction. Because of this, L2TP tunnel shared secrets should be chosen carefully. Their protective qualities should not be overestimated.

L2TP mutual authentication is accomplished as follows:

1. A randomly generated challenge is included in the SCCRQ.
2. A response based on the challenge from the SCCRQ is included in the SCCRP, and the peer provides its own challenge.
3. A response based on the challenge from the SCCRP is included in the SCCCN.

The SCCRQ sender therefore verifies that the peer agrees on the shared secret based on the response in the SCCRP. The SCCRP sender verifies that its peer agrees on the shared secret based on the response in the SCCCN.

There is no requirement that tunnel authentication be mutual; it may be that only one side verifies that the other side agrees with the shared secret. Whether or not a challenge is included in the SCCRP can therefore be considered separate from whether there is a challenge present in the SCCRQ.

It is required, however, that if a challenge is present in the SCCRQ, then a response must be present in the SCCRP (and that a response in the SCCRP must *not* be present if a challenge is not present in the SCCRQ). Likewise it is required that if a challenge is present in the SCCRP, then a response must be present in the SCCCN (and that a response in the SCCCN must *not* be present if a challenge is not present in the SCCRP).

A weakness of L2TP tunnel authentication is that it uses the same mechanisms as CHAP and is likely to have a text password. Because of this, a dictionary attack could be used to obtain the shared secret and break tunnel authentication. In the case of L2TP/IP, IPSEC could be used to secure the L2TP tunnel, and in this case cryptographically strong authentication is used. Tunnel authentication should be relied upon only when no better mechanisms exist.

5.3 Initiating a Tunnel

Let's look at an example of the messages exchanged and steps taken to establish the control connection (with tunnel authentication). Figure 5-2 shows the infrastructure for this example. Both the LAC and the LNS are configured to communicate with databases. These databases provide the mapping between peer hostname and L2TP tunnel configuration information that is necessary for the tunnel between the two to be established. In the case of the LAC device, the database is likely to be reachable through the RADIUS protocol, because RADIUS is the most popular database communication protocol in the remote access model, and the LAC will likely also be serving remote access connections. The database that the LNS is configured to communicate with can also be a RADIUS server. It is possible that either the LAC or the LNS could be communicating with a database using a protocol other than RADIUS. For example, the database could be available through a proprietary local configuration or through a different communication protocol such as Lightweight Directory Access Protocol (LDAP) to an X.500 database.

We will begin the example the LAC with hostname BigIspLac, having determined that a tunnel to the LNS with hostname LittleCompa-

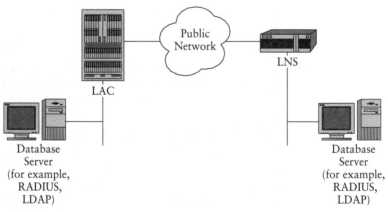

Figure 5-2 *LAC and LNS with separate external databases*

nyLns is desired (how this determination may have been made will be discussed in Chapter 7).

First, the LAC does a lookup for tunnel configuration to the peer LittleCompanyLns. From the database the LAC determines that there is a shared secret and discovers the reachability information for the LNS (for example, IP address if L2TP/IP).

Second, the LAC establishes a transport connection for the control connection, if necessary. For L2TP/IP this step is not necessary. For L2TP/ATM there may be a need to establish a Virtual Circuit (VC) over which the L2TP tunnel will be carried.

Next, the LAC sends the SCCRQ to the LNS.

```
SCCRQ ( challenge, hostname = "BigIspLac" )   LAC → LNS
```

The LNS then receives the SCCRQ, and it must determine information about the tunnel. It does this by performing a lookup in the database for tunnel configuration based on the peer hostname BigIspLac. After determining the shared secret, the LNS can calculate the response required in the SCCRP and send the SCCRP.

```
SCCRP ( response, challenge, hostname =
   "LittleCompanyLns" )                     LAC ← LNS
```

On receiving the SCCRP, the LAC verifies the response based on its view of the tunnel shared secret. If the shared secret matches, then a response to the challenge in the SCCRP is calculated for inclusion in the SCCCN, and the SCCCN is sent.

```
SCCCN ( response )                         LAC → LNS
```

The LAC control connection enters the ESTABLISHED state upon sending the SCCCN. The LNS control connection state machine enters the ESTABLISHED state upon receiving the SCCCN and verifying the response value in the message.

5.4 Tunnel Initiation Tiebreaker

In certain cases a tunnel endpoint may wish to ensure that only one tunnel is open between itself and a given peer. In most cases it is likely that one side or the other will initiate the tunnel and a single tunnel will be established. But it is possible that both tunnel endpoints may attempt to establish a tunnel at the same time. L2TP provides a mechanism to resolve this race condition so that only one tunnel is established between the tunnel endpoints, provided that at least one of the endpoints indicates that a single tunnel is desired. The winner of the tiebreaker continues normal operation of the tunnel establishment routine. As shown in Figure 5-1, if a tiebreaker is lost, then the initiator that lost tears down the losing tunnel and continues normal operation of tunnel establishment as the responder for the tunnel endpoint that won the tiebreaker.

It is important to note that the identification of an L2TP endpoint is done via the hostname for the endpoint that is provided during the message exchange. In order to provide the tiebreaker functionality, an implementation must be able to do a lookup for active or establishing tunnels based on the peer's hostname.

Here's how the tiebreaker works. An initiator's SCCRQ message can contain a tiebreaker value (see Chapter 6 for control message formats). If only one of the endpoints includes a tiebreaker in its SCCRQ, then that endpoint wins. If both ends include a tiebreaker value, then the tunnel associated with the tiebreaker with the lower value wins. If both endpoints include a tiebreaker and the tiebreaker values are the same, then both sides lose and both tunnels are torn down.

RFCl2tp recommends that either a physical network interface MAC address or a 64-bit random number be used as the tiebreaker value. Since interface MAC addresses are supposed to be globally unique, they provide a deterministic resolution to the tiebreaker process. The alternative of using a 64-bit random number makes it highly unlikely that both ends would include the same value for the tiebreaker. If both ends lose the tiebreaker because the values were the same then either end or both can attempt to bring up a tunnel again, including a new value.

Following is an example of tiebreaking in action. For simplicity, the tiebreaker values used in the example will be small, even though the tiebreaker value is a 64-bit quantity.

We will assume that the first two events happened simultaneously. What this means is that the LAC sent its SCCRQ before having received the LNS's SCCRQ, and the LNS sent its SCCRQ before receiving the LAC's SCCRQ.

```
SCCRQ ( tiebreaker = 1, hostname = "BigIspLac" )
                                        LAC → LNS
SCCRQ ( tiebreaker = 2, hostname =
   "LittleCompanyLns" )                 LAC ← LNS
```

Based on the tiebreaker rules, the peer sending the tiebreaker with the lower value wins. So in this case the LAC will be allowed to be the tunnel initiator because its tiebreaker value is lower than the value sent by the LNS. The following shows how this happens.

When the LAC receives the SCCRQ from the LNS, it determines if only a single tunnel to the peer is desired (if either a tiebreaker value is included in the SCCRQ, or through local configuration). If only a single tunnel is desired, then the LAC performs a lookup on all active and establishing tunnels to see if there is already a tunnel to the peer. If there is already an established tunnel to the same peer, then the LAC will drop the SCCRQ to avoid bringing up a second tunnel. If a tunnel is currently being established to the same peer (as in this case), then the LAC checks the tiebreaker values. In this case the LAC determines that there is an establishing tunnel and that based on it having the lower tiebreaker value, the LAC wins the tiebreaker, so the SCCRQ is dropped. Here is the pseudocode for this logic:

```
If ( single tunnel only to peer )
{
      If ( already established tunnel )
         Drop SCCRQ
      else
      {
         if ( currently initiating tunnel )
         {
             Perform tiebreaker decision on which
                side wins.
             If ( local win )
                Drop SCCRQ
             else
             {
                 Cleanup locally initiated tunnel.
                 Handle SCCRQ as normal
             }
```

```
        }
        else
        {
            if ( already responding to same peer )
                Drop SCCRQ
            else
                Handle SCCRQ as normal
        }
    }
}
```

For the LAC, the path that is made through this logic starts with determining that only a single tunnel to the peer is desired. An established tunnel is not found, but an initiating tunnel is found. The tiebreaker checking is then done, and a local win is indicated. The LAC therefore drops the SCCRQ from the LNS.

Meanwhile, the LNS receives the SCCRQ that the LAC sent and performs the same logic. In order for the tiebreaker mechanism to work, the LNS has to reach the conclusion that the LAC has won and the LNS has lost. Again, the starting point is the determination that only a single tunnel to the peer is desired. An established tunnel is not found, but an initiating tunnel is found. The tiebreaker checking is then done, and a local win is not the result. The LNS therefore cleans up the locally initiated tunnel and handles the SCCRQ as normal through a tunnel that is in the IDLE state.

The tunnel endpoint in the LNS handling the SCCRQ will then go through the normal tunnel establishment steps.

```
SCCRP          LAC ← LNS
SCCCN          LAC → LNS
```

The result is that the tunnel initiated by the LAC is established, and both the LNS and the LAC abandon the attempted tunnel initiated from the LNS.

Note that the tie-breaking mechanism works even if only one peer is configured with the single-tunnel policy. If the tiebreaker is not present in an SCCRQ, it is taken to mean that in a tiebreaker comparison the peer not sending a tiebreaker will lose.

5.5 Comparing L2TP to L2F and PPTP

L2TP, L2F, and PPTP all have overall tunnel state machines for the establishment, maintenance, and teardown of tunnels. The L2TP state machine is not quite like either the L2F or PPTP state machines, but in some ways it is a combination of the two. To establish tunnels, PPTP uses a single two-packet exchange—a start request and a start response. In L2F there is a double two-packet exchange. Part of the tunnel establishment message exchange for L2F is mandatory tunnel authentication. The mechanism is similar to the mechanism used in L2TP, although L2F specifies that there are two tunnel secrets; L2TP specifies that there is only one tunnel secret for tunnel authentication. The L2TP tunnel establishment three-way handshake is essentially an extension of the two-message exchange used in PPTP with the addition of a third message (SCCCN), which provides a message to complete the bidirectional tunnel authentication.

Both L2F and PPTP exchange messages in order to provide a keepalive mechanism for the tunnel. Since L2TP architecturally provides its own reliable delivery mechanism for the control channel, an explicit two-message exchange is not used. Instead, the detection of a reliable delivery failure of a HELLO indicates reachability failure between the tunnel endpoints (resulting in the CCTO event shown in Figure 5-1).

5.6 Implementation Tips

5.6.1 Handling Duplicate Received SCCRQ Messages

Generally, received control messages can be demultiplexed using the Tunnel ID that was assigned for the tunnel by the receiver. But since the SCCRQ is the first control message, the Tunnel ID in this message is sent as zero. In order to determine if an SCCRQ is a duplicate, an implementation must therefore check for duplication based on the transport mechanism being used for the L2TP tunnel and the Tunnel ID assigned to the tunnel by the sender of the SCCRQ (this is found in the Assigned-Tunnel-ID parameter of the SCCRQ).

For L2TP running over UDP/IP, checking for duplication requires taking a look at the source and destination UDP ports, the source and destination IP addresses, and the Assigned-Tunnel-ID. If a duplicate SCCRQ is detected, then, like all other duplicate control messages, it must be silently discarded. Note that normally the control channel uses sequence numbers to detect duplicate messages, but in this case the duplication check is more complex.

If this check is not done, an implementation may instantiate as many local tunnel endpoints as SCCRQ messages that are received. The practical consequences of this circumstance would generally be that one instance of the tunnel would remain, while the others would run out of time because their SCCRP messages would fail to be acknowledged. Why? Because each of the instances of the tunnel would send its SCCRP message to the same single instance located at the peer, and all but the first SCCRP message would be silently dropped by the peer because their sequence numbers would all be duplicates.

5.6.2 Considering Timeout Conditions

Although timeout values would not be needed in most cases based on the standards, they can be useful for handling situations where bugs may exist in peer implementations. For instance, an SCCRQ may be sent to an implementation that receives the SCCRQ, does not send an SCCRP, but continues to acknowledge HELLO messages. In this case, the implementation sending the SCCRQ would benefit from making use of a timer to be set when entering the WAIT-CTL-REPLY state so that the tunnel can be torn down if an SCCRP is not received within a reasonable amount of time.

A word of caution: such a timer is really used to attempt to catch a situation where the peer is never going to respond in the way specified by the operation of the protocol. Therefore the time setting should be generous enough that the time will not expire during the course of waiting for any normal operation to happen over the protocol (for instance, an SCCRP may be held up for some time while the peer performs a lookup in a database on the host name found in the received SCCRQ).

6

Data and Control Messages

In this chapter we outline the format of L2TP data and control messages. Data messages carry PPP frames and are said to be carried over a data channel. Control messages are carried over the control channel portion of the control connection and are used for communication between L2TP endpoints to establish, maintain, and tear down L2TP tunnels and data sessions.

6.1 Headers

Both control messages and data messages in L2TP begin with a commonly formatted header. The general header structure for L2TP data and control messages is shown in Figure 6-1. The first thirteen fields of the header are single-bit fields that specify processing options such as which of the optional header fields is present. A 3-bit L2TP protocol version number field follows these fields. The remainder of the header consists of the optional fields that are indicated as present.

```
0                   1                   2                   3
0 1 2 3 4 5 6 7 8 9 0 1 2 3 4 5 6 7 8 9 0 1 2 3 4 5 6 7 8 9 0 1
┌─┬─┬─┬─┬─┬─┬─┬─┬─┬─┬─┬─┬─┬─────┬───────────────────────────────┐
│T│L│0│0│F│0│S│P│0│0│0│0│0│ Ver │         Length (opt)          │
├─┴─┴─┴─┴─┴─┴─┴─┴─┴─┴─┴─┴─┴─────┼───────────────────────────────┤
│         Tunnel ID            │           Call ID             │
├──────────────────────────────┼───────────────────────────────┤
│         Ns (opt)             │           Nr (opt)            │
├──────────────────────────────┼───────────────────────────────┤
│     Offset Size (opt)        │      Offset pad...(opt)       │
└──────────────────────────────┴───────────────────────────────┘
```

Figure 6-1 *L2TP general message header*

Although in general the header used for control messages is flexible, it has a fixed format. Some of its optional header fields are specified as mandatory present, and others are specified as mandatory excluded from control messages. Figure 6-2 gives the format for the control message header. The use of each of the message header fields is explained in the following subsections.

6.1.1 T Bit

The T Bit field is used to specify whether a message is a control message or a data message. The T Bit is in the set state (value 1) for control messages and in the cleared state (value 0) for data messages.

6.1.2 L Bit

The L Bit field specifies whether or not the Length field of the L2TP header is present. If the T Bit is set, then the L bit also must be set, and the Length field is also present in the header. If the L Bit is cleared, then the Length field is not present.

In order to ensure that control messages can always be properly parsed independent of any transport mechanism, the presence of the Length field (and the requisite setting of the L Bit) in control message headers is required.

For data messages the sender may determine that the Length field is not required for the proper parsing of the data message by the receiver, and therefore the sender would opt not to include the Length field and to leave the L Bit cleared in a data message.

Because the Length field is optional in data messages, where possible, the data message receiver should not rely on the presence of the

```
0                   1                   2                   3
0 1 2 3 4 5 6 7 8 9 0 1 2 3 4 5 6 7 8 9 0 1 2 3 4 5 6 7 8 9 0 1
+-+-+-+-+-+-+-+-+-+-+-+-+-+-+-+-+-+-+-+-+-+-+-+-+-+-+-+-+-+-+-+-+
|1|1|0|0|1|0|0|0|0|0|0|0|0| Ver |           Length            |
+-+-+-+-+-+-+-+-+-+-+-+-+-+-+-+-+-+-+-+-+-+-+-+-+-+-+-+-+-+-+-+-+
|          Tunnel ID          |           Call ID            |
+-+-+-+-+-+-+-+-+-+-+-+-+-+-+-+-+-+-+-+-+-+-+-+-+-+-+-+-+-+-+-+-+
|             Ns              |             Nr               |
+-+-+-+-+-+-+-+-+-+-+-+-+-+-+-+-+-+-+-+-+-+-+-+-+-+-+-+-+-+-+-+-+
```

Figure 6-2 *L2TP control message header*

Length field for proper data handling to take place. Also, because the receiver cannot signal the sender that it requires the Length field to be present, the data message sender should be conservative in determining whether to exclude the Length field in the header. Keep in mind that as a transport protocol, UDP/IP transfers data in blocks as sent down from the application running over UDP. Proper operation of L2TP over UDP/IP does not require the presence of the Length field in the header of data messages.

6.1.3 F Bit

The F Bit specifies whether the Ns and Nr fields of the L2TP header are present. The Ns and Nr header fields are present if and only if the F Bit is set. For L2TP control messages, the F Bit must be set, and the Ns and Nr fields are always present. For L2TP data messages, the value of the F Bit depends on whether or not sequence numbers are being used for the session.

6.1.4 S Bit

The S Bit specifies whether or not the Offset Size field is present. If the S Bit is set, the Offset Size field is present. For L2TP control messages, the S Bit must be set to 0.

6.1.5 Control Bit Handling and Reserved Bits

As of the time of this writing, the remainder of the L2TP header control bits are reserved and must be set to 0. This is true for both data and control messages. It is possible that in the future some of the meanings of the control bits will depend on the settings of other control bits.

6.1.6 Version

The Version field is a 3-bit field specifying the version of L2TP. Currently the only valid value for this field in L2TP is 2 (see "Comparing L2F and PPTP" later in this chapter for an explanation).

6.1.7 Length

The Length field contains the total length of the L2TP message in octets, including the L2TP header itself. For control messages, the L Bit must be set, and this field is present in the header.

Since the Length field is 16 bits, the maximum size of a control message is 65,535 octets. When the Length field is present in data messages, the maximum data message size is also 65,535 octets, and when the Length field is not present in data messages there is no restriction on the maximum size of the data message by L2TP.

The minimum value for the Length field for control messages is 12 octets, representing a control message consisting of the control message header only. This construct is referred to in L2TP as a Zero Length Body (ZLB) message; it is used to send sequence acknowledgments to the peer.

6.1.8 Tunnel ID

The Tunnel ID field contains a unique identifier the receiver can use to identify the specific instance of a tunnel. The first message sent to establish a tunnel (the Start-Control-Connection-Request, or SCCRQ) is the only message for which the value of the Tunnel ID field can be 0. The value of the SCCRQ Tunnel ID is 0 because no Tunnel ID has been assigned for the tunnel by the SCCRQ receiver. When tunnels are established, each L2TP tunnel endpoint indicates to its peer the value for the Tunnel ID field that the peer should use when sending L2TP control and data messages.

6.1.9 Call ID

The Call ID field contains a value that is unique per tunnel. This value identifies a specific instance of a tunneled PPP session within a tunnel. A value of 0 in this field pertains primarily to control messages and specifically to control messages that are generic to the tunnel itself and are not specific to a session within the tunnel. There are two exceptions: the Incoming Call Request (ICRQ) and the Outgoing Call Request (OCRQ) covered in Chapter 8. These two messages are the first messages sent to establish incoming or outgoing call data session types, respectively. As with the SCCRQ sent with a Tunnel ID value of 0, the ICRQ is sent with a Call ID value of 0 and the OCRQ is sent with a Call ID value of 0.

6.1.10 Ns

Ns stands for "Next Sent" and is a field containing a number value that identifies the sequence number of a message. There is a single

---

Choosing Tunnel and Call ID Values

RFCl2tp specifies that the Tunnel ID and Call ID values be chosen in an unpredictable manner so as to protect against blind attacks against active L2TP tunnels when no other security protections for the L2TP tunnel are being used. If a malicious host can predict the Tunnel ID and Call ID values, then if the malicious host can spoof L2TP packets it can inject control or data messages that can be used to inject data messages into a session, terminate a session, or terminate the tunnel.

---

sequence number state for the L2TP control channel that is independent of the L2TP data messages. For L2TP data messages, each session within the tunnel has its own sequence number state. The first message sent contains an Ns value of 0 with the counter sequentially increasing for each message that is subsequently sent. In the case of the L2TP control channel, retransmitted control messages contain the same Ns value as the original message that was transmitted.

For control messages, the F Bit must be set and the Ns and Nr fields must be present. For data messages, whether the F Bit is set and the Ns and Nr fields are present depends on whether sequencing was specified for the specific session within the tunnel while the session was being established.

6.1.11 Nr

Nr stands for "Next Received." This field consists of a number value identifying the sequence number that the sender of the message is next expecting to receive. For example, a value of 0 for Nr would specify that the sender of the message is expecting to receive a message with an Ns value of 0 next. By sending a value of n in the Nr field, the sender of the message is acknowledging receipt of messages with Ns values through $n - 1$.

Since only sequencing and not flow control is specified for data messages, the Nr field for data messages is present if the F Bit is set, but the value is ignored. RFCl2tp specifies that the Nr value should be sent as 0 for data messages.

6.1.12 Offset Size

The Offset Size field is present if the S Bit is set. For control messages the S Bit must not be set, but for data messages whether or not the S Bit is set and the value of the Offset Size field is up to the sender of the message. The sender can attempt to align data following the L2TP header by using the Offset Size field. The Offset Size field can be present and have a value of 0, indicating that the L2TP message starts directly after the Offset Size field. If the Offset Size field contains a non-zero value, the L2TP message starts that many octets past the Offset Size field.

The main use of the Offset Size field is to align the tunneled data in data messages. Technically the offset field could contain a maximum value of 1,023, yielding an unnecessarily large L2TP data packet. Setting the S Bit and varying the Offset Size field from 0 to 1,023, the L2TP header can be padded from 2 to 1,025 bytes.

6.1.13 Offset Pad

If the Offset Size field is present and contains a non-zero value, then an Offset Pad exists between the end of the Offset Size field and the beginning of the L2TP message, and the size of the Offset Pad in octets is equal to the value specified in the Offset Size field. It is recommended that the Offset Pad be initialized to 0 by the sender. A robust receiver will ignore the contents of the Offset Pad, and a generous sender will set the value of the Offset Pad to 0.

6.2 Control Message Format

6.2.1 Attribute Value Pairs

The L2TP control message consists of the L2TP packet header followed by a non-zero set of Attribute Value Pair (AVP) instances. An AVP is an extensible format for containing a message field. Instead of defining control messages to consist of static fields, the L2TP protocol defines control messages to consist of lists of AVPs.

By using AVPs instead of defining a fixed field format, the L2TP control messages can easily support optional fields simply by including or not including the AVP in the message.

Using the AVP definition also makes future extensions to the L2TP control messages as easy as defining a new AVP to be contained in the message. For backward compatibility, the AVP contains a bit describing what a receiver should do if an AVP is unrecognized (the M Bit, detailed in the next section).

A mechanism is also provided whereby individual AVPs in a control message can be encrypted. This process is known as *AVP Hiding* and will work properly only if the L2TP peers agree on a shared secret. To verify agreement on the shared secret, the L2TP peers authenticate with each other using the shared secret during tunnel establishment. If tunnel authentication is done in only one direction, then the tunnel endpoint that sent the challenge is able to hide AVPs, because the endpoint that sends a challenge receives a response and can verify that its peer agrees on the shared secret.

Figure 6-3 shows the L2TP AVP format. Two control bits are used to specify how the AVP should be treated if it is unrecognized and if the AVP is hidden. The AVP instance is specified by the combination of the Vendor ID and Attribute fields, and the Value field size depends on the value of the Overall Length field.

6.2.2 M Bit

The "Mandatory Bit" in the AVP is referred to as the M Bit. The M Bit specifies how the receiver should behave if it does not recognize the combination of the Vendor ID and Attribute fields as a valid AVP instance. If the value of the M Bit is 1, the AVP is mandatory. Therefore a receiver that does not recognize this AVP must, upon discovering the unrecognized AVP, tear down either the specific session associated with the control message or the tunnel.

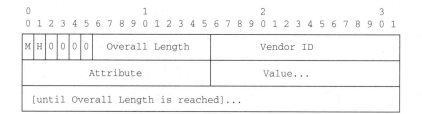

Figure 6-3 *L2TP AVP format*

If the Call ID field in the L2TP header is a non-zero value and an unrecognized AVP is received with the M Bit set to 1, then the session associated with the Call ID value is torn down. If the Call ID field in the L2TP header is 0, the message is not an ICRQ or OCRQ, and an unrecognized AVP is received with the M Bit set to 1, then the tunnel is torn down. If the M Bit is set to 0, then the receiver can ignore the AVP as if it hadn't been included in the control message.

It is very important to recognize the distinction between an AVP with the M Bit set and an AVP that must be included in a particular control message. It is possible that for a given control message an AVP is present optionally, but when it is present the M Bit must be set. This specifies that the AVP is optional for the message but the peer for proper operation must recognize the AVP if it is included.

6.2.3 H Bit

The Hidden Bit in the AVP is referred to as the H Bit. The H Bit specifies whether or not the AVP is hidden. If the H Bit is set to 1, then the AVP is hidden and the receiver must unhide the AVP before recovering the original AVP value. With the H Bit set to 1, the Value field of the AVP is encrypted and when unencrypted contains a Length field for the value itself, the original value, and optional padding. Figure 6-4 shows the AVP format, including the Hidden AVP subformat for the AVP Value field. While the Value field of the AVP is encrypted, the Value Length, Original Value, and Padding fields are all hidden.

Note that when an AVP is described as hidden it is only the subformat in the AVP Value field that is hidden. The other AVP fields are still present in the clear, including the Vendor ID and Attribute fields that identify the type of AVP. Figure 6-5 shows the entire structure of a hidden AVP, essentially combining the contents of Figures 6-3 and 6-4.

```
 0                   1                   2                   3
 0 1 2 3 4 5 6 7 8 9 0 1 2 3 4 5 6 7 8 9 0 1 2 3 4 5 6 7 8 9 0 1
+---------------------------------+-------------------------------+
|     Length of Original Value    |      Original Value ...       |
+---------------------------------+-------------------------------+
|              ...                |         Padding ...           |
+---------------------------------+-------------------------------+
```

Figure 6-4 *L2TP hidden AVP value subformat*

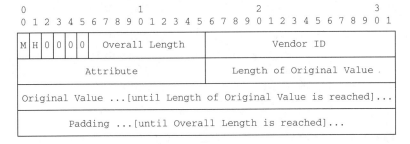

Figure 6-5 *Entire L2TP hidden AVP with subformat shown*

The first six octets of the AVP are not hidden, but the remainder of the AVP would be hidden.

6.2.4 Control Bit Handling and Reserved Bits

Currently there are four control bits in the AVP definition that are reserved for future use and whose value must be set to 0. If one of these bits is set to a value of 1, an implementation must treat the AVP as unrecognized. What the receiver does next follows the rules we have already described for treating unrecognized AVPs depending on whether or not the M Bit is set to 1 in the AVP.

6.2.5 Overall Length

The Overall Length field of the AVP specifies the length of the AVP in octets, including the AVP header itself. The minimum value for this field is therefore 6, specifying an AVP with a zero-length Value field.

6.2.6 Vendor ID

The Vendor ID field is one of the fields that specifies the identity of an AVP. The Vendor ID value is set to 0 for AVPs that are defined by the IETF. Vendors may add proprietary AVPs to L2TP messages by using a Vendor ID value equal to their Structure of Management Information (SMI) Network Management Private Enterprise Code as assigned by the Internet Assigned Numbers Association (IANA) (RFC1700) in network byte order. Because these values must be unique, the combination of Vendor ID and Attribute (see next subsection) provides a globally unique identity for AVPs.

6.2.7 Attribute

The Attribute field is used with the Vendor ID field to uniquely identify the AVP instance. The value of the Attribute field does not have a globally unique value; it can be used to identify the AVP globally only when paired with the Vendor ID field value in the AVP.

6.2.8 Value

The Value field of the AVP contains the actual value of the attribute. The valid sizes and values for an AVP depend on the identity of the AVP as provided by the combination of Vendor ID and Attribute. The length of the Value field is calculated by taking the Overall Length field of the AVP and subtracting 6, the aggregate size of the other AVP fields.

As shown in Figure 6-4, if the AVP is hidden, the actual value of the AVP is found only when the Value field is unencrypted and the Hidden AVP subformat is inspected.

It is useful for an implementation to classify the AVPs into specific types, since most specific AVPs naturally fall into classes, depending on the specified size of their values. Some useful classes for AVPs are 16-bit AVPs, 32-bit AVPs, and variable-length string AVPs.

6.3 AVP Hiding and Unhiding Algorithms

6.3.1 AVP Hiding Algorithm

To hide AVPs, the Message-Digest 5 (MD5) algorithm (RFC1321) is used, based on the existence of a shared secret between the tunnel endpoints. To provide the uniqueness of MD5 hashing and make the shared secret more difficult to break, there needs to be a random component to the MD5 hashing. For this purpose, whenever a hidden AVP is found in a control message, there must have first been a Random Vector AVP found in the control message.

Whether or not an implementation sequentially parses the AVPs found in a control message, the Random Vector value used in the hiding and unhiding of AVPs is taken from the Random Vector value that would have most recently been parsed if the AVPs were inspected sequentially. Multiple Random Vector AVPs can be found in a control message, allowing different AVPs to have different randomized values for MD5 hashing. Multiple AVPs may also be hidden using the same Random Vector AVP value.

The use of the MD5 algorithm for AVP hiding should be convenient for most implementations because the MD5 algorithm is also used in PPP for CHAP. Because it is likely that implementations containing L2TP also contain a PPP implementation, most L2TP implementations should have easy access to the MD5 library functions.

Here is the algorithm for hiding an AVP value:

1. Produce a random value. This value will be sent in the Random Vector AVP preceding this hidden AVP.
2. Perform an MD5 hash over the concatenation of the two-octet AVP Attribute ID, the shared secret, and the random value from step 1.
3. Perform an exclusive OR operation (XOR) on the result of the MD5 hash from step 2 with the first sixteen octets to be hidden.
4. Save the result from step 3 as the first sixteen octets of hidden data. Note that this result can be saved to the same location as the first sixteen octets to be hidden, since the unhidden octets are no longer needed in the hiding calculations.
5. Move on to the next sixteen octets to be hidden.
6. Perform an MD5 hash over the concatenation of the shared secret and the preceding sixteen octets as they were hidden (that is, the results of the hiding, not the value before hiding).
7. XOR the result of the MD5 hash from step 6 with the current sixteen octets to be hidden.
8. Save the result from step 7 as the next sixteen octets of hidden data. Note that this result can be saved to the same location as the corresponding unhidden octets, since the unhidden octets are no longer needed in the hiding calculations.
9. Repeat steps 5 through 8 until the input is exhausted (that is, all data has been hidden).

Note that the final XOR (either in step 3 or in step 7) is done with the remaining octets that need to be hidden, which may be less than sixteen octets. The MD5 hashes are always performed in the same manner regardless of how many octets remain to be hidden in the last iteration; the only difference in the process when there are less than sixteen octets remaining is that the XOR is performed only over the actual octets that remain to be hidden.

To make it easier for implementations to check their hiding algorithms, let's look at an example of hiding an AVP. The Vendor Name AVP (Vendor ID of 0 [IETF], Attribute ID of 8) will be used since the Value field is flexible. The Vendor Name (without parentheses) of (AN EXAMPLE HIDDEN MESSAGE.) will be used (including the "."). This string is 26 (1A) bytes long and is encoded as the following series of hexadecimal octet values:

```
41 4E 20 45 58 41 4D 50 4C 45 20 48 49 44 44 45
4E 20 4D 45 53 53 41 47 45 2E
```

The subformat of the Value field for the AVP will therefore be the octets 00 1A (encoding the length of this value as 1A) followed by the encoding of the string itself. Figure 6-6 shows the encoding of the entire AVP. Using Figure 6-5 as a guide to the encoding, the first byte encodes that the AVP is mandatory and hidden. The second byte gives the overall length of the AVP, which is 22 hexadecimal (34 decimal). The third and fourth bytes encode the Vendor ID of the AVP as 0. The fifth and sixth bytes encode the Attribute ID as 8. The first two bytes of the Value field, the seventh and eighth bytes of the AVP, encode the length of the actual value of the AVP. The remainder of the Value field is the actual value to be hidden (in this case the vendor name [AN EXAMPLE HIDDEN MESSAGE.]).

Note that the entire AVP Value field is hidden, including the length of the actual value. The data to be hidden is therefore

```
00 1A 41 4E 20 45 58 41 4D 50 4C 45 20 48 49 44
44 45 4E 20 4D 45 53 53 41 47 45 2E
```

Other values needed for the AVP hiding are the tunnel shared secret and the random vector AVP that came before this Vendor Name AVP. The tunnel shared secret we will use is the four-octet string "test," which is

```
74 65 73 74
```

The random vector for this example is the ten-octet value

```
55 89 E5 81 EC 84 04 00 00 57
```

0	1	2	3
0 1 2 3 4 5 6 7 8	9 0 1 2 3 4 5 6	7 8 9 0 1 2 3 4	5 6 7 8 9 0 1

C0	22	00	00
00	08	00	1A
41 'A'	4E 'N'	20 ' '	45 'E'
58 'X'	41 'A'	4D 'M'	50 'P'
4C 'L'	45 'E'	20 ' '	48 'H'
49 'I'	44 'D'	44 'D'	45 'E'
4E 'N'	20 ' '	4D 'M'	45 'E'
53 'S'	53 'S'	41 'A'	47 'G'
45 'E'	2E '.'		

Figure 6-6 *Vendor Name AVP before hiding Value field*

The first calculation (from step 2 of the algorithm process) is to do the MD5 hash over the two-octet AVP attribute ID (00 08), the shared secret, and the random vector value. For the values in this example, this yields the sixteen-octet value

```
3C 6E 5B A3 78 7C 86 FB 91 66 70 0E F7 B5 33 75
```

In step 3 this value is XORed with the first sixteen octets to be hidden. This is

```
00 1A 41 4E 20 45 58 41 4D 50 4C 45 20 48 49 44
  XOR
3C 6E 5B A3 78 7C 86 FB 91 66 70 0E F7 B5 33 75
```

which is

```
3C 74 1A ED 58 39 DE BA DC 36 3C 4B D7 FD 7A 31
```

Step 4 is to save this value as the first sixteen octets of hidden value. Moving on to the next sixteen octets of hidden data, an MD5 hash is performed over the concatenation of the shared secret and the preceding sixteen octets as they were hidden. This yields the sixteen-octet MD5 digest

```
E6 30 86 EE B7 4A 8D 9F CF FC DC DB 1E E3 6B 61
```

Step 7 of the algorithm then XORs this value with the next sixteen octets to be hidden. In this case there are less than sixteen octets left, so the XOR is performed over the remaining octets. This is

```
E6 30 86 EE B7 4A 8D 9F CF FC DC DB 1E E3 6B 61
  XOR
44 45 4E 20 4D 45 53 53 41 47 45 2E
```

which is

```
      A2 75 C8 CE FA 0F DE CC 8E BB 99 F5
```

In this example the algorithm then terminates because the input is exhausted. Repeating steps 5 through 7 should be trivial if longer values need to be hidden. The entire hidden data in this example is

```
3C 74 1A ED 58 39 DE BA DC 36 3C 4B D7 FD 7A 31
A2 75 C8 CE FA 0F DE CC 8E BB 99 F5
```

The hidden AVP in the message would be encoded with the first six octets being identical to those of Figure 6-6, followed by the twenty-eight octets of hidden data shown above as the Value field for the AVP.

6.3.2 AVP Unhiding Algorithm

Next we explore a straightforward algorithm for unhiding AVP data. This algorithm requires the use of a second storage area separate from the area from which the hidden data is read, because there needs to be a place to store the results of the unhiding. The subsection immediately following this one shows an alternate algorithm that does not require a second, separate area for storing the results of the unhiding.

This first algorithm for unhiding AVP data processes sixteen-octet chunks in order, much in the same way that the AVP hiding algorithm does.

1. Obtain the random vector from the most recently processed Random Vector AVP that precedes the AVP to be unhidden.

2. Perform an MD5 hash over the concatenation of the two-octet AVP Attribute ID, the shared secret, and the random value from step 1.

3. XOR the result from step 2 with the first sixteen octets of hidden data.

4. Save the result from step 3 in an area that is separate from the first sixteen octets of hidden data. This is necessary because the first sixteen octets of hidden data will be used in the unhiding of the next sixteen octets of hidden data.

5. Move on to the next sixteen octets to be unhidden.

6. Perform an MD5 hash over the concatenation of the shared secret and the preceding sixteen octets of hidden data (but not the results of unhiding the preceding sixteen octets).

7. XOR the result from step 6 with the current sixteen octets to be unhidden.

8. Save the result from step 7 as the next sixteen octets of unhidden data in an area that is separate from the area containing the current sixteen octets of hidden data. This is necessary because the current sixteen octets of hidden data will be used in the unhiding of the next sixteen octets of hidden data.

9. Repeat steps 5 through 8 until the input is exhausted (that is, all data has been unhidden).

At the conclusion of the operation of this algorithm the unhidden data will reside in the separate storage area. Depending on the design of the implementation, the unhidden data may then need to be copied so as to overwrite the hidden data.

It should be noted that this algorithm can be optimized to unhide only as much of the data as is needed. Because the Length of Original Value field of the hidden data subformat is among the first sixteen octets that are unhidden, it is possible to detect how many octets really need to be unhidden and to shortcut the process to avoid unhiding unnecessary data.

To illustrate the steps in unhiding an AVP value, we will unhide the hidden AVP Value field from the preceding section.

Again, the tunnel shared secret is

74 65 73 74

and the random vector for this example is the ten-octet value

```
55 89 E5 81 EC 84 04 00 00 57
```

As we saw in the result of the example of hiding AVP in the previous section, the data to be unhidden is the twenty-eight octets

```
3C 74 1A ED 58 39 DE BA DC 36 3C 4B D7 FD 7A 31
A2 75 C8 CE FA 0F DE CC 8E BB 99 F5
```

Step 2 of the unhiding algorithm is identical to step 2 of the hiding algorithm. Since the tunnel shared secret is agreed on by both sides and the random vector used is the same, the MD5 hash of the AVP Attribute ID (8), the shared secret, and the random vector is once again

```
3C 6E 5B A3 78 7C 86 FB 91 66 70 0E F7 B5 33 75
```

Following step 3 of the unhiding algorithm, this value is XORed with the first sixteen octets to be unhidden. This is:

```
3C 6E 5B A3 78 7C 86 FB 91 66 70 0E F7 B5 33 75
  XOR
3C 74 1A ED 58 39 DE BA DC 36 3C 4B D7 FD 7A 31
```

which is

```
00 1A 41 4E 20 45 58 41 4D 50 4C 45 20 48 49 44
```

One can already see that this is indeed the original first sixteen octets that were hidden by the peer as it went through the hiding algorithm. Moving on to the next sixteen octets of hidden data, an MD5 hash over the concatenation of the shared secret and the previous (in this case first) sixteen octets of hidden data is performed. This yields the sixteen-octet MD5 digest

```
E6 30 86 EE B7 4A 8D 9F CF FC DC DB 1E E3 6B 61
```

In step 7 this value is XORed with the current sixteen octets to be unhidden. In this case there are less than sixteen octets left, so the result is less than sixteen octets. The operation is

```
E6 30 86 EE B7 4A 8D 9F CF FC DC DB 1E E3 6B 61
  XOR
A2 75 C8 CE FA 0F DE CC 8E BB 99 F5
```

which is

```
44 45 4E 20 4D 45 53 53 41 47 45 2E
```

It can be seen that we come out with the original last twelve octets. Putting the results of the algorithm together for this example yields the result

```
00 1A 41 4E 20 45 58 41 4D 50 4C 45 20 48 49 44
44 45 4E 20 4D 45 53 53 41 47 45 2E
```

which is exactly the same as the Value field we originally hid in the previous section, the value originally encoded by the peer. The Value field for the hidden AVP is then decoded so that the (00 1A) is taken to be the length of the actual value, and the remaining twenty-six octets are the actual Vendor Name.

6.3.3 AVP Unhiding Algorithm with No Separate Storage Area

As opposed to the AVP unhiding algorithm given in the preceding subsection, the algorithm here does not require that the unhidden data be saved in an area that is separate from the hidden data. The general idea behind this algorithm is that by starting at the end of the hidden data and working backward, the sixteen octets preceding the octets that are to be unhidden are always available (that is, not yet overwritten), and the result of each unhiding can overwrite the octets being unhidden.

Here is the algorithm (if less than sixteen octets are being unhidden go directly to step 7):

1. Move to the last group of octets that were hidden. Note that this may mean that less than sixteen octets are unhidden in this first part of the algorithm. The important thing is to make sure that all subsequent groups of octets to be unhidden are exactly sixteen bytes.
2. Perform an MD5 hash over the shared secret and the preceding sixteen octets of hidden data.
3. XOR the result from step 2 with the sixteen octets to be unhidden.
4. Save the results from step 3 over the sixteen octets of hidden data.
5. Back up sixteen octets in the hidden data.

6. Repeat steps 2 through 5 until you arrive at the first group of sixteen octets to be unhidden.

7. Obtain the random vector value from the most recently processed Random Vector AVP preceding the AVP to be unhidden.

8. Perform an MD5 hash over the concatenation of the two-octet AVP Attribute ID, the shared secret, and the random vector value from step 7.

9. XOR the result from step 8 with the sixteen octets to be unhidden.

10. Save the results from step 9 over the sixteen octets of hidden data.

At the conclusion of the operation of this algorithm the unhidden data is in the same location as the originally hidden data.

This algorithm does not optimize the unhiding when padding is present at the end of the real data. But this optimization can be achieved by starting in the same way as in the first unhiding algorithm to recover the first sixteen octets, which includes the length of the original value. Then the no-copy version of the algorithm can be used with the modification that you start only as close to the end of the hidden data as necessary to unhide the actual original value.

6.3.4 Restrictions on Hiding AVPs

There are some AVPs that cannot be hidden because of how they are used or because they are implicitly part of the AVP hiding process, making unhiding logically impossible.

- The Message Type AVP must be the first AVP in a control message. Because of this, it cannot be preceded by a Random Vector AVP, and therefore the Message Type AVP may not be hidden.

- Because the Random Vector AVP is a crucial part of the AVP hiding process, the Random Vector cannot be hidden, even if it has been preceded in the message by another instance of the Random Vector AVP.

- The Host Name AVP found in the SCCRQ and SCCRP messages also must not be hidden. This is because the Host Name AVP is used to identify the tunnel endpoints so that the shared secret for the tunnel can be established through tunnel authentication.

- The Assigned Tunnel ID AVP in the SCCRQ, SCCRP, and StopCCN messages also must not be hidden, because this value must be guaranteed to be communicated to the peer regardless of whether or not agreement of a shared secret has been reached.
- The Result Code AVP in the StopCCN also must not be hidden, because the value of this AVP must be guaranteed to be recognizable to the peer independent of whether or not an agreement has been reached on the shared secret.

6.4 Comparing L2TP to L2F and PPTP

The header formats for the data messages of L2TP, L2F, and PPTP are all based on the same principle as the Generic Routing Encapsulation (GRE) header. The headers for all three of these protocols have the same format for the first sixteen bits (as does GRE). This means that the Version field lies in the same place. This factor is significant when one is considering L2TP and L2F, since they share the same transport mechanism (for example, when either is run over UDP). The Version field can be used to distinguish L2TP from L2F. For L2F, the Version field value is 1, and for L2TP the Version field value is 2. Both L2F and L2TP share a remarkable numerical association with GRE: both run over UDP port 1701, and the specification for GRE is RFC1701. At least there is one less number to have to remember.

L2TP and L2F packet formats and transport mechanisms are different than those used in PPTP in three respects: in-band management, transport mechanism independence, and the ability to trivially work through Network Address Translation (NAT) devices when run over IP. By defining the control channel to run over TCP/IP, PPTP is effectively tied to running over IP networks. At the same time, PPTP defines the data to be encapsulated in GRE/IP, thus splitting it from the control channel.[1] By contrast, L2TP and L2F both define the control and data to be run over the same transport with a bit in the header specifying whether the message is a control message or a data message. NAT devices operate on UDP and TCP protocols simply by manipulating port numbers (UDP or TCP) in packets and keeping state to translate the IP

---

1. Actually, Enhanced GRE.

addresses in the IP header for traffic flows. Because both L2TP and L2F run over UDP, L2TP and L2F tunnels are able to run with a simple NAT device sitting in the middle.[2] Although the PPTP control channel is TCP and it can be handled easily by NAT devices, the GRE header used for PPTP data traffic makes running PPTP tunnels through a NAT more difficult and requires special PPTP awareness (such NAT devices do exist).

6.5 Implementation Tips

There are several key points to remember and some subtle or not so subtle things to keep in mind when one is implementing the processing of L2TP headers and control message AVPs. In the following subsections we give some useful guidance on what issues to look out for.

6.5.1 Meaning of AVP Mandatory Bit

While reading through RFCl2tp for the first time (or first few times!) it is easy to lose track of what it is that the M Bit (Mandatory Bit) in the AVP represents. This is because some AVPs are optional in messages while other AVPs are required in some control messages. Section 6 of RFCl2tp lists the L2TP control messages and the AVPs found in each control message. This list also shows which of the AVPs must be present in the particular control message and which of the AVPs are optional.

Keep in mind that the M Bit defines whether or not it is mandatory that an implementation understand what the AVP is. The M Bit has nothing whatsoever to do with defining whether the presence of the AVP in the particular message is mandatory or not.

6.5.2 The Order of AVPs

With few exceptions, RFCl2tp does not specify that the AVPs in a control message be arranged or ordered in any set way. It is reasonable to implement AVP encoding so that the AVPs are found in the order in which they are listed in the RFC.

When receiving control messages, however, an implementation should not make assumptions about the order of AVPs in a control

---

2. Using IPSEC Transport Mode to secure L2TP traffic makes running through NAT devices all but impossible except in the simplest of cases.

message, except for those noted for proper protocol behavior. The only assumptions that can be made are that at least one Random Vector AVP must precede an AVP with the H Bit set, and that the Message Type AVP must be the first AVP in a message.

6.5.3 SCCRQ, SCCRP, and SCCCN AVPs Can Be Hidden

Keep in mind that other than the exceptions given in this chapter, the SCCRQ, SCCRP, and SCCCN messages can all have AVPs that are hidden. If this consideration is not heeded, proper tunnel establishment can be compromised.

Unless deemed absolutely necessary for security purposes, an implementation should shy away from hiding AVPs in the SCCRQ, SCCRP, and SCCCN messages. Otherwise, the peer implementation doing the unhiding may not have a matching shared secret and will decode the hidden AVPs incorrectly. This could result in unexpected behavior and a confusing diagnosis of the tunnel establishment failure.

6.5.4 Odd AVP Conditions

The M Bit is specified to decide behavior if an unrecognized AVP is received. The logic of this bit should also be used in the case of other unexpected AVP events. Three such conditions are (1) the presence of a hidden AVP without a preceding Random Vector (RV) AVP, (2) the reception of an AVP that is recognized in a message in which it is not expected to be found, and (3) an unexpected value in an AVP.

7

Control Channel Dynamics

The L2TP control channel is responsible for the orderly passing of control messages between tunnel endpoints. This chapter explains how the L2TP control channel acts as a transport layer for the reliable delivery of control messages and tunnel keepalive services for the tunnel.

7.1 An Overview of the Control Channel

The logical structure of the control channel can be split into two interacting parts, the sender portion and the receiver portion. To send control messages, the L2TP state machines pass the control messages down to the control channel to be delivered. The sender portion of the control channel then transports these messages to the peer's receiver, retransmitting as necessary until receipt is acknowledged by the peer's control channel receiver. If the maximum number of retransmissions is reached for a message before an acknowledgment of receipt is made by the receiver, then the tunnel state machine is notified that the control channel timed out and the tunnel is subsequently torn down. On the receiver side, messages are received and may be queued if reordering is necessary. Acknowledgments are sent for the sequence number of the most recently received message that the receiver was able to send up to the L2TP state machines.

When the tunnel is established, each end of the tunnel can include a receive window size for its control channel using the Receive Window AVP in the SCCRQ and SCCRP control messages. The sender looks at the receive window size of the peer to determine how many control messages may be simultaneously outstanding. If the peer's receive window size is not communicated explicitly to the sender, then the receive window size is taken to be four control messages.

The behavior of the control channel is leveraged to provide a keepalive mechanism for the tunnel. Since failure to receive acknowledgment of a message results in the tunnel being torn down, an explicit Echo-Request/Echo-Reply mechanism is not required. Instead, a message called the HELLO message can be sent to the peer. If receipt of an acknowledgment for the HELLO message is received, this is an implicit reply to the request. Reliable delivery and acknowledgment of a HELLO message therefore provides the means to detect if a tunnel is still established between two endpoints.[1]

Both the sending and the receiving portions of the control channel access two state variables:

- *Ss.* The Ss state variable is the value that is plugged in the Ns field of the next outgoing control message to be sent. After a control message is assigned an Ns value from Ss, the Ss state variable is incremented. The Ss state variable is initialized at tunnel setup to the value of 0 so that the first tunnel message (SCCRQ) is sent with the Ns value set to 0. Retransmitted messages keep the original Ns value sent with the message.
- *Sr.* The Sr state variable is the value expected in the Ns field for the next control message that is received. This value is sent in the Nr field of control messages as an acknowledgment of received control messages. The Sr state variable is initialized to the value of 0, indicating that a message with an Ns value of 0 is the first message that can be sent up to the state machines after the message has been received from the peer. The value of Sr only changes as messages with sequential Ns values are received. The state variable Sr also dictates what value will be put into the Nr control field on messages sent to the peer.

Note that much of the terminology in this chapter is not found in RFCl2tp.[2] The purpose of the terminology and figures is to illustrate the specifications found in the RFC in a different light.

---

1. This single-message HELLO keepalive procedure is borrowed from Border Gateway Protocol (BGP).
2. Ss and Sr were used in versions of the draft preceding RFCl2tp.

7.2 Sequence Number Handling

The orderly delivery of control messages between L2TP peers is made possible by the use of sequence numbers assigned to control messages. Each control message sent out has a control header as described in Chapter 6. The control header has two fields that are used to convey sequence number information. The Ns field of the control header contains the sequence number assigned to the message. The Nr field of the control header contains a value used for acknowledging receipt of control messages. As already mentioned, each peer has two sequence number state variables that are used to set the values of Ns and Nr in outgoing messages.

The sequence number space of the L2TP control channel is a 16-bit unsigned number space. Sequence numbers start at 0 and increase sequentially, wrapping at 65,535 ($2^{16} - 1$) back to 0. A sequence number is said to be less than (or come before) another sequence number if the first number is within the previous 32,767 ($2^{15} - 1$) values of the second. Otherwise, unless the two sequence numbers are equal, the first sequence number is said to be greater than (or come after) the second sequence number. For example, for the sequence number 15, the sequence number values 0 through 14 as well as the values 32,784 through 65,535 are all considered to be less than 15. The values 16 through 32,783 are all considered to be greater than 15.

A Zero Length Body (ZLB) message can also be sent to a peer. The sole purpose of a ZLB is to communicate sequence number information. The sending of a ZLB is essentially the sending of an acknowledgment. A ZLB is identified by the fact that the value in the Length field (12) of the control header is equal to the size of the control header. This indicates that the message consists of nothing more than the control header itself. Note that the Ns value in the header of a ZLB is equal to the Ns value that will be in the header of the next non-ZLB message.

7.3 The Reliable Delivery Sender

The job of the sending portion of the reliable delivery mechanism of the control channel is to receive messages from the L2TP state machines that need to be sent to the peer and ensure reliable delivery of these messages. Messages are retransmitted to the peer until they are acknowledged or the control channel times out trying to send the messages.

7.3.1 The Sender Window

Similar to TCP, the L2TP control channel uses a sliding window of messages on transmission. The purpose of using a send window is to provide for the smooth delivery of control messages and to avoid overwhelming the receiving peer in the case of a message storm (for example, many calls being brought up or torn down at once).

In this chapter we describe a model of interaction between the L2TP state machines and control channel sender in which these two entities are tightly coupled. The L2TP state machines check the control channel send window before handing a message down to be delivered. The control channel therefore does not need to queue any messages beyond those in the send window. This causes the state machines to stall in the case where the window is full. If the state machines were not so tightly coupled to the send window, messages could get sent down by multiple call state machines to the control channel sender, causing resources to be wasted by keeping messages on queues in the control channel sender until the send window opened up.

RFCl2tp recommends that slow-start and congestion-avoidance mechanisms be used in L2TP as in TCP, because if this is done, the size of the send window actually changes with time. The lower bound of the send window size is 1, and the upper bound on the send window size is whatever size the peer specifies for the receive window.

The similarities and differences between the operation of the L2TP control channel and the operation of TCP are discussed later on in this chapter in the section entitled "Comparing L2TP to TCP."

7.3.2 Sender Actions

Figure 7-1 illustrates the actions performed by the reliable delivery sender. In this diagram, states are shown as rectangles and actions taken without a change of state are represented by circles. The third symbol used is diamonds, which are used to represent predicates (Boolean decision points). The data needed for the operation of the control channel is

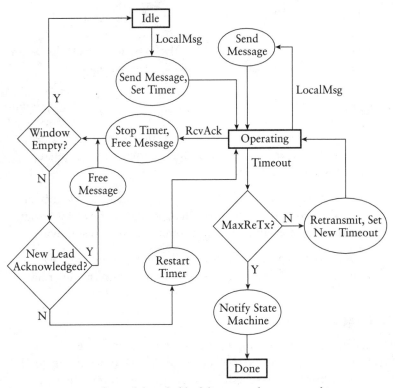

Figure 7-1 *Logic flow of the reliable delivery sender state machine*

- *WindowQueue*. This is a queue of the control messages sent to the peer that are currently unacknowledged. The maximum number of messages queued on WindowQueue is equal to the receive window size of the peer.
- *MaxReTx*. The value for this factor indicates the maximum number of times that the control channel will attempt to retransmit a control message. When the acknowledgment timeout occurs and a message has already been retransmitted MaxReTx number of times, the L2TP tunnel state machine is notified so that the tunnel can be torn down.
- *ReTx*. The value for this factor is the number of times a control message has been retransmitted.

- *TimeoutValue.* This is the amount of time for the control channel sender to wait before retransmitting a message.
- *Timer.* A timer is required so that the control channel sender can be notified when specific intervals of time have elapsed.

There are only a small number of events that the control channel sender has to process. These are

- *LocalMsg.* This event occurs when a control message has been received from an L2TP state machine and needs to be reliably delivered to the L2TP peer.

- *RcvAck.* This event occurs when a control message or ZLB message is received for the control channel that acknowledges some outstanding messages that are currently in the transmit window.

- *Timeout.* This event occurs when the timer has expired. A timeout indicates that the amount of time set on the timer has elapsed.

7.3.3 The IDLE State

The reliable delivery sending state machine is in the IDLE state when there are no unacknowledged control messages outstanding to the peer, and no control messages have been given to the state machine to be delivered to the peer. The purpose of the IDLE state is essentially to wait for control messages from the L2TP state machines to kick off the reliable delivery state machine. The IDLE state is the initial state for the reliable delivery sender state machine.

Each time the IDLE state is entered there is an implicit resetting of sending state information. Specifically, the retransmit time is reset to the initial timeout period of one second (TimeoutValue = 1), and the number of retransmits is reset to zero (ReTx = 0).

7.3.4 Send Msg, Set Timer Actions

The Send Msg, Set Timer actions are taken when the sender state machine is leaving the IDLE state because of a LocalMsg event, which indicates that a control message has been given to the state machine to be delivered.

The control message is prepended with the L2TP control message header; the Ns field value becomes the current value of Ss, and the Nr field value becomes the current value of Sr for the control channel. Once the control message header is complete, the control message is given to the transport mechanism being used for the tunnel. When the Ns field value is set to Ss, the value of Ss is incremented. The control message is appended to the WindowQueue so that the message may be freed or retransmitted as necessary as processing continues. The retransmission timer is then started and the Operating state is entered.

7.3.5 The Operating State

The Operating state is the main state of the state machine. Most of the state machine is essentially a flow chart based on events occurring while in this state. There are three events that can occur while the state machine is in this state: LocalMsg, Timeout, and RcvAck.

The LocalMsg event indicates that a control message has been sent down to the reliable delivery mechanism from an L2TP state machine while at least one other unacknowledged control message has been sent to the L2TP peer. Because the assumption is that the state machines check to see if the sender has a slot in the window, the message is added to the window and is sent to the L2TP peer without checking the window first.

When the Timeout event occurs in the Operating state, the first control message in the window is generally retransmitted. But if the maximum number of retransmissions has already been reached, then the control channel notifies the main L2TP tunnel state machine that the control channel has timed out, and the control channel enters the Done state.

When a RcvAck event occurs while the state machine is in the Operating state, this means that the peer has acknowledged one or more of the control messages that are currently in the transmit window of the sender. If the peer acknowledges a message not yet sent or acknowledges messages already removed from the window, the acknowledgment is ignored. When the RcvAck event occurs, all of the acknowledged messages are removed from the window and freed. If there are no more messages in the window, the reliable delivery sender reenters the IDLE state. If there are still messages that are unacknowledged, the state machine remains in the Operating state as shown in the state machine diagram.

7.3.6 Send Msg Actions

Send Msg actions occur after the state machine receives the LocalMsg event while in the Operating state. The actions taken are the same as those taken to send a message when the LocalMsg event is received in the IDLE state, except that no retransmission timer is set.

The control message is prepended with the L2TP control message header; the Ns field value takes on the current value of Ss, and the Nr field value takes on the current value of Sr for the control channel. Once the control message header is complete, the control message is given to the transport mechanism being used for the tunnel. When the Ns field value is set to Ss, the value of Ss is incremented. The control message is appended to the WindowQueue so that the message may be freed or retransmitted as necessary as processing continues.

7.3.7 The MaxReTx? Predicate

This predicate is reached when the Timeout event occurs while the state machine is in the Operating state. The MaxReTx checks to see whether or not the control message at the head of the window has already been retransmitted the maximum number of times. The evaluation of this predicate is achieved by checking the value of ReTx against the value of MaxReTx. If ReTx is equal to the value of MaxReTx, then the result is Yes (Y). If ReTx is not equal to the value of MaxReTx, then the result is No (N), and the control flow retransmits the message.

7.3.8 Retransmit, Set New Timeout Actions

The Retransmit, Set New Timeout actions are encountered when a Timeout event occurs while the state machine is in the Operating state and the maximum number of retransmissions has not yet been reached.

These actions start with the control message at the head of WindowQueue being resent to the transport mechanism for the tunnel. Before this is done, the Nr field in the control message is updated with the current value of Sr for the tunnel. It is important to note that this is the only aspect of the L2TP control message that potentially changes between retransmissions.

After the control message is retransmitted, the timeout value is adjusted upward based on the current value. The back-off mechanism for control message retransmission specifies an exponential back-off. Until a maximum retransmission timeout value is reached (a minimum value for the maximum timeout is specified to be 8 seconds), the timeout value (which we have represented as TimeoutValue) is doubled. Once the value of TimeoutValue has been adjusted, the timer is set using this value, and the state machine remains in the Operating state waiting for an event.

RFCl2tp specifies that the minimum number for the maximum retransmission threshold (the minimum value of MaxReTx) is five (that is, a total of six transmissions). The value of TimeoutValue is specified to begin at 1 second and double each time a retransmission occurs until a maximum TimeoutValue is reached. The minimum maximum threshold for TimeoutValue is specified to be 8 seconds. Based on this information it is possible to calculate the minimum amount of time that it can take the reliable transmission mechanism of the control channel to reach its timeout limit and reach the Done state. In order to wait the full time intervals for the acknowledgment of the first transmission and five retransmissions, six retransmission intervals are necessary. The minimum time that it may take a control channel reliable delivery mechanism to timeout is therefore $1 + 2 + 4 + 8 + 8 + 8 = 31$ seconds.

7.3.9 Notify State Machine Actions

The Notify State Machine actions occur when the maximum number of retransmissions for a control message has been reached without an acknowledgment from the peer. The Notify State Machine actions are the tunnel state machine's method of signifying that the control channel reliable delivery mechanism has timed out. These actions cause the CCTO event for the control connection state machine explained in Chapter 6. The state machine then enters the Done state.

7.3.10 The Done State

The state machine enters the Done state after a Timeout event has occurred in the Operating state and the upper-level control channel state machine has been notified that a control channel timeout has occurred. When the Done state is entered, the resources taken up by any queued control messages on the WindowQueue can be cleaned up.

7.3.11 Stop Timer, Free Msg Actions

The Stop Timer, Free Msg actions are taken when the RcvAck event occurs while the state machine is in the Operating state. First the retransmission timer is stopped, since at least the first message in the window has been acknowledged. The head of the WindowQueue can then be removed, and the resources associated with that control message can be cleaned up.

7.3.12 The Window Empty? Predicate

The Window Empty? decision point is reached after a message has been removed from the transmit window because there has been a RcvAck event in the Operating state. This can be evaluated by checking if the WindowQueue is empty.

If the window is found to be empty (following the "Y" branch), then the control flow goes on to the IDLE state. If the Window Empty? query results in a No (N), then the control flow goes on to check if the control message at the head of the WindowQueue has been acknowledged (since multiple control messages may be acknowledged at once).

7.3.13 The New Lead Ack'd? Predicate

The New Lead Ack'd predicate evaluates whether or not the control message at the lead position in the transmit window has been acknowledged. First the last value of Nr received in a control message is checked. If this value is greater than the value of Ns used in the control message at the head of the WindowQueue, then the control message at the head of the WindowQueue has been acknowledged and the result of the query is Yes (Y); otherwise the answer is No (N). In the case of a Y result, control moves on to free the message at the head of the WindowQueue. In the case of an N result, control moves on to the Restart Timer actions.

7.3.14 Free Msg Actions

The Free Msg actions are encountered upon the state machine's evaluating the New Lead Ack'd predicate and arriving at a value of Yes (Y). Since the control message at the head of the WindowQueue has been acknowledged in this case, this control message is removed from the WindowQueue and its resources can be cleaned up. Control then goes back to the Window Empty? predicate. The value of WindowRoom is incremented as part of these actions, to take into account that a slot has become available in the transmit window.

7.3.15 Restart Timer Actions

These actions are encountered after one or more messages have been acknowledged and there is a new message at the head of the window. The value of ReTx is set to zero, and the value of TimeoutValue is set to 1 second so that the retransmission limit checking can be restarted. The timer is then set to expire after an interval of TimeoutValue, and the state machine remains in the Operating state.

7.4 The Reliable Delivery Receiver

The job of the receiver portion of the control channel is to receive messages sent by the peer over the network and send these up to the control channel state machines. The receiving logic is tied to the sending logic. Control messages (including ZLBs) received from the peer include acknowledgments for messages that the peer has received. This information is communicated in the Nr field of the control message header. Control messages that are received before or within the receive window have their Nr value passed on to the sender to be processed as an acknowledgment.

If a nonzero receive window was specified and the network between the L2TP peers can lose packets, then an implementation should queue messages received in the window that aren't the expected message. For this purpose, the following two state variables are used in Figure 7-2:

- *RecvQueue*. This is a queue for out-of-order received messages until the expected message is received.
- *RecvWindowSize*. This value represents the size of the receiver's window. The receive window is the same size as the send window. This value is either explicitly communicated to the peer during tunnel establishment (via the Receive Window AVP in SCCRQ or SCCRP) or if not explicitly sent this value is assumed to be set to 4.

Figure 7-2 is the logic flow diagram for the control channel reliable delivery receiver, showing the logic flow followed upon receipt of a control message. Unlike the reliable delivery sender, the receiver does not require a state machine to express its operation. Instead, there is a

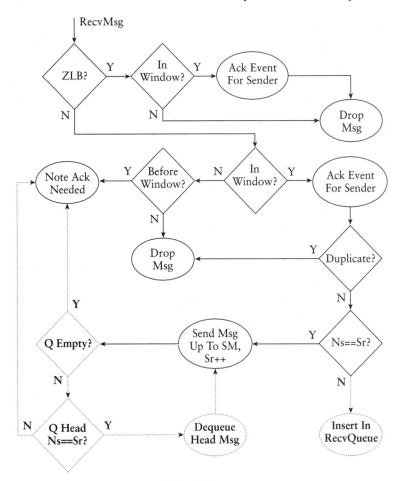

Figure 7-2 *Logic flow of the reliable delivery receiver*

single event: RecvMsg, the reception of a control message. The symbols used in Figure 7-2 are the same as those used in Figure 7-1.

7.4.1 The RecvMsg Event

The RecvMsg event occurs when the transport layer the tunnel is running over receives a message on the network and sends it up to the control channel.

7.4.2 The ZLB? Predicate

The purpose of the ZLB predicate is to split the logic flow according to whether or not the received control message is a Zero Length Body (ZLB) message. ZLB messages are used solely to send acknowledgments for control messages. Whether or not a message is a ZLB can be determined by comparing the value of the Length field in the control header with the length of a control header. If the Length field is equal in value to the size of the control header, that means that the message contains nothing but the message header itself, making it a ZLB. In this case, the predicate evaluates to Yes (Y). If the value of the Length field of the control header is greater than the size of the control header, then the predicate evaluates to No (N).

7.4.3 The In Window? Predicate

The purpose of this predicate is to decide whether or not the current message being received is within the control channel receive window. If the value of the Ns field in the received message is less than the value of Sr for the control channel or greater than or equal to the value of (Sr + RecvWindowSize), then the message is not within the control channel window and the predicate evaluates to No (N). Otherwise the predicate evaluates to Yes (Y).

For non-ZLB messages, upon detecting that the control message is not in the window, the logic flow moves on to check whether the message is before the receive window or after the receive window. If the non-ZLB control message is in the window, then the logic flow goes on to check if the message is a duplicate of a message that has already been received.

For ZLB messages, if the Ns field in the control message header of the ZLB indicates that the ZLB is not in the receive window, then the logic flow moves on to drop the message. If the ZLB is indicating that it is within the receive window, then the logic flow moves on to actions that indicate the acknowledgment to the sender portion of the control channel reliable delivery.

7.4.4 ACK Event for Sender Actions

These actions are taken when both a ZLB and a non-ZLB message are received and are evaluated to be received within the current receive window. To work correctly with the logic in Figure 7-1, for the reliable delivery sender state machine the value of the Nr field of the message must be evaluated to be greater than the previous acknowledgment value indicated to the reliable delivery sender state machine. If the Nr field is deemed to be a new acknowledgment, then a sender state machine RcvAck event is generated and the value of the Nr field is communicated along with this event.

7.4.5 The Duplicate? Predicate

The purpose of this predicate is to check whether the non-ZLB message being received has already been received (that is, a control message with the same control header Ns field value has been received).

The RecvQueue is checked to see if there is already a message with the same Ns value as the Ns value of the message currently being processed. If a message already exists in the RecvQueue with the same Ns value, then this predicate evaluates to Yes (Y). If no entry is found in the RecvQueue for the value of Ns found in the control header Ns field of the message currently being processed, then the predicate evaluates to No (N).

Upon detecting that the message is a duplicate the logic flow moves on to drop the message. If the message is not a duplicate, then the logic flow moves on to check if the message currently being processed is the message that is expected to be the next one to be received.

7.4.6 The Ns == Sr? Predicate

The evaluation of whether the message currently being processed is the message that the receiver is expecting to be the next one to be received is decided by this predicate. If the value of Sr for the control channel is equal to the Ns field value in the control header of the message, then the result is Yes (Y). If the Sr value for the control channel is not the same as the Ns field value in the control header of the message, the result is No (N).

If the current message is the expected one, then the logic flow goes on to send the message up to the L2TP tunnel or call state machines. If the current message was not the one that was expected, the logic flow goes (optionally) on to queue the message on the RecvQueue (sorted by Ns value). Note that it is acceptable for the receiver to drop instead of queue any messages for which Ns does not equal Sr since retransmission will be attempted by the peer sender.

7.4.7 Insert in RecvQueue Actions

These actions are taken by an implementation that has the policy that
messages received within the receive window will be queued so that
once the expected message is received, retransmission of subsequent
messages will be minimized.

A message is inserted into the RecvQueue according to the Ns
value in the message compared to the Ns values of messages that are
already in the queue. The RecvQueue is an ordered queue ranging
from the message with the lowest Ns value (sequence-space-wise) at
the head of the queue to the highest Ns value (sequence-space-wise) at
the tail of the queue.

7.4.8 Send Msg up to SM, Sr++ Actions

These actions are taken when the receiver is in possession of a message
that is the next one that is to be delivered to the L2TP state machines.
As part of these actions the message is sent up to the state machines,
and the control channel Sr value of the message is incremented. The
sequence number of the next message that will be sent up to the state
machines is changed to a value one greater than the value of the current message being sent up.

Which state machine the message is passed up to depends on the
Call ID value in the control header of the message. If the value of the
Call ID field in the control message header is 0 and the message is not
an Incoming Call Request (ICRQ) or Outgoing Call Request (OCRQ),
then the control message is sent up to the tunnel state machine. If the
value of the Call ID field is nonzero, the local call matching that Call
ID for the tunnel is found and the message is sent up to the respective
state machine.

If the incoming message is an ICRQ or OCRQ, then resources to
handle a call are allocated and the message is handed to a call state
machine in the initial state (call setup is covered in Chapter 8).

7.4.9 The Q Empty? Predicate

The purpose of this predicate is to determine if the RecvQueue is
empty. If there are no messages queued to the RecvQueue, then this
predicate evaluates to Yes (Y); otherwise, it evaluates to No (N). If the
queue is empty, there is no more for the receiver to do, except send out
an acknowledgment regarding the control messages received and sent

up to the state machines. If the queue is not empty, the receiver goes on to check if the messages next expected to be received from the peer have been placed in queue.

7.4.10   The Q Head Ns == Sr? Predicate

This point in the logic flow determines whether the message at the head of the RecvQueue contains the Ns value matching the value of the control channel Sr. If the value of the Ns value of the control message at the head of the RecvQueue is the same as the value of Sr for the control channel, then this predicate evaluates to Yes (Y). If the Ns value of the message at the head of the RecvQueue is not the same as the control channel Sr value, then this predicate evaluates to No (N). If the message at the head of the RecvQueue is not the next expected message from the peer then the receiver simply goes on to send an acknowledgment to the peer for all of the messages that were received and sent up to one of the state machines. If the head of the RecvQueue is the next expected message from the peer, then the receiver goes on to send that message up to the control channels.

7.4.11   Dequeue Head Msg Actions

These actions are taken after it is determined that the message queued at the head of the RecvQueue is the next message expected to be sent up to the L2TP state machines. The message at the head of the RecvQueue is simply dequeued and then sent to the correct state machine.

7.4.12   The Before Window? Predicate

This predicate is encountered after it has been determined that a non-ZLB control message is not within the current receive window. If the value of the Ns field in the control header of the message is less than the value of Sr for the control channel, then this predicate evaluates to Yes (Y); otherwise the evaluation is No (N).

If the message is determined to be before the current receive window, then the receiver goes on to set in motion actions that will send an acknowledgment to the peer. If the message is determined not to be before the current receive window, then the receiver moves on to simply drop the packet. The packet is dropped in lieu of sending an acknowledgment. When an unexpected future message is received in the receive window, more than likely it means that either the peer's sending logic is in error or the message is extremely old. In either case the peer sender is not helped by the reception of an acknowledgment.

7.4.13 Drop Msg Actions

The Drop Msg actions are taken when the receiver has determined that no further processing of the message is necessary. The receiver simply frees the resources associated with the message and then waits for another instance of the RecvMsg event to begin the logic flow for a newly received control message.

7.4.14 Note Ack Needed Actions

These actions prepare the way for an acknowledgment to be sent to the peer. When an acknowledgment is sent, the Nr value in the message header is set to the current value of Sr. The actual acknowledgment may take the form of a ZLB, or it may be sent along with the next control message sent by the local control channel sender.

A robust implementation should set a timer for a ZLB to be sent. If the control channel sender does not send a control message before this timer expires, then a ZLB should be sent. If the control channel sender does send a control message in time, then the acknowledgment is said to be "piggybacked" on the sent control message and a ZLB transmission is not necessary.

7.5 The Message Delivery Process: An Example

In order to illustrate the operation of the reliable delivery sender state machine and the reliable delivery receiver mechanism as well as the interaction between the two, let's work through an example of a single message being sent from Peer A to Peer B. To mix things up a little bit we will make the acknowledgment of the message by Peer B take a little longer than expected, causing a retransmission of the message by Peer A. We will then continue the example by showing a message being sent from Peer B back to Peer A.

In the example we will assume that the tunnel has already been established and is in the steady state (no other messages except the ones in the example exist on either end). We will start with Peer A's Ss value set as 58 and Peer B's Ss value set as 37. Correspondingly, Peer

	Peer A	Peer B
Ss	58	37
Sr	37	58

Figure 7-3 *The initial state (T = 0) of Ss and Sr for Peer A and Peer B*

A's Sr value will then be 37, and Peer B's Sr value will be 58 (that is, Peer A is sending message 58, and Peer B is expecting to receive message 58; and Peer B is sending message 37, and Peer A is expecting to receive message 37). This initial state is shown in Figure 7-3. For both peers an initial retransmission time of 1.0 (units not specified) and a ZLB transmission wait time of 0.5 will be used. The time for a message to be delivered by the underlying transport between A and B will be taken to be 0.1.

7.5.1 T = 0, LocalMsg for Peer A

The first step in our example is at time T = 0 , where the Peer A sender gets a LocalMsg event with a message from the state machines that needs to be delivered to Peer B. The sender state machine then takes the following steps:

1. From the IDLE state, the LocalMsg event transitions the state machine to the Send Msg, Set Timer actions. These actions cause the Ns and the Nr for the control message to get set and the control message to get sent out. The Ns value for the message is set to the value of Ss, which is 58. The Nr value gets set to the value of Sr, which is 37. After setting the Ns for the control message to the value of Ss for the tunnel, the value of Ss for the tunnel is incremented. The new state for the session is shown in Figure 7-4.

	Peer A	Peer B
Ss	59	37
Sr	37	58

Figure 7-4 *The state of the session after Peer A sets Ns in the non-ZLB message to 58*

2. After sending the message and setting the timer, the Peer A sender state machine is transitioned to the Operating state awaiting an event.

For the sake of this example we will have the underlying transport drop this message and have Peer B not receive it.

7.5.2 T = 1.0, Peer A Retransmits

Because the message sent to Peer B did not make it to its destination, Peer B obviously has not acknowledged receipt of the message with Ns of 58. The retransmission timer set when the message was first sent (at T = 0) now expires at T = 1.0. This causes the following sequence of events to occur in the Peer A sender state machine:

1. In the Operating state, the Timeout event is encountered, and the result is the "MaxReTx?" predicate. The current value of ReTx is 0, since no retransmissions have taken place. As long as the value of MaxReTx is configured to be a nonzero value (which we will take to be the case in this example) the predicate evaluates to "N."

2. The Retransmit, Set New Timeout actions are then taken. Peer A retransmits the message with the same value of Ns and the value of Nr equal to the current value of Sr (which in this example has not changed since the last transmission). A new timeout is then set. Transmission timeouts back off exponentially, and since the first timeout value was 1.0, the value will now be set to 2.0. This means that if the message is not acknowledged by T = 3.0, the Timeout event will occur again. It is also at this point that the send window would be adjusted down due to the timeout.

3. The state machine stays in the Operating state waiting for an event.

7.5.3 T = 1.1, Peer B Receives Message with Ns = 58, Nr = 37

Peer B now receives the message, and a RecvMsg event is triggered at the receiver. The following logic flow takes place:

1. First the ZLB? predicate is put into action. Because the received message was not a ZLB, this predicate evaluates to "N" in this case.

2. Next the In Window? predicate is carried out. Because the Sr value of Peer B at this time is 58, this predicate will evaluate to "Y" no matter what value the receive window size is set at.

3. The Ack Event for Sender actions are then taken. These actions would cause the receiver to give the local sender portion of the control channel a "RcvAck" event if the Nr value of the packet is greater than a previously received Nr value, but this doesn't occur in this example.

4. The Duplicate? predicate is then encountered. The RecvQueue is checked for a queued message with an Ns value that is the same as the Ns value of the message currently being found. Peer B does not find such a message, so the result is "N."

5. The "Ns == Sr?" predicate is then evaluated as "Y" since the Ns for the message is 58 and the Sr value for Peer B's control channel is 58.

6. The next steps in processing are therefore the Send Msg up to SM, Sr++ actions. Based on the Call ID found in the message, the message is handed up to the corresponding state machine. Figure 7-5 shows the state of the session after Peer B leaves the Send Msg up to SM, Sr++ actions.

7. The Q Empty? predicate then evaluates to "Y" since, as we have already said, the tunnels were starting from a steady state idle.

8. The Note Ack Needed actions are then taken. A timer is set for a ZLB message to be sent. If a message is not sent from Peer A to Peer B before this timer expires (at T = 1.6), a ZLB will be sent.

7.5.4 T = 1.5, LocalMsg for Peer B

We now continue the example with a message from the Peer B state machines to be sent over to Peer A. Upon Peer B receiving the LocalMsg event, the following occurs:

	Peer A	Peer B
Ss	59	37
Sr	37	59

Figure 7-5 *State after Peer B sends message up to state machine*

1. From the IDLE state, the LocalMsg event transitions the state machine to the Send Msg, Set Timer actions. These actions cause the Ns and the Nr for the control message to get set and the control message to get sent out. The Ns value for the message is set to the value of Ss, which is 37. The Nr value gets set to the value of Sr, which is 59. After the Ns for the control message is set to the value of Ss, the value of Ss for the tunnel is incremented. The new state for the tunnel is shown in Figure 7-6.

2. After sending the message and setting the timer, the Peer B sender state machine is transitioned to the Operating state, awaiting an event. The timer set to send a ZLB can now be cleared, since the sending of this message contained a piggybacked acknowledgment of the message earlier received by B.

7.5.5 T = 1.6, Peer A Receives Message, Ns = 37, Nr = 59

Upon receiving the message sent by Peer B in the previous step, the following logic takes place for the Peer A receiver:

1. A RecvMsg event occurs and the ZLB? predicate is evaluated. The current message is not a ZLB, so the result of the evaluation is "N."

2. The non-ZLB In Window? predicate then goes into action, checking the message Ns value with the Peer A control channel Sr value. In this case both the message Ns value and the control channel Sr value are 59, so the message is in the window and the evaluation is "Y."

3. Next the Ack Event for Sender actions are encountered. The receiver in this case can check the value of Nr in the message

	Peer A	Peer B
Ss	59	38
Sr	37	59

Figure 7-6 *The state of the session after Peer A sets Ns in a non-ZLB message to 37*

and see if the value for Nr is greater than what has previously been received. In this case the Nr value of 59 is newer, so the RcvAck event for the sender is carried out.

4. The Duplicate? predicate is next evaluated to "N" because there are no messages in the RecvQueue with an Ns value of 37 (in fact, the RecvQueue is empty in our present example).

5. The Nr == Sr? predicate evaluates to "Y" here, because the Ns value of 37 is the same as the Peer A control channel Sr value of 37.

6. The Send Msg up to SM, Sr++ actions are then taken. As indicated, the message is sent up to the proper L2TP state machine (depending on the value of Call ID in the message). The Sr value for the control channel is then incremented, indicating the value for the next new message that will be sent up to the local L2TP state machines. Figure 7-7 shows the Ss and Sr values for Peer A and B after these actions have been completed.

7. The result of the Q Empty? predicate is then determined to be "Y" in this case because the RecvQueue is empty.

8. The Note Ack Needed actions are then taken. A timer is set for 0.5 from the current time (T = 2.1) in order to send a ZLB to acknowledge this message, if this notification is not first sent as part of a subsequent message.

7.5.6 T = 2.1, Peer A Sends ZLB, Ns = 59, Nr = 38

The timer set back at T = 1.6 when Peer A received a message from Peer B now expires. Because this functionality straddles the receiver and sender portions of the control channel, it is not represented explicitly in the diagrams. The action taken simply involves a ZLB being sent to the peer with the current values of Ss and Sr as the values for Ns and

	Peer A	Peer B
Ss	59	38
Sr	38	59

Figure 7-7 *Sequence number states after Peer B receives message with Ns = 37*

Nr in the ZLB header, respectively. In this case, the result is a ZLB sent from Peer A to Peer B with Ns = 59 and Nr = 38.

7.5.7 T = 2.2, Peer B Receives ZLB, Ns = 59, Nr = 38

When Peer B receives the ZLB from Peer A the following actions occur:

1. The ZLB? predicate is evaluated. Because the message is in fact a ZLB, the evaluation is "Y."
2. The In Window? predicate is then evaluated by comparing the value of Ns in the ZLB to the current receive window sequence numbers for the receiver. Because the receiver is next expecting a message from Peer B with an Ns value of 59 (that is, Sr = 59), the evaluation is "Y" regardless of the actual size of the receive window.
3. The Ack Event for Sender actions are then carried out in order to inform the sender portion of reliable delivery mechanism of any messages that are acknowledged by the ZLB. Because the Nr value in the ZLB is greater than any previously received messages, a RcvAck event is generated for the sender state machine (see the next list for a description of sender actions).
4. After giving the local sender state machine a RcvAck event, the Drop Msg actions are begun, and any resources taken up by the ZLB are freed.

In step 3 of the preceding list, a RcvAck event was generated for the local sender state machine. This causes the sender state machine to do the following:

1. The RcvAck event transitions the state machine toward the Stop Timer, Free Msg actions. The Timer is stopped (since no retransmissions are necessary), and any resources taken up by the message can be freed.
2. The Window Empty? is then evaluated based on whether there are other messages from Peer A that have not yet been acknowledged by Peer B. In this case there are no other messages, so the evaluation is "Y."
3. The IDLE state is entered, in which the state machine waits for another occurrence of the LocalMsg event.

7.6 Packet Trace Summary

A packet trace for our example data session would look like this:

T = 0	Message from A to B	Ns = 58, Nr = 37
T = 1.0	Message from A to B	Ns = 58, Nr = 37
T = 1.5	Message from B to A	Ns = 37, Nr = 59
T = 2.1	ZLB from A to B	Ns = 59, Nr = 38

7.7 Comparing L2TP to TCP

The reliable delivery of data (messages) is a common goal of TCP and the L2TP control channel. One may even ask why TCP was not chosen to carry the control channel instead of reinventing (that is, respecifying) mechanisms for reliable delivery for L2TP. The main reason that new mechanisms were created was to keep L2TP self-reliant. If L2TP relied on TCP for its operation, then L2TP implementations would be confined to running over TCP/IP networks.

It is useful to compare and contrast the operation of the L2TP control channel with the operation of TCP if for no other reason than that understanding the similarities and differences of the two can aid in the partial porting of TCP code for control channel implementations.

7.7.1 Three-way Handshake Initiation

The L2TP control channel is established via the exchange of three messages: SCCRQ, SCCRP, and SCCCN. This is somewhat similar to the three-way handshake used in TCP: SYN, SYN-ACK, ACK. The receiver window size is advertised during the L2TP three-message exchange, as is done with TCP.

7.7.2 Initial Sequence Numbers

Whereas TCP chooses the initial sequence numbers on a per session basis, the L2TP sequence numbers for a tunnel always start at 0. This makes L2TP messages easier to spoof without access to the traffic in between if the tunnel and session identifiers are not chosen randomly.

7.7.3 The Meaning of Sequence Numbers

In TCP the sequence numbers represent bytes of data. In contrast, L2TP sequence numbers specify a message. The meaning of the sequence number fields Ns and Nr for L2TP have the same general meaning as the sequence number and acknowledgment number fields of TCP. Similar to the acknowledgment field of TCP specifying the next byte of data expected from the peer, the Nr field of the L2TP control header specifies the next message expected from the peer.

7.7.4 Sliding Window

L2TP control messages are sent according to a sliding window, as are bytes of data in a TCP session. RFCl2tp recommends that the slow start and congestion avoidance algorithms of TCP be used to control the size of the send window.

Control of the window in L2TP is handled completely by the sender by detecting lost packets. In contrast, in TCP the current size of the receive window is sent to the peer. This is a significant limitation of L2TP since the receiver cannot give adequate feedback to the sender to slow down and do buffering. Since the role of the L2TP control channel is not to handle bulk data transfer, the behavior of the receiver is believed to be reasonable and acceptable.

7.8 Comparing L2TP to L2F and PPTP

Both L2F and PPTP provide reliable delivery of control channel messages. How they achieve this is quite different from how L2TP achieves reliable delivery of control channel messages. In PPTP the control channel runs over TCP. The reliable delivery mechanism for control messages in PPTP is entirely defined by the dynamics of TCP. In L2F the control channel reliable delivery mechanism is defined by the protocol itself, but the dynamics are different from those of L2TP.

In L2F the reliable delivery mechanism is very simple. Control messages are exchanged in lockstep, and retransmission is not required to be done in a back-off manner. The sequence number space for L2F is also modulo 256, compared with the modulo 65,536 sequence number space of L2TP. The drawback of only exchanging messages in lockstep is that there will be only one message unacknowledged at any one time. For example, if the round-trip time between tunnel endpoints is 1 second, then in L2F it will take 4 seconds to send four L2F control messages from one endpoint to the other. By contrast, in L2TP if the window size is equal to or greater than 4, then all four messages could be sent without getting an acknowledgment. Note that using a window size of 1 in L2TP degenerates the L2TP behavior to that of L2F in this regard. The practical drawback of using a window size of 1 is that the rate at which multiple calls can be set up within a tunnel will be degraded.

7.9 Implementation Tip: Checking Sequence Number Ordering

As explained earlier in the chapter, sequence numbers start from 0 and sequentially increase to 65,535. After 65,535 the sequence numbers wrap back to 0. Checking the order of sequence numbers (that is, which one comes first) is therefore not as simple as straightforwardly checking if one is greater than the other. Because the sequence number space wraps, the 32,767 sequence number values preceding a sequence number are considered to come before it (or be less than it). All other sequence number values, except the sequence number value itself of course, are considered to come after (or be greater than) that particular sequence number.

The following macro has been used in both TCP implementations and in Multilink PPP implementations to calculate sequence number ordering:

```
#define SEQ_LT(a,b)   (((a)-(b))&0x8000)
```

This macro works assuming that the previous 32,768 sequence number values for b are considered to be less than those for sequence number a. For all conditions except very strict conformance testing this should be ignored. For the pedantic, an inefficient modification such as the following could be made:

```
#define SEQ_LT(a,b)  ((a)!=(b) && ((((a)+1)-(b))&0x8000))
```

8

Session Setup

So far we have examined the state machines for establishing a tunnel, the manner in which control messages are constructed, and the dynamics of the control channel used to transport messages from one L2TP endpoint to another. This final chapter on the control portion of L2TP describes the state machines used to establish sessions within an L2TP tunnel.

There are two types of sessions in L2TP—sessions for incoming calls and sessions for outgoing calls. Incoming calls are the result of a PPP session having been started involving an LAC (for example, over the LAC's ISDN lines). In the case of an incoming call the LAC signals the LNS that a new session is desired. Outgoing call sessions are the result of an LNS desiring a PPP session to be initiated by the LAC to a remote system. In the case of an outgoing call the LNS signals the LAC that a new session on the tunnel is desired.

This chapter also includes important information on how LCP information should be treated for data sessions for both incoming and outgoing calls.

8.1 Incoming Calls

There are two cases in which an incoming call construct is used. The first is in the case of an actual call incoming to an LAC that is to be tunneled to an LNS. The second involves an L2TP client. The common practice for an L2TP client model is for the client to act as an LAC with an incoming call. LNS devices are then able to terminate both real incoming calls from LAC devices and also L2TP client connections. Although the protocol handshakes will be the same for LAC connections and client connections, the demands on the LNS in the two cases will be different. In the case of client connections there is a single session within the tunnel. In the case of tunnel connections via an LAC there are typically many sessions within a tunnel, coming and going often. In the case of the client connection it is the entire tunnel that is coming and going often.

As discussed earlier, an LAC may use various methods to decide whether a call should be tunneled and to determine the LNS. The decision can be based on information that is external to PPP (such as the number dialed to or the number dialed from), or it can be based on authentication information presented by the incoming PPP such as a domain name in the username.

When an incoming call is made, a connection is established at both L2TP endpoints via a three-way handshake of control messages. The LAC sends an Incoming Call Request (ICRQ), the LNS responds with an Incoming Call Reply (ICRP), and the LAC completes the exchange with an Incoming Call Connected (ICCN) message. The following subsections describe the state machines that come into play for the LAC and for the LNS in the event of an incoming call.

8.1.1 Incoming Call LAC State Machine

Figure 8-1 shows the state machine used by the LAC to respond to an incoming call. The following events are part of this state machine:

- *CallDetect.* This event occurs when the LAC device detects that a call needs to be tunneled. In this state machine the LAC has already determined the LNS that the call is to be tunneled to as well.
- *TunnelFail.* This event occurs when the LAC is unable to bring up a tunnel to the LNS.
- *TunnelEstablished.* The TunnelEstablished event indicates that the tunnel is established between the LAC and the desired LNS for a call, and call establishment within the tunnel can be attempted.
- *BadICRP.* This event occurs when an Incoming Call Reply (ICRP) is received from the LNS for a call indicating that this call cannot be established.
- *GoodICRP.* The GoodICRP event is triggered when an ICRP is received from the LNS indicating that call establishment can continue.

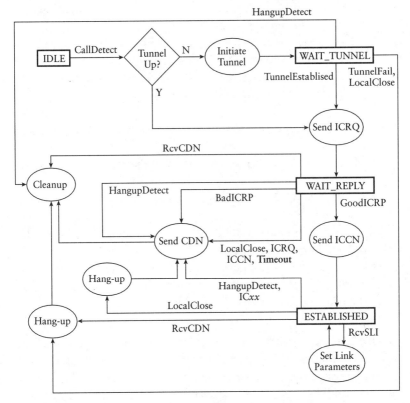

Figure 8-1 *LAC incoming call state machine*

- *RcvCDN.* The RcvCDN event indicates that a Call Disconnect Notify (CDN) for a call was received from the LNS.
- *LocalClose.* This event is encountered when the LAC device initiates the termination of a call for some reason generally external to the call itself. For example, the tunnel containing the call may be terminated.
- *HangupDetect.* The HangupDetect event is the result of the LAC detecting that the connection between the original call endpoint and the LAC has been broken. In the case of an ISDN call to the LAC, this event would happen when the LAC detects that the ISDN call has been terminated.
- *RcvSLI.* The RcvSLI event indicates that a Set Link Info (SLI) message was received from the LNS. Generically speaking, the

LNS sends SLI messages to the LAC to pass on information regarding the settings on the link between the LAC and the remote system that are negotiated during LCP between the LNS and the remote system. RFCl2tp specifies that currently only ACCM values (discussed in the "Asynchronous Control Character Map" section later in this chapter) are contained in the SLI message.

- *ICRQ.* The ICRQ event simply indicates that an ICRQ has been received.
- *ICRP.* The ICRP event simply indicates that an ICRP has been received.
- *ICCN.* The ICCN event simply indicates that an ICCN has been received.
- *ICxx.* The ICxx event indicates that any one of an ICRQ, ICRP, or ICCN has been received.
- *Timeout.* The Timeout event indicates that a timer expired. This event is a suggestion and is not present in the RFCl2tp text or in the LAC incoming call state machine.

The IDLE State: The IDLE state is the state in which processing of the LAC incoming call state machine begins. Reentering the IDLE state from any of the other states is a figurative representation that may or may not indicate an actual instance of an L2TP call and all of its resources reentering the IDLE state.

The Tunnel Up? Predicate: The Tunnel Up? predicate is used to detect whether or not there is already a tunnel up between the LAC and the LNS to which the call is to be tunneled. The actual manner in which this is determined depends on the implementation and isn't presented here.

Initiate Tunnel Actions: The Initiate Tunnel actions are taken when the state machine detects that there is not yet a tunnel established between the LAC and the LNS within which the session for the call can operate. Looking back to Chapter 5, this is accomplished by giving a Local-Open-Req event to the tunnel state machine in the IDLE state.

The Wait_Tunnel State: The purpose of the Wait_Tunnel state is to wait for an indication as to whether or not the tunnel (that is, the control connection) to the LNS has been established. This means that the data session must be informed of the results of running the control connection state machine covered in Chapter 5.

The three normal events that occur in the Wait_Tunnel state are either the TunnelFail event, the TunnelEstablished event, or the HangupDetect event. If the TunnelFail event is encountered, the state machine goes back to the IDLE state after hanging up the call and cleaning up any extraneous call resources. If the TunnelEstablished event is received, the state machine is transitioned to the Wait_Reply state after going through the Send ICRQ Actions. In the event that the actual call hangs up before the state of the tunnel can be determined (that is, before the HangupDetect event can take place), the state machine is transitioned back to the IDLE state after going through the Cleanup actions.

Send ICRQ Actions: The state machine arrives at the Send ICRQ actions when it has been determined that a tunnel exists for the call. This determination is made when the state machine receives a TunnelEstablished event while in the Wait_Tunnel state or the "Tunnel Up?" predicate evaluates to Yes (Y) upon the state machine leaving the IDLE state.

The Send ICRQ actions involve simply sending an Incoming Call Request (ICRQ) to the LNS to request that this call be added to the tunnel. The form for the ICRQ is shown in full in section 6.6 of RFCl2tp. The ICRQ in general contains AVPs that communicate information about the physical connection to the LNS. The ICRQ also contains the Call ID that the LAC will be using for the call. The information contained in the ICRQ can include the Dialing Number, Dialed Number, Physical Channel ID, and Bearer Type for the call.

After sending the ICRQ, the state machine transitions to the Wait_ Reply state to wait for an Incoming Call Reply (ICRP) from the LNS.

It would also be useful to set a timer after sending the ICRQ. The timer value should be very large compared to the retransmission interval being used. The purpose of the timer is to detect problems with LNS implementations that may have received the ICRQ but not done anything with it. Setting a timer is a proactive step that can be taken to make sure a connection will operate well in the case of a bug existing in the peer implementation.

The Wait_Reply State: The state machine enters the Wait_Reply state to wait for an Incoming Call Reply (ICRP) from the LNS indicating whether or not the call session will be allowed to be established.

If the GoodICRP event is received, indicating that an ICRP was received from the LNS and that the LNS has accepted the session, the state machine is transitioned toward the ESTABLISHED state through the Send ICCN actions.

If the BadICRP event is received, indicating that an ICRP was received from the LNS and that the session was not acceptable, the state machine is transitioned toward the IDLE state through the Send CDN actions. If the state machine receives either a LocalClose or a HangupDetect event while in this state the state machine is also transitioned toward the IDLE state through the Send CDN actions.

If a CDN is received from the LNS for a session while the state machine is in the Wait_Reply state, the state machine is transitioned toward the IDLE state, passing through the Cleanup actions.

Send ICCN Actions: The purpose of the Send ICCN actions is to send an Incoming Call Connected (ICCN) message to the LNS after the state machine has received a good ICRP from the LNS and the state machine is going into the ESTABLISHED state. The full format for the ICCN is given in section 6.8 of RFCl2tp.

The sending of the ICCN by the LAC completes the three-way handshake (ICRQ, ICRP, ICCN) used to establish incoming call sessions within a tunnel. In the case where LCP negotiation was done between the LAC and the remote system before the data session was established with the LNS, the LCP information for the LAC remote system negotiation should be passed on to the LNS in the ICCN. See the "LCP Considerations" section later in the chapter for details on how LCP should be handled by both the LAC and the LNS in incoming call sessions.

The ESTABLISHED State: Once the LAC incoming call state machine has reached the ESTABLISHED state the call is established and the LAC simply forwards PPP data received from the remote system over the tunnel to the LNS, and PPP data from the LNS in the tunnel to the remote system.

While in the ESTABLISHED state the LAC state machine may receive SLI messages from the LNS. These messages are indicated by an RcvSLI event. When this event occurs the state machine stays in the ESTABLISHED state, but the SLI is parsed and information from the SLI is used to set physical parameters for the connection between the LAC and the remote system. The only information specified in RFCl2tp to be included in the SLI is the receive and send ACCM values for an Asynchronous HDLC connection.

Any of the events associated with RcvCDN, LocalClose, or HangupDetect can transition the state machine out of the ESTAB-LISHED state. When the RcvCDN event is received, the state machine is transitioned toward the IDLE state through both the Hang-up actions and the Cleanup actions. When a LocalClose event is encoun-tered while the state machine is in the ESTABLISHED state, the state machine is transitioned toward the IDLE state through the Hang-up actions and then the Send CDN actions, so that the LNS can be informed of the call going away. In the case of a HangupDetect event, the state machine again transitions toward the IDLE state, but this time it goes directly to the Send CDN actions.

Set Link Parameters Actions: These actions are taken when an SLI message is received from the LNS while the LAC incoming call state machine is in the ESTABLISHED state. The purpose of the SLI message is to pass PPP-negotiated physical link parameters from the LNS to the LAC so that the LAC can set the appropriate parameters on the con-nection between it and the remote system. In RFCl2tp the only infor-mation conveyed in the SLI is the Receive and Send ACCM for the physical connection between the LAC and the remote system when the physical connection is an AHDLC connection. The sending of such information is necessary any time the ACCM values need to change. Generally the completion or initiation of an LCP negotiation between the LNS and remote system causes the SLI to be sent.

The state machine remains in the ESTABLISHED state while these actions are being performed. If the information found in the SLI is not appropriate (for example, Send/Receive ACCM is indicated for a non-AHDLC connection) they are to be ignored.

Send CDN Actions: The Send CDN actions are entered when the LAC has decided to tear down the session, and the LNS must be informed of this state of affairs. The actions taken involve sending a CDN to the LNS indicating the reason that the session is being torn down. Section 6.12 of RFCl2tp gives the AVPs found in the CDN.

Hang-up Actions: The exact actions performed in the Hang-up actions depend on the implementation and media used. The purpose of these actions is for the state machine to indicate that the connection between the LAC and the remote system is to be broken.

Cleanup Actions: The Cleanup actions are entered in all cases before the state machine transitions back into the IDLE state. The purpose of these actions is to clean up any resources used by the session (and call) that are not needed while the state machine is in the IDLE state. The exact amount of cleanup done while the state machine is in this state depends to a great extent on the implementation.

8.1.2 Incoming Call LNS State Machine

Figure 8-2 shows the state machine used by the LNS for an incoming call session. The following events are part of this state machine:

- *GoodICRQ*. This event occurs when an Incoming Call Request (ICRQ) is received from the LAC and the session is acceptable. The judgment of what is acceptable to the LNS depends on the implementation. (Some examples may be whether or not the maximum allowed number of connections has been reached on the LNS, whether or not the LNS is willing to accept calls of a given bearer type, and so forth.)

- *BadICCRQ*. This event occurs when an ICRQ is received from the LAC that is not acceptable. See the discussion of GoodICRQ under "Wait_Reply State" for examples of the criteria for acceptable ICRQ messages.

- *GoodICCN*. This event occurs when an Incoming Call Connected (ICCN) message is received from the LAC and the LNS determines that the data session is acceptable. Again, the criteria for determining an acceptable ICCN depend on the implementation. Because the ICCN may contain information

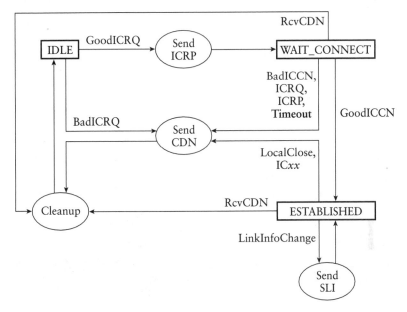

Figure 8-2 *LNS incoming call state machine*

regarding LCP negotiation between the LAC and the remote system, this information may be used by the LNS to determine whether or not the ICCN is acceptable.

- *BadICCN.* A BadICCN event indicates that an ICCN message was received from the LAC that was not acceptable to the LNS. Refer to the discussion of GoodICCN.
- *RcvCDN.* A RcvCDN event is received when a CDN message is received by the LNS for a given session.
- *LocalClose.* This event indicates that some entity external to the state machine is initiating a teardown of the session.
- *LinkInfoChange.* This event indicates that the LNS has detected that some physical characteristics of the link between the LAC and the remote system need to be changed.
- *ICRQ.* The ICRQ event simply indicates that an ICRQ has been received.
- *ICRP.* The ICRP event simply indicates that an ICRP has been received.

- *ICxx*. The IC*xx* event indicates that any one of an ICRQ, ICRP, or ICCN has been received.
- *Timeout*. A Timeout event indicates that a timer has expired. This event is a suggestion and not present in the RFCl2tp text or LNS incoming call state machine.

The IDLE State: The initial state of the LNS incoming call state machine is the IDLE state. Depending on the implementation, this state may represent an actual instantiation of L2TP session data structures or it may be a figurative state for pre-instantiated L2TP sessions. Most dynamic situations have sessions for incoming calls created as the result of the LNS having received an ICRQ.

Send ICRP Actions: The Send ICRP actions are encountered when an Incoming Call Reply (ICRP) is to be sent by the LNS. These actions are reached when the LNS receives an ICRQ from the LAC and LNS find the data session to be acceptable. The criteria for such acceptance depends on the implementation, but they may rely on factors such as whether or not the LNS has reached a condition where its resources have been fully allocated (memory, bandwidth, and so forth). The Send ICRP actions then transition the state machine into the Wait_Connect state.

It would also be useful to set a timer after sending the ICRP. The timer value should be very large compared to the retransmission interval being used. The purpose of the timer is to detect problems with LAC implementations that may have received the ICRP but not done anything with it. Setting a timer is a proactive step that can be taken so that a data session can operate well in the case of a bug existing in the peer implementation.

The Wait_Connect State: The purpose of the Wait_Connect state in the state machine is for the LNS to wait for an Incoming Call Connected (ICCN) message from the LAC. If a good ICCN is received from the LAC while the LNS is in this state, the tunnel is transitioned into the ESTABLISHED state. If a bad ICCN is received from the LAC while the LNS is in this state, the tunnel is transitioned toward the IDLE state through the Send CDN actions. If a CDN is received while the LNS is in this state, the machine transitions toward the IDLE state through the Cleanup actions.

The ESTABLISHED State: While in the ESTABLISHED state for a data session, the LNS tunnels a PPP session between a local instance of PPP and the LAC. During the lifetime of the tunneled PPP session it may become necessary for the LNS to inform the LAC of changes in the physical link characteristics between the LAC and the remote system based on PPP negotiation performed by the PPP implementation on the LNS. In this case a LinkInfoChange event is received by the state machine, prompting the Send SLI actions to be taken. When this happens the LNS state machine remains in the ESTABLISHED state. All other events in the ESTABLISHED state cause the state machine to transition out of the ESTABLISHED state and into a mode where the session is to be torn down.

The LNS reaches the ESTABLISHED state when an ICCN is received from the LAC that is acceptable to the LNS. The criteria for what makes an ICCN acceptable to an LNS depend on the implementation. One possibility is that the LNS looks at the negotiated LCP information between the LAC and the remote system (perhaps including proxy authentication information), which may be present in the ICCN, and makes a decision based on that. Note that it is not necessary for the LNS to reject a session based on negotiated LCP parameters between the LAC and the remote system that the LNS does not agree with, since the LNS may simply renegotiate LCP between itself and the remote system after the data session has been established. There is a common bug in some LNS implementations when it comes to LCP renegotiations done after completion of authentication—the connection tends to be terminated. Therefore it is strongly recommended that LNS implementations avoid LCP renegotiations after full authentication (note that this does not include LCP renegotiations in the middle of authentication, which is not a problem).

Send SLI Actions: The Send SLI actions are taken as a result of the LinkInfoChange event occurring while the LNS is in the ESTABLISHED state. These actions send an SLI to the LAC including physical link information to be used between the LAC and the remote system.

The SLI message is defined in RFCl2tp to contain only the ACCM AVP. For AHDLC, the ACCM AVP contains the receive and transmit Asynchronous Control Character Map (ACCM) values to be used on the physical link between the LAC and the remote system. For non-AHDLC connections between the LAC and the remote system, the SLI with ACCM values does not need to be sent since the ACCM is not applicable. If the SLI is sent with ACCM for non-AHDLC connections, the LAC should ignore it anyway.

Send CDN Actions: The LNS state machine gets to take Send CDN actions when the data session is to be disconnected by the LNS. After these actions are completed the state machine moves on to the Cleanup actions. Reasons for performing these actions are BadICRQ from the IDLE state, BadICCN from the Wait_Connect state, and LocalClose from the ESTABLISHED state.

Cleanup Actions: The Cleanup actions are entered in all cases before the LNS state machine transitions back into the IDLE state. The purpose of these actions is to clean up any resources used by the session that are not needed while the session is in the IDLE state. The exact amount of cleanup done while the state machine is in this state depends to a great degree on the implementation.

8.2 Outgoing Calls

An outgoing call is a construct whereby an LNS can signal an LAC to initiate a connection to a remote system PPP. Among other applications, an outgoing call can be used when the LNS wants to initiate a PPP callback to a peer.

Although the L2TP outgoing call uses three messages, these three messages do not create a three-way handshake as they do in the case of an incoming call. For an outgoing call, the initiation is done via an Outgoing Call Request (OCRQ) from an LNS to an LAC. The second message is the Outgoing Call Reply (OCRP) sent by the LAC to the LNS to indicate that the LAC will attempt to make the outgoing call to the remote PPP. The third message, again sent from the LAC to the LNS, is the Outgoing Call Connected (OCCN) message, which indicates that the call to the remote PPP peer has been established.

8.2.1 Outgoing Call LNS State Machine

The LNS state machine for outgoing calls is shown in Figure 8-3. If a successful connection is established, the state machine starts in the IDLE state, moves to the Wait_Reply state (possibly after going through the Wait_Tunnel state), the Wait_Connect state, and then to the ESTABLISHED state. Following are the events that transition the state machine:

- *LocalOpen.* The LocalOpen event is an indication for the LNS to bring up a data session to an LAC and for the LAC to establish an outgoing call to a remote system.
- *TunnelEstablished.* This event occurs when the state machine is in the Wait_Tunnel state waiting for the tunnel establishment to

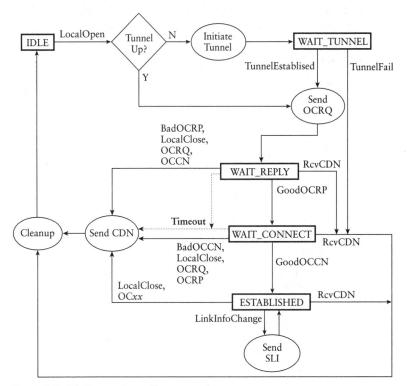

Figure 8-3 *LNS outgoing call state machine*

either fail or succeed. The TunnelEstablished event indicates that the tunnel establishment was successful.

- *TunnelFail.* This event occurs when the state machine is in the Wait_Tunnel state waiting for the tunnel establishment to either fail or succeed. The TunnelFail event indicates that the tunnel establishment was not successful.

- *GoodOCRP.* The GoodOCRP event occurs when the LNS receives an Outgoing Call Reply (OCRP) message from the LAC indicating that call establishment is continuing, and the LNS has no problems with any AVP values present in the OCRP.

- *BadOCRP.* The BadOCRP event indicates that the LNS has received an OCRP from the LAC that is not acceptable for some reason. The OCRP may be unacceptable because it contains an unrecognized mandatory AVP (that is, AVP with the M Bit set), or because the LNS may check the Session ID that the LAC has assigned and find another session in the same tunnel with the same Session ID assigned by the peer.

- *GoodOCCN.* This event indicates that an OCCN was received and the LNS determined that all values in the OCCN were acceptable.

- *BadOCCN.* This event is an indication that an unacceptable OCCN was received. This can happen, for example, in the case of the LNS receiving an unrecognized mandatory AVP.

- *RcvCDN.* The RcvCDN event indicates that the LNS has received a CDN from the LAC.

- *LocalClose.* The LocalClose event indicates that some entity outside of the state machine has requested that the call be torn down.

- *LinkInfoChange.* This event indicates that some LCP-negotiated option may have changed the connection settings for the connection between the LAC and the called PPP (remote system).

- *OCRQ.* This indicates that an OCRQ has been received.

- *OCRP.* This indicates that an OCRP has been received.

- *OCCN.* This indicates that an OCCN has been received.

- *OCxx.* This indicates that one of an OCRQ, OCRP, or OCCN has been received.

- *Timeout.* The Timeout event indicates that a timer has expired. This event is a suggestion and not present in the RFCl2tp text or LNS outgoing call state machine.

The IDLE State: The LNS outgoing call state machine begins in the IDLE state. An outgoing call has not yet been started. When an outgoing call session needs to be started, a LocalOpen event is generated to the state machine, and the state machine operation begins with the Tunnel Up? predicate.

The Tunnel Up? Predicate: The Tunnel Up? predicate is used to determine if the tunnel to the LAC needed for this outgoing call session has already been established. The mechanism by which an implementation detects that a tunnel is already established is specific to the implementation. The predicate evaluates to Yes (Y) if a tunnel has already been established. The predicate evaluates to No (N) if there is not already a tunnel established.

Initiate Tunnel Actions: These actions are taken if a tunnel has to be established before the outgoing call session can be initiated. Looking back at Chapter 5, Figure 5-1, the required action is for a Local-Open-Req event to be given to the tunnel state machine when it is in the IDLE state.

The Wait_Tunnel State: The purpose of the Wait_Tunnel state is for the state machine to wait for tunnel establishment to succeed or fail. If the tunnel establishment fails, then the resources for the session thus allocated can be cleaned up and the state machine enters the IDLE state. If the tunnel is successfully established, a TunnelEstablished event is generated and the state machine can move on to the Send OCRQ actions.

Send OCRQ Actions: The Send OCRQ actions come into play when there is a tunnel within which the session is to be established. The actions involve sending an OCRQ to the LAC. The Session ID field of the control header for the OCRQ is set to 0, since the LAC has not had a chance to assign the Session ID for the call yet. All subsequent Outgoing Call messages (that is, OCRP, OCCN) have a nonzero Session ID field in the control header.

In general, the important information in the OCRQ is the bearer and framing type for the call as well as the information needed by the LAC so that it can place the call to the desired target.

Once the OCRQ has been sent, the state machine transitions into the Wait_Reply state.

It would also be useful to set a timer after sending the OCRP. The timer value should be very large compared to the retransmission interval being used. The purpose of using a timer is to detect problems with LAC implementations that may have received the OCRP but not done anything with it. Setting a timer is a proactive step that can be taken to ensure that the connection operates well in the case of a bug existing in the peer implementation.

The Wait_Reply State: The Wait_Reply state is where the state machine waits for an OCRP before session establishment can proceed. If an unacceptable OCRP is received, the state machine is transitioned toward the IDLE state through the Send CDN actions. If an acceptable OCRP is received, the state machine is transitioned to the Wait_Connect state to wait for an OCCN message to complete outgoing call establishment.

The reception of the OCRP indicates that the LAC has accepted the responsibility to place the outgoing call and is attempting the call. It isn't until an OCCN is received that an outgoing call session can be considered established by the LNS.

If a CDN is received while the state machine is in the Wait_Reply state, it indicates that the LAC did not accept the responsibility to place the outgoing call. In this case the state machine is transitioned toward the IDLE state through the Cleanup actions.

It would also be useful to reset a timer after receiving the GoodOCRP event while the state machine is in the Wait_Reply state. The timer value should be very large compared to the retransmission interval being used. The purpose of the timer is to detect problems with LAC implementations that may not be sending the OCCN. Setting a timer is a proactive step that can be taken to help ensure that a connection operates well in the case of a bug existing in the peer implementation.

The Wait_Connect State: The LNS state machine waits in the Wait_Connect state for an OCCN message from the LAC. If the state machine receives an acceptable OCCN, a GoodOCCN event is generated while the state machine is in the Wait_Connect state and the state machine is transitioned to the ESTABLISHED state. If the LNS state machine receives an unacceptable OCCN from the LAC, a BadOCCN event is generated and the state machine heads toward the Send CDN actions to start the transition back into the IDLE state.

If the LAC was unable to make the outgoing connection on behalf of the LNS, the LNS state machine will receive a CDN. In this case the state machine is transitioned toward the IDLE state through the Cleanup actions.

The ESTABLISHED State: The ESTABLISHED state for the LNS outgoing call state machine is similar to the ESTABLISHED state for the LNS incoming call state machine. Once this state is reached the LNS forwards PPP data back and forth between itself and the remote system.

The LinkInfoChange event indicates that some LCP-negotiated option that affects the configuration of the physical connection may have changed and this change needs to be communicated to the LAC. In this case the state machine remains in the ESTABLISHED state but it sends an SLI message to the LAC with the required information.

The ESTABLISHED state is only terminated when the session is going to be torn down. This can happen because the LNS state machine received either a CDN or a LocalClose event. The ESTABLISHED state can also be exited if an unexpected event occurs (that is, the state machine receives an OCRQ, ORCP, or OCCN).

Send SLI Actions: The Send SLI actions are invoked when the LNS state machine is in the ESTABLISHED state and some link-specific LCP-negotiated option changes that requires the LAC set characteristics on the connection between the LAC and the remote system. See the "LCP Considerations" section later in the chapter for more information regarding the proper use of the SLI message.

Send CDN Actions: These actions are taken when the LNS has decided that an outgoing call session is being torn down and the LAC needs to be notified. A CDN is sent to the LAC and the state machine moves on to the Cleanup actions.

Cleanup Actions: The Cleanup actions are pretty much the same actions that occur in all the other state machines. The purpose of the actions is to clean up any resources used by a particular outgoing call session that will not be needed once the state machine returns to the IDLE state.

8.2.2 Outgoing Call LAC State Machine

The LAC state machine is started when it receives an OCRQ message. The LAC decides if the session can be initiated and sends an OCRP if it can. The LAC then attempts to place the outgoing call and sends an OCCN to the LNS once the call is successfully established. Note that in the case of an outgoing call there is no way by which LCP negotiation can be done between the LAC and the remote system because there is no mechanism to inform the LNS of such negotiations. Figure 8-4 shows the LAC outgoing call state machine.

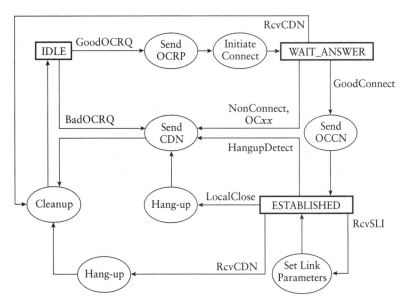

Figure 8-4 *LAC outgoing call state machine*

Following are the actions found in this state machine:

- *GoodOCRQ*. This event is given to the LAC state machine when an OCRQ is received from an LNS and it is determined that the outgoing call can be attempted. The decision to attempt a call is based on the dialing information found in the OCRQ as well as local policy regarding the allowance of outgoing calls.
- *BadOCRQ*. This event occurs when the LAC receives an OCRQ from an LNS and the outgoing call cannot be attempted. This typically will happen either because the dialing information in the OCRQ is invalid or because there is some policy restricting the initiating of outgoing calls at the LAC.
- *GoodConnect*. The GoodConnect event occurs when the outgoing call placed by the LAC is connected and the LAC detects that it can send and receive PPP frames on the connection.
- *NonConnect*. The NonConnect event is given to the LAC state machine either because the outgoing call could not be connected at all or else the call was connected but the framing could not be synchronized over the connection.
- *HangupDetect*. This event occurs when the LAC detects that a connection between the LAC and the remote system has been broken.
- *LocalClose*. The LocalClose event occurs when some entity outside of the state machine requests that the call be torn down.
- *RcvCDN*. When the LAC receives a CDN from the LNS, the RcvCDN event is triggered in the LAC state machine.
- *RcvSLI*. When the LAC receives an SLI from the LNS, the RcvSLI event occurs in the state machine.
- *OCxx*. This event indicates that either an OCRQ, OCRP, or OCCN has been received.

The IDLE State: When the LAC state machine is in the IDLE state it means that an outgoing call on the LAC has not yet been started. When the LAC state machine receives an OCRQ from the LNS, the LAC state machine actions are set in motion, depending on whether a GoodOCRQ or BadOCRQ event is generated.

Send OCRP Actions: These actions occur when the LAC has accepted the OCRQ from the LNS and will be attempting to initiate the outgoing call on behalf of the LNS. The information conveyed in an OCRP is minimal; essentially the LAC is simply acknowledging that it will be attempting to place the outgoing call.

Initiate Connect Actions: The Initiate Connect actions involve placing the outgoing call. The manner in which these actions are carried out is specific to the type of connection being made. Communication between the LAC state machine and the other functional components in order to have the call placed depend to a great degree on the implementation.

After initiating the connection, the LAC state machine enters the Wait_Answer state to wait for the outgoing call to either succeed or fail. The outgoing call is considered to be successful when PPP frames can be transferred over the call.

The Wait_Answer State: The purpose of the Wait_Answer state is for the LAC state machine to wait for an initiated outgoing call either to be successfully connected or to fail. If the connection fails, the NonConnect event is generated and the state machine moves on to the Send CDN actions. If the connection is successful, the state machine moves on to the Send OCCN actions so that the LNS can be notified that the outgoing call was successful.

Send OCCN Actions: Send OCCN actions are taken when an OCCN is to be sent to the LNS to indicate that the outgoing call made on behalf of the LNS was successful. The general contents of the OCCN are AVPs that give the final physical connection characteristics. It is notable that unlike the ICCN, the OCCN does not contain any LCP information. It is not within the construct of the outgoing call for LCP to be negotiated between the LAC and the remote system. See the "LCP Considerations" section later in this chapter for more information on the treatment of LCP options for both incoming and outgoing calls.

The ESTABLISHED State: The ESTABLISHED state of the LAC outgoing call state machine is essentially the same as that of the incoming call state machine. The state machine remains in the ESTABLISHED state until it is time for the session to be torn down. If the peer tears down the session, the LAC state machine is notified by a CDN. If the session is torn down locally owing to loss of connection between the LAC and the remote system or owing to some other local action, then a CDN is sent and the call is cleaned up.

If an SLI is received while the LAC state machine is in the ESTAB-LISHED state, then information from the SLI is used to set physical connection characteristics for the connection between the LAC and the remote system if applicable.

Set Link Parameters Actions: The purpose of the Set Link Parameters actions is to establish connection characteristics communicated by the LNS in the SLI to the connection between the LAC and the remote system. RFCl2tp only specifies the ACCM to be present in the SLI message for AHDLC connections.

Send CDN Actions: These actions are entered when a CDN needs to be sent to the LNS. After the CDN is sent, the Cleanup actions are taken and the state machine reenters the IDLE state.

Hang-up Actions: The purpose of the Hang-up actions is to disconnect the outgoing call that has already been placed. The details of how this connection is broken depends on both the type of connection made and on the implementation's method for handling such connections.

Cleanup Actions: The Cleanup actions are taken to prepare the LAC state machine to be returned to the IDLE state. Any resources that a particular session does not need while in the IDLE state can be reclaimed. For some implementations this can mean that the entire session is removed, representing a figurative return to the IDLE state. An implementation should have a policy (or potentially a configuration) for what to do to the tunnel when the last session is brought down (see the "Tunnel Teardown" section at the end of this chapter).

8.3 LCP Considerations

As we learned in Chapter 2, PPP can be described as consisting of three sublayers: a media-dependent sublayer, a services sublayer (consisting of, for example, compression and encryption), and a multiplex sub-layer responsible for configuring and passing traffic between PPP and various layer 3 protocols. It was further explained that the LAC retains some of the media-dependent responsibilities of PPP operation during the life of the PPP session.

The handling of LCP options must be considered carefully both by LAC implementations and by LNS implementations so that a successful and transparent tunneling service to remote system PPP sessions can be provided. There are several LCP options that must be treated carefully by the LAC and LNS because these options affect media-dependent behavior over the physical connection between the LAC and the remote system, but these options may also be negotiated in LCP between the LNS and the remote system. These options are

- Asynchronous Control Character Map (ACCM)
- FCS Alternative
- HDLC Address and Control Field Compression (ACFC)
- Maximum Receive Unit (MRU)
- Multilink Endpoint Discriminator (ED)
- Quality Protocol
- Protocol Field Compression (PFC)
- Self-Describing Pad (SDP)
- Numbered Mode
- Multilink Procedure
- Compound Frames
- Link Discriminator

There are three general scenarios regarding LCP negotiation between the remote system and the LAC and the remote system and the LNS. Each of these scenarios requires separate consideration.

In the first scenario LCP negotiation between the remote system PPP and the LAC occurs and the LCP information is passed on to the LNS when the session is established. The only possible instance of this is an incoming call session with LCP information passed between the LAC and the LNS as part of the ICCN message. This scenario will be referred to as *proxy LCP*.

In the second scenario LCP negotiation does not occur between the remote system and the LAC at all. This is the usual way that outgoing calls are handled, but incoming calls can also be handled this way when the LAC is able to pick the LNS to tunnel to based on information external to PPP (for example, DNIS).

In the third scenario LCP negotiation between the remote system and the LAC occurs and the LCP information is not passed on to the LNS when the session is established. This mode of operation is not recommended since the LNS is guaranteed to have to renegotiate LCP with the remote system in this case, and there is no way for the LNS to avoid attempting to negotiate options that are inconsistent with options previously negotiated by the LAC. This scenario will be referred to as *blind proxy LCP* because the LNS is blind to the LCP negotiated between the LAC and the remote system.

8.3.1 LAC Frame Inspection and Negotiation/Translation

RFCl2tp does not specify that the LAC do any more than blindly forward PPP frames between the LNS and the remote system once the data session is established. At the same time, there is no specification dictating that the LAC cannot be more active and inspect frames transiting between the LNS and the remote system, perhaps injecting, dropping, or modifying PPP frames in the process. In fact, such functions can be used to isolate the LNS from the details of the physical connection between the LAC and remote system. Also, if connections between the LAC and remote system other than HDLC are to be supported, at least some simple inspection and processing must be done by the LAC.

Because the LNS assumes operation of HDLC and includes HDLC framing bytes in at least the LCP frames (and in all frames if ACFC is not negotiated), the LAC has to translate between this framing and whatever framing is appropriate for the connection to the remote system if it is non-HDLC. Figure 8-5 shows a tunneled PPP frame sent from the LNS to the LAC and the PPP frame as it is sent between the LAC and the remote system.

To truly keep the details of the connection between the LAC and remote system transparent to the LNS, the LAC can translate LCP negotiation between the LNS and the remote system. Figure 8-6 shows where such a scenario would be useful.

RFC 2364 specifies the operation of PPP over ATM AAL5 and prohibits the negotiation of ACCM and ACFC (as well as FCS Alternative, which is not present in the example of Figure 8-6). Figure 8-6 shows a simple LCP negotiation in one direction between the LNS and

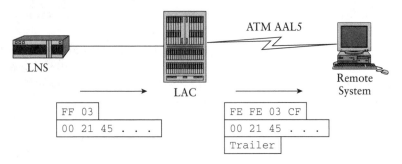

Figure 8-5 *Framing translation between L2TP and ATM AAL5*

the remote system. The LNS, not aware of the restrictions that apply to the connection between the LAC and remote system, requests an ACCM, a CHAP authentication, and an ACFC. When the LAC receives this tunneled PPP frame it checks the PPP protocol field to check for LCP in case LAC needs to translate the frame. In this case the LAC sees that the frame is an LCP frame and that it is a CONFREQ that contains two options that are not appropriate to the remote system. The LAC then decides to keep state as to what options were originally in the CONFREQ but sends the CONFREQ along with the ACCM and ACFC options removed. The remote system then receives a CONFREQ with just the CHAP authentication option present. Figure 8-6 shows the remote system then sending an LCP CONFACK of CHAP authentication. In this direction the LAC has to recognize that the original options have to be restored into the CONFACK before it is forwarded to the LNS. The example shows that in addition to mapping the framing back to HDLC framing, the ACCM and ACFC are inserted into the CONFACK in their original positions, and this information is forwarded back to the LNS.

Figure 8-7 shows how the same negotiation would occur between the LNS and the remote system if the LAC were not translating the LCP negotiation.

Note the difference in the result of the negotiations shown in Figures 8-6 and 8-7. First, the negotiation of Figure 8-7 took longer because two exchanges were necessary instead of one. Also the results were different. The difference in the result in the case of ACCM in this example is inconsequential since the LNS doesn't do any framing and

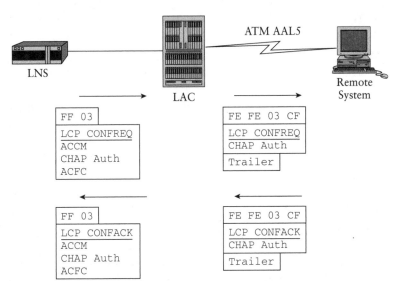

Figure 8-6 *An example of negotiation/translation with CONFREQ/CONFACK exchange*

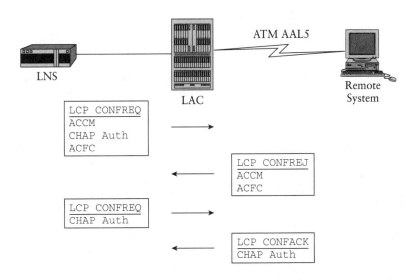

Figure 8-7 *An LCP negotiation between LNS and the remote system with no LAC translation*

the LAC doesn't use ACCM for this type of connection. The difference in the result of ACFC does have some impact, however. In Figure 8-7 the LNS will have to prepend all PPP frames with two bytes of HDLC framing when tunneling to the LAC. In Figure 8-6 the LNS can leave off the two bytes of HDLC framing for non-LCP frames tunneled to the LAC (but the LAC will still include the proper framing when forwarding these frames to the remote system).

The following subsections examine each of the special LCP configuration options and describe the treatment implications of each. Note that the future may bring more LCP options that need special treatment. These subsections also include information on how LAC frame inspection can be used in relation to these LCP configuration options to improve transparent tunneling, as well as how the option should be handled assuming no LAC inspection (since the LCP doesn't know if LAC translation is occurring or not) and a subsection on how translation at that LAC can improve handling of the option.

Asynchronous Control Character Map: The Asynchronous Control Character Map (ACCM) LCP option is found in RFC1662, "PPP in HDLC-like Framing." Over Asynchronous HDLC (AHDLC) links characters may be escaped so that characters used for control over the physical connection do not get interpreted as actual PPP data. Both ends of the connection have a transmit ACCM and a receive ACCM. An ACCM is a bit mask with each numbered bit corresponding to an ASCII value. The least significant bit of the least significant octet is bit number 0 and corresponds to an octet of value 0. As octets are transmitted on an AHDLC link, each octet is checked against the transmit ACCM, and if the corresponding bit is set, then the octet is escaped before being transmitted. As octets are received on an AHDLC link each octet is compared against the receive ACCM, and if the corresponding bit is set, then the octet is dropped (since the transmitter on the other end should have escaped the octet if it was a valid octet) and processing continues for the next octet. Each end can negotiate the value of its 32-bit receive ACCM. The default receive ACCM and default least significant 32 bits of the transmit ACCM are all bits set to 1 (32-bit unsigned value 0xFFFFFFFF). For non-AHDLC connections there is no ACCM handling, and receive ACCM LCP option negotiation is not performed.

In L2TP the LAC maintains the receive ACCM and transmit ACCM and performs octet escaping and unescaping between the LAC and the remote system if the connection is an AHDLC connection. If the connection between the LAC and the remote system is not AHDLC, then ACCM and octet escaping are not used.

The problem created by ACCM negotiation is that the LNS needs to decide what value for receive ACCM it should request and accept and what values for the peer's receive ACCM the LNS should accept if the LNS needs to perform any LCP negotiation with the remote system. There is also the further issue of communicating negotiated receive ACCM values to the LAC should the LNS negotiate LCP.

The L2TP SLI message is used to communicate ACCM changes to the LAC from the LNS. Any time the LNS believes the send or receive ACCM needs to change, it sends an SLI message with the ACCM AVP specifying the values that the LNS has to use on the call.

The proxy LCP scenario, in which the LAC negotiates LCP with the remote system and the LCP information is communicated to the LNS in the ICCN message, is the best scenario for optimal treatment of ACCM. In this case, the LNS learns what either end of the link negotiated for its receive ACCM. The LNS can then set its desired receive ACCM and its peer's acceptable receive ACCM to be the same values negotiated by the LAC with the remote system. This scenario would also cover the case where the ACCM was not negotiated. If a receive ACCM was not negotiated, then the LNS should set itself up not to allow negotiation of the receive ACCM for that direction. Then the LNS will be in a position to negotiate LCP to the same results with the remote system that the LAC initially negotiated with the remote system, if in fact LCP renegotiation is performed by the LNS.

The blind proxy LCP and non-LAC LCP cases are both equally unhelpful to the LNS in determining how it should negotiate receive ACCM LCP options between itself and the remote system. In these cases the implementation can decide how it wants to default behavior. On one end of the spectrum the least optimal but safest method is to use 0xFFFFFFFF ACCMs in each direction, although there are probably no circumstances where this is necessary. Instead it is common practice to default to receive ACCM values where only the ASCII XON (0x11) and XOFF (0x13) characters are set (ACCM = 0x000A0000) to allow for the operation of connections using software flow control. Also an LNS could use the ACCM values that the remote system is negotiating as a hint for what to negotiate. Unfortunately this method results in tying together the two directions of negotiation, complicating the LCP logic, but this option allows for correct operation of data sessions over links such as PPP over Telnet.

If the LNS is not given proxy LCP information by the LAC, the LNS should base its decision about whether to negotiate receive ACCM values at all on the framing type of the call. The framing type is communicated to the LNS from the LAC using the Framing Type AVP that must be present in the ICCN and OCCN messages. In RFCl2tp the framing type is specified as either asynchronous or synchronous. If the framing type for a call is asynchronous, the connection type is AHDLC, and LNS may negotiate ACCM.

It is recommended that proxy LCP information should take precedence over decisions made based on call framing type should there be a discrepancy (that is, the framing type is not asynchronous but the proxy LCP in ICCN specifies that ACCM was negotiated in one or both directions).

The nature of the ACCM is really such that only the LAC should be deciding what acceptable values are. By inspecting frames between the LNS and remote system and translating LCP negotiations, the LAC can conduct a negotiation of the ACCM values that it wants for the connection to the remote system. This process may involve injecting frames into the negotiation. For example, sending a CONFNAK to a remote system for an ACCM value that the LAC wants the remote system to request. If the LAC is performing such actions for the ACCM, then the ACCM values in the SLI message received from the LNS can simply be ignored.

Another good reason for the LAC to be proactive where ACCM is involved is so that the ACCM values used by the LAC are known when they should be. If the LAC is learning ACCM values from the SLI messages sent by the LNS, the SLI messages may lag when the ACCM transition should actually be made. This can result in needlessly dropped frames.

Frame Check Sequence Alternative: The FCS Alternative is defined among the extensions found in RFC1570, "PPP LCP Extensions." The FCS Alternative LCP option allows a different FCS to be negotiated for use with non-LCP frames. (Initial LCP frames have the default FCS, and LCP frames in renegotiations have both the default and previously negotiated alternative FCS included.)

The negotiation and use of FCS Alternative with tunneled PPP sessions is essentially nonfunctional for a number of reasons. To properly handle this option would require additions to the L2TP protocol as specified in RFCl2tp. The first problem is that unlike with ACCM, there is no mechanism for communicating a negotiated FCS alternative between the LNS and the remote system to the LAC. Such communication could be arranged in a fashion similar to that used for ACCM, through the creation of a new FCS Alternative AVP that could be included in the SLI message sent from the LNS to the LAC, but no such construct yet exists in RFCl2tp.

In addition there is also the problem that the FCS Alternative is to be applied selectively to traffic depending on whether PPP is in the LCP negotiation phase. Again, the correct application of FCS Alternative could be accomplished by communicating the transitions into and out of LCP negotiation phase to the LAC from the LNS so that the correct FCS could be used if such a construct were added.

Because of these problems, in no case should the LNS negotiate the use of alternative FCS.

An NAS that only acts as an LAC and does not inspect/translate frames between the LNS and remote system should simply never negotiate the use of FCS Alternative. If an NAS device acts as a noninspecting/translating LAC that does proxy-LCP and also terminates legacy remote access connections, there are two choices:

1. Never negotiate FCS Alternative. That means that the use of FCS Alternative for the legacy remote access connections is precluded as well.

2. If FCS Alternative is negotiated and a connection is going to be tunneled, renegotiate LCP without FCS Alternative before beginning to tunnel to the LNS. By this means legacy remote access connections can use FCS Alternative, and tunneled PPP sessions, which are not able to use FCS Alternative, will not have to.

Although FCS Alternative cannot be made to work properly within the constructs of L2TP, an LAC performing inspection of frames can make FCS Alternative work easily. Of course, if the LAC is capable of also doing translation then it can make sure that any requests from the LNS for FCS Alternative do not reach the remote system, and LAC can also reject requests from the remote system for FCS Alternative.

If FCS Alternative is negotiated for the connection between the remote system and the LAC, then the LAC can simply inspect frames sent by the LNS to detect transitions into and out of the LCP negotiation phase (using LCP CONFREQs to detect entrance into LCP negotiation and LCP CONFACKs to detect exit from LCP negotiation).

Address and Control Field Compression: The use of Address and Control Field Compression (ACFC) is specified in RFC1661, "The Point-to-Point Protocol (PPP)." RFC1661 specifies that PPP frames be transmitted with address and control fields appropriate to the link layer of the connection. An ACFC LCP option is defined in order to negotiate the omission of address and control fields on PPP frames when possible. For LCP frames, however, address and control fields are required to be included, independent of whether ACFC was negotiated or not.

The use of ACFC is not permitted at all over some link layers. For example RFC1973, "PPP in Frame Relay," specifies that ACFC must not be negotiated for PPP connections running over frame relay. There is not enough information signaled from the LAC to the LNS indicating in general whether ACFC is permitted over the connection between the LAC and the remote system. But negotiation by a well-behaved LNS will result in proper ACFC configuration.

The overarching consideration regarding ACFC is that it is not fatal to request it. As long as the LNS treats ACFC as an option and not as a requirement, there should be no problem in asking for ACFC. This is true even in the case where the actual connection between the LAC and the remote system does not support ACFC (the remote system should send an LCP CONFREQ for the option if it does not support it).

An LNS should still try to avoid requesting options that are bound to get rejected. To this end, in the proxy LCP scenario, the LNS should use the information for the LCP negotiation between the LAC and remote system to decide its own ACFC policy.

The ACFC is interesting, because it affects both the PPP frames between the LNS and the LAC and the PPP frames between the LAC and the remote system. As shown in Figure 8-6, by performing translation the LAC can have ACFC negotiated from the LNS's point of view, even if ACFC is not allowed (or desired) for the connection between the LAC and remote system.

Negotiating ACFC can be useful even when HDLC is used but ACFC is allowed but not desired on the LAC–remote system connection. In this case the LAC can have the negotiations carried out from the point of view of the LNS include ACFC while the point of view of the remote system would not have ACFC. This results in saving two octets per non-LCP PPP frame within the L2TP tunnel for the session while still providing for non-ACFC operation on the LAC–remote system connection.

Maximum Receive Unit: Negotiation for the maximum receive unit (MRU) for each direction of a PPP connection is also defined in RFC1661, "The Point-to-Point Protocol (PPP)." An implementation can negotiate the maximum size of a PPP frame that it wishes to receive. The transmitter of the peer then conforms to the negotiated MRU.

With blind proxy LCP and non-LAC LCP, the LNS has no way of knowing what the MRU and maximum transmission unit (MTU) capabilities or preferred values are for the LAC. In these cases the LNS should either be preconfigured with this information or not negotiate MRU so that the default value of 1,500 will be used.

With proxy LCP the LNS should use the information from the LCP negotiation between the LAC and remote system to determine valid MRU values for each direction. It is recommended that in lieu of further configuration an LNS pick the lower of the MRU value negotiated by the LAC (1,500 if the LAC did not negotiate MRU) and the MRU value desired by the LNS. The decision should be made in a consistent manner for the allowed MRU negotiated with the remote system.

The proper handling of the MRU when the LAC is doing inspection/translation is trivial. The LAC can simply decrease the MRU value included in LCP CONFREQs sent by the LNS if the LAC cannot or does not want to handle the MRU requested by the LNS. Also if the LNS does not include the MRU option in the CONFREQ, the LAC could add it to the CONFREQ forwarded to the remote system in the case where the LAC would like to negotiate an MRU with a value less than 1,500 bytes.

There may also be limitations on the LAC's MTU. These limitations can be communicated to the LNS by requesting an MRU value for the remote system in a CONFREQ to the LNS.

Multilink Endpoint Discriminator: As part of the multilink PPP negotiation in LCP defined in RFC1990, "The PPP Multilink Protocol (MP)," negotiation of an endpoint discriminator (ED) is defined. The ED (if any) is used along with the authenticated peer name (if there is any) to uniquely identify an MP instance so that multiple PPP connections made to the same endpoint can be grouped together into one multilink "bundle." The handling of the ED option by the LNS will depend on the manner in which an LNS is being used in the multilink picture.

There are two ways to handle the Multilink ED at the LNS. The first method is to use an ED specific to the LNS to identify the PPP implementation instance in the LNS. The problem with this method is that if the remote system has already undergone LCP negotiation with the LAC and received the LAC multilink ED, the implementation may be disagreeable to the multilink ED value changing when the LNS renegotiates LCP (although technically this should not be a problem). Also a connection made to an LAC that advertises an ED different than the one advertised on previous links will likely cause the calling remote system to drop the connection as a mismatched link. The second method for handling Multilink ED in proxy LCP is to use the multilink ED used by the LAC. The problem with this method is that it requires the LAC (or a set of LACs) to present the same MP ED to the remote systems initially in order for MP to configure correctly.

Clearly if no LCP is done between the LAC and the remote system, the MP ED must be chosen by the LNS.

Blind LCP proxy is the worst case because the LAC may negotiate an MP ED with the remote system and then the LNS will renegotiate LCP with the remote system and likely put forth a different MP ED.

The LCP proxy case is the most versatile because the LNS can choose to inherit the MP ED previously presented by the LAC to the remote system. Here, if desired, the LNS does not change the value of the MP ED advertised to the remote system, and the connection will operate successfully if the LACs dialed by a remote system all present the same ED initially.

Unfortunately it is difficult to decide within the confines of L2TP signaling and inference about previously negotiated LCP values which MP ED value the LNS should use. The best strategy is likely to be free to choose to make this behavior configurable so that the LNS can work in different environments depending on the required behavior of the LNS in order for MP to configure correctly. It is even conceivable that there may be a policy defined on the LNS on a per LAC basis so that tunnels to a given LAC will have their own default behavior.

In the case of MP ED, LAC inspection/translation as thus far described is not that useful, because it is the LNS that is best able to correlate what MP ED should be used for its links. For example, an LNS may bring up an outgoing call session to an LAC to add a link into an existing bundle. In this case the LNS wants to present the same MP ED value to the remote system that it presented in the other links for the bundle. If the LAC then translates the MP ED into a value that the LAC thinks is correct, it will break this operation.

Going beyond the simple LAC inspection/translation that has been described so far, an LAC implementation could hide the details of MP operation from the LNS by tunneling a session for a bundle to the LNS instead of to each link individually. For this to work multiple NAS devices potentially would have to tunnel links to a single NAS operating as an LAC so that MP could be terminated at the NAS and the bundle tunneled to an LNS. Because the rules for negotiating LCP on MP bundles are different than the rules for LCP negotiation on ordinary PPP links, the LAC has to translate the LCP negotiations appropriately. Also the LAC may have to translate some of the other negotiations on the MP links onto the bundle. Authentication of links in the case of translating multilink is not straightforward. If PAP authentication is done initially, then the LAC can cache the PAP password and proxy the PAP authentication. If CHAP authentication is being done, then the LAC has to have access to the same authentication database that the LNS does, or LAC has to be otherwise configured with the correct password. Authentication on PPP multilink links should not be done on the multilink bundle; otherwise a link that fails authentication will cause the entire bundle to be torn down.

8.3.2 Proxy LCP

In the case of incoming calls, the LAC may negotiate LCP with the remote system before tunneling the PPP session through to the LNS. In this case, the ICCN message should contain information about the LCP negotiation between the LAC and the remote system. This information is used by the LNS both to learn the desired LCP media-dependent option values from the LAC, and also to skip LCP renegotiations with the remote system if all of the LCP negotiated options are agreeable to the LNS.

The ICCN can include the following optional AVPs:[1]

- Initial Received (by LAC) LCP CONFREQ
- Last Sent (by LAC) LCP CONFREQ
- Last Received (by LAC) LCP CONFREQ

The Initial Received LCP CONFREQ (IRREQ) informs the LNS about how the remote system started LCP negotiation. This information is especially useful when it is compared with the contents of the Last Received LCP CONFREQ (LRREQ). If the IRREQ contains LCP options that are not present in the LRREQ, it means that the options must have been removed by the remote system because a NAK or a REJ was received from the LAC PPP. If there are options such as these that the LNS PPP would not NAK or REJ, then the LNS PPP can make the decision as to whether the options are important enough to merit the LNS PPP's renegotiating LCP with the remote system so that the options in the IRREQ can be accepted.

The Last Sent LCP CONFREQ (LSREQ) indicates what the LAC PPP was able to negotiate with the remote system. The LNS PPP can learn a great deal from this AVP about what the LAC is able to support for media-dependent LCP options such as those described in the sec-

---

1. Note that the AVPs are defined to provide the CONFREQ form of the packets as opposed to the equivalent CONFACK messages. It is important to note that it is understood that the Last Sent LCP CONFREQ and Last Received LCP CONFREQ are not sent in the ICCN unless the associated LCP CONFACK messages were also exchanged between the PPP client and LAC.

tions above. For example, the lack of an ACCM in the LSREQ indicates that it is not mandatory for the connection between the LAC and the LNS that an ACCM be negotiated. It is also from the LSREQ than the LNS PPP learns information such as what MP ED or MRU value was negotiated by the LAC. Beyond the media-dependent options, the LNS PPP also should examine the other LCP options to determine if it wants to negotiate LCP with the remote system itself. For example, the lack of an authentication option or the presence of an authentication option that the LNS PPP does not accept should trigger the LNS PPP to negotiate LCP with the remote system itself.

The LRREQ contains the LCP options that the remote system negotiated with the LAC PPP. As noted above, the LRREQ can be used in combination with the IRREQ to determine what the LAC PPP did not find acceptable. For media-dependent options, the goal of the LNS PPP is to accept exactly the same media-dependent options that the LAC PPP did if LCP renegotiation ever occurs. For the media-dependent options present in the LRREQ, the LNS PPP should initialize its acceptable values for those options to the values found in the LRREQ. For any media-dependent options not present in the LRREQ, the LNS PPP should initialize to reject those options. From the non-media-dependent options in the LRREQ the LNS should learn through the negotiated values or through the lack of options what the preferences of the remote system are.

Clearly if any LCP options that the LNS does not support are present either in the LSREQ or the LRREQ, then the LNS PPP must renegotiate LCP with the remote system. Not doing so would be just as bad as acknowledging an unrecognized (or sending an unrecognized!) option during LCP negotiation. The LNS PPP can also decide to renegotiate LCP based on other criteria such as those noted earlier, based on MRU, for instance. Also since there is no such thing as an "Initial Sent LCP CONFREQ" AVP, the LNS PPP may decide to renegotiate if there is some option not present in the LSREQ that the LNS PPP deems important enough to attempt negotiation for. Also the LNS PPP doesn't know what option values were attempted by the LAC PPP that may have resulted in a NAK from the remote system. Because of this the LNS PPP can attempt to negotiate a different preferred value for an option found in the LSREQ.

8.4 Proxy Authentication

Another PPP shortcut similar to proxy LCP that can be used in the case of incoming calls is the use of proxy PPP authentication. This is achieved through the use of five optional AVPs in the ICCN during establishment of an incoming call. The purpose for including proxy authentication information during incoming call establishment is to provide an optimized connect path for the case where the LAC is using authentication information to establish the tunneled call. Because the LAC bases the decision of whether and where to tunnel a PPP session on the PPP authentication ID when using proxy authentication, half of the PPP authentication transaction has been done between the LAC PPP and the remote system already. If both the proxy LCP options in the ICCN are acceptable to the LNS (including the authentication type negotiated) and the LNS wishes to use the proxy authentication information, then the LNS PPP simply needs to send the requisite PPP authentication response in order to finish the authentication phase. In this case a single packet from the LNS PPP is all that is required in order to enter the network protocol phase, because the rest of the negotiation has been done by the LAC.

There are five optional AVPs in the ICCN related to proxy authentication:

- Proxy Authen Type
- Proxy Authen Name
- Proxy Authen Challenge
- Proxy Authen ID
- Proxy Authen Response

RFCl2tp specifies five values for the Proxy Authen Type AVP: Textual username/password, CHAP, PAP, None, and MSCHAP version 1. In order for any of the other proxy authentication AVPs to be present this AVP must be present in the ICCN and must have a value other than "None."

For proxy PAP authentication the Proxy Authen ID contains the Identifier value sent in the Authenticate Request from the remote system. The PAP UID is found in clear text in the Proxy Authen Name AVP, and the PAP password is found in clear text in the Proxy Authen Response AVP. Because the PAP UID and PAP password are in clear text in the proxy authen AVPs it is highly recommended that these AVPs be hidden when they are used with proxy authentication of PAP. Note that hiding does not account for the fact that the remote system may end up retransmitting the PAP Authenticate Request and this would be tunneled to the LNS by the LAC unhidden.

For proxy CHAP and MSCHAP version 1 authentication the same AVPs are used. The Proxy Authen ID contains the ID value sent by the LAC in the CHAP/MSCHAPv1 challenge. The Proxy Authen Challenge contains the challenge sent by the LAC in the CHAP/MSCHAPv1 challenge. The Proxy Authen Name and Proxy Authen Response contain the name and response value from the CHAP/MSCHAPv1 response sent back to the LAC PPP from the remote system.

The addition of MSCHAPv2 to the L2TP proxy authentication scheme would be trivial. The only required addition would be a new value for Proxy Authen Type reflecting MSCHAPv2. Although MSCHAPv2 specifies changes to the interpretation of the response and success messages, the overall packet format is the same as CHAP, and therefore all of the proxy authentication AVPs could be used the same way as with CHAP and MSCHAPv1.

Currently there is no support for proxy authentication of the Extensible Authentication Protocol (EAP) in L2TP. In order for the LNS to use EAP to the remote system, LCP renegotiation of EAP as the authentication type for the PPP session is required.

8.5 Comparing L2TP to L2F and PPTP

In comparing the call setup features of L2F and PPTP with those of L2TP there are several striking differences and also some resemblance. The call setup area is probably the clearest example of the best aspects of both L2F and PPTP being inherited by L2TP, with some L2TP-specific additions.

L2TP gets the concept of outgoing calls from PPTP, because there is no such construct as an outgoing call in L2F. This is probably the most striking difference between L2F and L2TP in call setup.

From a high level the state machines are reminiscent of the PPTP state machines as well. The incoming call in PPTP is also handled via a three-way handshake as is done in L2TP. For outgoing calls, however, PPTP has only a two-way handshake compared to the three-message OCRQ, OCRP, OCCN sequence in L2TP.

The L2TP SLI message is a direct descendant of the PPTP SLI message. Of course, in PPTP the ACCM is hard-coded in the form of fields in the SLI message instead of using the flexible AVP construct of L2TP. The absence of an SLI mechanism to set the ACCM in the L2F equivalent of the LAC is an important drawback in L2F unless the L2F implementation performs stateful inspection of LCP. Without the SLI construct, the LAC would not be informed of ACCM changes. Because LCP requires transmit ACCM values to go back to 0xFFFFFFFF, this means that L2F does not do the right thing with ACCM values based on negotiation between the remote system and the L2F equivalent of the LNS. Also if the remote system and LNS equivalent were to negotiate different ACCM values than the L2F NAS was using, then AHDLC communication would fail.

Although L2F lacks the SLI mechanism of PPTP and L2TP, it does have the same LCP proxy and authentication proxy mechanism bestowed to L2TP, which is absent in PPTP. This means that for PPTP tunnels the LNS-equivalent cannot be informed of the results of LCP negotiation between the LAC equivalent and the remote system or even be informed that LCP negotiation was done. In the best case this means that PPTP call setup for incoming calls cannot be optimized via the presence of proxy LCP and proxy authentication information. In the worst case this mode of operation causes connectivity problems because the LNS equivalent is not able to learn anything about the MP ED, MRU, ACCM, and so forth, negotiated by the LAC equivalent.

Of course, PPTP and L2F implementations equivalent to the L2TP LAC can both perform the inspection/translation logic we have discussed in terms of L2TP, and they can overcome the absence of proxy LCP information and ACCM mismatching.

8.6 Implementation Tips

8.6.1 Including Last-Sent LCP CONFREQ AVPs

When the LAC includes the Last-Sent LCP CONFREQ AVPs in the ICCN message it is important that the associated LCP CONFACKs were received from and sent to the remote system. The reason for this is that the LNS uses the values from these AVPs to infer valid configuration information about the physical connection between the LAC and the remote system.

8.6.2 Proxy CHAP Not Secure to LNS

It is important for an LNS implementation to recognize that using the proxy CHAP information without issuing its own challenge is not a secure mode of operation. The reason for this is because a malicious party operating as an LAC could provide the LNS with proxy CHAP information with a challenge previously sent by the LNS and a response previously sent by a remote system. If the LNS is not free to choose its own CHAP challenge value on every authentication attempt, it is possible that old authentication information could be used. Note that the attacker does not need to know the password to authenticate with the LNS; it just needs to know the contents of a previously successful authentication exchange.

An LNS implementation should use the proxy CHAP information for an incoming call only if trust between the LAC and LNS can otherwise be established.

8.6.3 Tunnel Teardown

Implementations should have some policy for when a tunnel will be torn down if there are no sessions within the tunnel. There are three obvious choices for a tunnel teardown policy (configuration could even be provided on which policy to use):

1. Tear down the tunnel immediately when no more sessions are within tunnel.
2. Tear down the tunnel after a period of time in which there are no sessions within tunnel.
3. Leave the tunnel up indefinitely.

Under normal circumstance the first two choices are the more desirable. For client implementations of L2TP the first choice is likely to make sense. Also LNS devices that terminate mostly client implementations may also want to choose the first choice. The second choice makes sense for tunnels involving LAC devices. An LAC may not be able to predict when a connection will come in that is to be tunneled to a particular LNS, so it makes sense to go with the second option and leave the tunnel up for a bit when there are no sessions running within it in case a new remote system connection is established to be tunneled within a reasonable period of time. Of course, if the LNS is following the first policy, then the tunnel will come down anyway (that is, whichever end has the more restrictive policy for tunnel teardown will govern when the tunnel actually is torn down).

The third choice, leaving the tunnel up indefinitely, is probably appropriate only as an explicit configuration item; it would not be the best default choice for an implementation. In some circumstances it may be fine to leave the tunnel up indefinitely because an idle tunnel uses minimal resources and leaving a tunnel established allows a new session to be established more quickly. This option can also be used as an explicit means of abdicating control to the peer implementation, which will then decide when the tunnel should be brought down.

8.6.4 LCP Issues

As noted in the previous sections, it is very important that LNS implementations pay particular attention to the details of LCP negotiation. As a rule of thumb, for LCP options tied to connection characteristics between the LAC and the PPP client, the LNS should use known values from the LAC if possible (through proxy LCP AVPs) and otherwise be conservative.[2]

For its part, the LAC should detect whether it needs to worry about issues surrounding the ACCM, ACFC, FCS Alternative, and MRU/MTU and decide if the logic of inspecting and/or translating PPP traffic between the LNS and remote system is desirable.

---

2. See Chapter 6 for information on new AVPs being defined to communicate LCP values from the LAC to the LNS for incoming and outgoing calls.

9

Data Handling

Up to this point only the control portion of the L2TP has been covered. This chapter explains the handling of data by the LNS and the LAC, which is at the heart of operation of the connection—tunneling PPP frames.

When we consider the tunneling of PPP frames there are two classes of issues to examine. The first arises out of the splitting of responsibility between the LAC and the LNS for framing and PPP negotiation. The second class of issues arises from L2TP's ability to tunnel PPP frames over networks with traffic characteristics different from those assumed on actual point-to-point connections. The most obvious example of this is tunneling over an IP network, where packets may be silently lost, delayed, or duplicated, or a stream of packets may be reordered. Because PPP assumes operation over a point-to-point connection where duplication and reordering are not present, it is the task of L2TP to provide these characteristics.

9.1 PPP Frame Handling

The handling of PPP frames by the LAC and the LNS can be broken down as follows:

1. Operation of PPP over HDLC is assumed by the LNS.
2. The LNS performs HDLC Address and Control field processing.
3. Besides HDLC Address and Control field processing, all other framing (for example, FCS, character escaping) is handled by the LAC.

4. For non-HDLC connections, the LAC is responsible for translating between the addressing method being used on the physical connection and the HDLC addressing that the LNS is using (as shown in Figure 8-5).

9.1.1 Synchronous versus Asynchronous Framing

The operation of L2TP is defined in RFCl2tp to be specific to the tunneling of PPP over HDLC, especially from the perspective of the LNS. When a data session is established for a call, the LNS assumes that the call is HDLC-based. The major distinction made by the LNS is whether the call is an HDLC or AHDLC (that is, synchronous framing versus asynchronous framing) call. The LNS gets this information from the LAC via the Framing Type AVP found in both the ICCN and OCCN control messages.[1]

If LNS detects that a call is in asynchronous framing, then LNS uses AHDLC operation. The LNS may attempt to negotiate PPP Protocol Field Compression (PFC), PPP HDLC Address and Control Field Compression (ACFC), and values for receive Asynchronous Control Character Map (ACCM).

If LNS detects that a session is in synchronous framing, LNS uses HDLC operation. For such a connection there is no negotiation of ACCM. Non-asynchronous HDLC connections are generally defined as also not negotiating ACFC or PFC. Again, on LCP frames at the minimum, there is also the assumption that PPP HDLC addressing will be present.

Notice that with both synchronous framing and asynchronous framing the PPP HDLC Address and Control field processing is handled by the LNS. There is also no way that the LAC can indicate to the LNS that HDLC or AHDLC is not being used.

9.1.2 LNS Frame Handling

Once LCP negotiation is complete, the operations the LNS performs on tunneled PPP frames is a subset of the work normally done by an NAS on a PPP connection over HDLC. Encapsulated PPP frames

---

1. In the case of an outgoing call, the LNS also indicates which types of framing it will support in the Framing Type AVP included in the OCRQ message.

received on a data session have the framing stripped, the control characters unescaped, and the FCS removed. The only lower-level framing potentially present is the HDLC Address and Control fields. The PPP frames encapsulated in L2TP sent to LAC are in a similar state. They may have HDLC Address and Control fields present, but no framing, character escaping, and FCS have been done.

The processing of the encapsulated PPP frame received at the LNS is simple. The PPP code usually used in the HDLC receive path can be used, skipping the removal of framing, escape sequences, and FCS. If ACFC was not negotiated and the first two octets of the decapsulated PPP frame are not `FF 03` then the frame is dropped.

The processing of PPP frames that are to be encapsulated into an L2TP session and sent to an LAC is straightforward. The usual HDLC Address and Control field processing is done for a PPP-over-HDLC connection, and the frame is then encapsulated in an L2TP data message and sent to the LAC. If ACFC was not negotiated for the session, each outbound frame simply gets `FF 03` prepended to it. If ACFC was negotiated for the session, each outbound LCP frame gets `FF 03` prepended to it, but the LNS can decide if any non-LCP frames get `FF 03` prepended to them as well.

9.1.3 LAC Frame Handling for HDLC

When the LAC is handling PPP frames for an L2TP session that is associated with a physical connection that is operating as a PPP-over-HDLC connection, processing as specified in RFCl2tp is simple. As described above, the HDLC Address and Control field processing is either already done (for L2TP encapsulated frames received by the LAC) or will be done (for frames received on the connection that will be L2TP-encapsulated and sent to the LNS). The LAC is responsible for framing, escaping (if AHDLC), and FCS calculation/checking.

As PPP frames are received by the LAC on the physical connection to the remote system, the LAC removes escaping and framing and checks the FCS. Once this work is done, the PPP frame can be encapsulated in L2TP and sent to the LNS. Here is pseudocode for this operation:

```
LACInboundFromRemoteSystem()
{
  Remove Framing;
```

```
    Remove Escaping;   /* if AHDLC */
    Check FCS, exit if incorrect;
    Output to LNS;
}
```

If the LAC is doing LCP inspection and translating or negotiating, then this work can be done following the FCS check and before the LAC proceeds to the output path to the LNS. The FC check simply requires looking for the specification of LCP in the Protocol field per frame. If the frame is an LCP frame, then logic is performed based on the state of LCP negotiations and the options present in the frame. For an HDLC connection, only the FCS Alternative and ACCM would require special treatment.

For PPP frames received on the L2TP session from the LNS, work of an opposite nature is done. The FCS is calculated on the PPP frame, if over AHDLC then control character escaping is performed, and the proper framing is done. This processing is presented in the following pseudocode:

```
LACInboundFromLNS()
{
    Calculate and append FCS;
    Perform character escaping;   /* if AHDLC */
    Perform framing and output to remote system;
}
```

If the LAC is doing LCP inspection and translating or negotiating, then an additional step for LAC is first to check the specification of LCP in the Protocol field in the pseudocode for `LACInboundFromLNS()`. If the frame is an LCP frame, then logic based on the state of LCP negotiations between the LNS and remote system is performed. For an HDLC session the processing potentially involves the modification, removal, or addition of ACCM, FCS Alternative, or Numbered Mode options for CONFREQ frames. The PFC or ACFC options may also be treated specially in the HDLC case, although this isn't as important.

9.1.4 LAC Frame Handling for Non-HDLC

If the connection between the LAC and the remote PPP system is not over HDLC and the PPP session is being tunneled in L2TP, then the

LAC is required to perform more logic than in the case of PPP being tunneled over HDLC. As noted previously, this is because the LNS does PPP tunneling over HDLC, and the LAC is responsible for making the connection look to the LNS like it is an HDLC connection while performing the right actions for the actual connection type on the physical connection (see Figure 8-5).

When frames are received from the remote system in the case of a non-HDLC connection, the logic is given in the following pseudocode:

```
LACInboundFromRemoteSystem()
{
  Remove Framing;
  Check FCS (if applicable), exit if incorrect;
  Map Addressing from physical connection to HDLC;
  Output to LNS;
}
```

As in the case of HDLC, the LAC can also do inspection and translation of LCP negotiations by performing a check for LCP frames after checking the FCS and before outputting the frames to the LNS (before or after mapping addressing doesn't matter).

The pseudocode for the logic when the LAC is receiving frames from the LNS to be forwarded to the remote system over a non-HDLC connection is also similar to the logic in the HDLC case:

```
LACInboundFromLNS()
{
  Map addressing from HDLC to physical connection;
  Calculate and append FCS (if applicable);
  Perform framing and output to remote system;
}
```

Again, the LAC performing inspection, translation, and negotiation can perform the check for LCP as the first step, before mapping HDLC addressing to the addressing appropriate to the remote system connection. The processing work is likely to include the removal of ACCM and ACFC options in the negotiations from the point of view of the remote system. The LAC can make it look to the LNS like such options were acceptable for the connection.

9.2 Tunnel Substrate Considerations

L2TP can run on top of transports with characteristics that are not consistent with the characteristics of a point-to-point connection. Because of this, the L2TP protocol includes mechanisms to provide the same characteristics as a point-to-point connection for PPP where necessary. The usual network to consider is an IP network. L2TP is defined to run on an IP network using UDP, which is a connectionless protocol. Because of this, the characteristics of the IP network will be exposed to L2TP. The non–point-to-point properties that we consider are silent packet loss, packet reordering and duplication, packet delay (that is, packets held up in an intermediate router), and fragmentation.

9.2.1 Packet Delay

Let's consider the property of a packet being delayed first. This property isn't really new to PPP, so we can dismiss it as something that we don't need to worry about. To illustrate this fact, consider an LNS sending a PPP frame to an LAC encapsulated in L2TP and sent on an IP network. On the way the IP datagram gets delayed in an intermediate router. This likely happened because the intermediate router in question was overloaded with other packets that were also being sent. Now consider an NAS with packets to send over a legacy PPP connection (for example, an AHDLC modem connection). Once transmission is begun on the physical connection, some intermediate buffering on the point-to-point connection is possible. Buffering in software does occur both outbound at the NAS and inbound at the remote PPP system. The delay of a packet is therefore possible if either NAS or the remote PPP system is overloaded. So there is nothing new in the possibility of packet delay occurring, except there are other places where packet delay can possibly occur. This difference does have an implication for performance, but functionally there is nothing new introduced.

9.2.2 Fragmentation

Fragmentation potentially introduces a higher exposure to packet loss and packet reordering, which affects performance. Given that packets can be lost in different ways (in groups, with a pattern, randomly) there is no way to quantify the effect that fragmentation has on packet loss. A worst-case scenario is a network that drops every other datagram sent between the LAC and the LNS, and every single L2TP data message being sent from the LNS to the LAC needs to be fragmented. In this case the network has a real packet loss rate of 50 percent (every other packet). The L2TP data session between the LNS and the LAC is experiencing 100 percent loss rate, however, since every L2TP data message is getting fragmented and none of the L2TP data messages is able to get all of its fragments to the other side.

9.2.3 Silent Packet Loss

In contrast to the previous two effects, the probability of silent packet loss is generally nil on a point-to-point connection (for example, an HDLC connection) as compared to a much greater probability on an IP network. The fact that packet loss can be silent really affects the operation of only one PPP protocol. RFC1144 "Compressing TCP/IP Headers for Low-Speed Serial Links" defines a protocol (called VJ Compression after the author of the RFC, Van Jacobson) for compressing TCP/IP headers on a per TCP connection basis. Essentially, instead of sending the whole TCP/IP header for every packet, this protocol has only the differences from the previous packet's header sent so that the receiver can reconstruct the header. On this protocol lost packets are detected at the link level (generally packets are only lost as a result of an FCS error) and the VJ engine is notified of the packet loss. RFC1144 explains that there is at least a 1 in 2^{16} chance that a TCP segment with incorrect contents is forwarded to the receiver if a packet is silently lost. Increasing the probability that packets can be lost brings the probability that incorrect TCP contents will be processed, causing applications to receive incorrect data.

9.2.4 Reordering and Duplication

The other non–point-to-point properties introduced by the operation of L2TP over an IP network are packet reordering and duplication. Because of the dynamic nature of IP routing, it is possible that IP datagrams will not be received in the same order in which they were originally sent. Because PPP is a point-to-point protocol, it contains no provisions for reordering packets. Some PPP protocols specify sequence numbers in order to detect lost packets (most notably compression and encryption protocols). Since these protocols are run over PPP, however, they will view the late-arriving packet as having been dropped, and when it does come in they will treat it as an old packet. Of course, in the case of VJ TCP/IP header compression there is no loss or order checking so the effect of processing an early-arriving packet is the same as having dropped the late-arriving packet.

Both the problems of detecting packet loss and of handling disordered packets are solved by the use of sequence numbers on the L2TP data session. The Ns field of the data message header (shown in Figure 5-1) contains the sequence number of the data message. As explained in Chapter 5, L2TP uses a 16-bit sequence number space. The 32,768 (modulo 2^{16}) values preceding a sequence number are considered "less than" or "before" the sequence number, and the 32,767 (modulo 2^{16}) values following a sequence number are considered to be "greater than" or come "after" a sequence number. L2TP can therefore detect lost messages as long as fewer than 32,768 consecutive messages are not lost. It is straightforward for L2TP to detect lost packets simply by checking whether the sequence number on a received message is the next consecutive message expected.

An implementation can also use the sequence numbers in data message headers to reorder messages if necessary. But a balance needs to be maintained between checking on the order of messages and proceeding with the next step of processing the packets so that the performance of the connection will not suffer. To reorder messages, the implementation has to queue received messages while waiting for the late-arriving message(s). Once the late-arriving messages are received, all of the messages can then be decapsulated and processed by the PPP layer in the order in which they were originally sent from the L2TP peer. An implementation does not generally know whether a message has been lost or if it will be arriving out of order, but it should limit the amount of time it will wait for a misordered message before declaring it lost. (The tradeoff between message loss and message reordering will be discussed later on in this chapter in the section entitled "Performance.")

In general, under heavy reordering conditions (which should be rare) queuing can be used to reorder messages. Under normal conditions, however, the expense incurred in terms of packet delay when packets are merely lost and not reordered (a more common scenario in properly functioning networks) will be more than it is worth, and performance will be needlessly lower.

9.3 Multilink PPP

There are two ways in which the operation of Multilink PPP (MP) interacts with L2TP. We will call the first way *coincidental MP tunneling* and the second *multibox multilink*. *Coincidental* refers to the fact that PPP sessions are getting tunneled to an LNS from an LAC or a set of LACs as normal and it just so happens that some of the PPP sessions are running MP. In this case the LACs do not pay attention to the fact that MP is being run on the links.

The multibox multilink operation of MP and L2TP involves using L2TP specifically as a tool to solve the problem of MP links originating from the same system but terminating on more than one system. For MP to work, a single system has to be on either end of the MP connection so that the MP links can be joined together into one bundle on either end.

9.3.1 Coincidental MP Tunneling

Multilink PPP is tunneled coincidentally when the PPP sessions that are tunneled from the LAC to the LNS negotiate the MP LCP options, although the LAC has given the PPP sessions running on MP no special treatment; the LAC has simply passed the sessions along as normal. The operation of coincidentally tunneled MP is no different than the usual processing of MP by an NAS. It is beyond the scope of the discussion here to go into the operation of MP beyond the introduction provided in Chapter 3 and Figure 3-1. Chapter 3 also shows the communication model for coincidental MP tunneling in Figure 3-2.

There are two issues that arise in L2TP relative to coincidental MP tunneling. The first is the problem of how to identify the MP endpoint at the LNS; this is done via an MP Endpoint Discriminator (MP ED) negotiated in LCP. If a particular deployment is such that the LAC is not involved in any LCP negotiation, then LNS's handling of MP ED is straightforward. The LNS can simply use whatever it wants as an MP ED, the same way that any directly connected NAS would. But if the LAC is involved in LCP negotiation with the remote system at the beginning of the PPP session, there is a potential problem because the LAC will have initially negotiated an MP ED with the remote PPP system. If the LNS renegotiates LCP with its own MP ED, the remote PPP system implementation may become confused and drop the connection (not because renegotiation is disallowed but because it is unexpected in normal circumstances). In this case the LNS should negotiate an MP ED for the PPP session that is the same as the MP ED negotiated by the LAC. When a set of LACs is being used, the issue of MP ED assignment becomes a deployment issue because it is up to the LAC devices to present a common MP ED to the remote PPP system initially. This latter strategy should not be a problem practically, since most remote access installations have to deal with the "multibox multilink" problem discussed in the following section.

The second issue introduced with coincidental MP tunneling is that it is another source of fragmentation. It is likely that the realized loss rate of data traffic for a coincidental MP tunnel session will be greater than if the data messages contained whole PPP frames (as opposed to MP fragments).

Coincidental MP tunneling also seriously degrades performance as compared with terminating the multilink "closer" to the remote system, because the MP is sensitive to variance in delay among the links in a bundle. The greater the amount of the network the MP fragments have to traverse (for example, the addition of tunneling across an IP network), the higher the delivery variance between fragments received on links is likely to be. Although no public tests have been done specifically testing performance of MP over L2TP tunnels, testing of MP over ISDN connections has shown that its performance over two-line unclean connections quickly degrades to the performance level of running PPP over a single connection.

9.3.2 Multibox Multilink

Remote access installations typically have multiple NAS boxes that can be reached via the same phone number. As a result, remote MP devices may end up with their MP links being terminated at physically separate NAS devices. This situation is sometimes called the *multibox* (or multichassis) *multilink* problem (in RFC12tp it is referred to as the "multilink hunt-group splitting" problem). Chapter 3 provides a description of how L2TP can be used to solve this problem, and the communication model for this solution is shown in Figure 3-3.

The first step in the solution is that an NAS receives a new connection for an MP link and learns that a bundle has already been established for the remote PPP system MP ED on a different NAS. The NAS receiving the new connection then plays the role of the LAC for that connection and tunnels the session to the NAS containing the associated bundle head for the incoming MP link. As shown in Figure 3-3, the NAS device containing the bundle is capable of combining MP links that are connected directly along with MP links that are tunneled from other NAS boxes. The actual MP processing done in the box is exactly the same as if all of the links were directly physically connected. An Internet Draft specifying this procedure is draft-ietf-mmp-discovery-01.txt by Gary Malkin.

It is conceivable that LAC devices could use a procedure such as MMP to terminate links locally at a single NAS and then tunnel the bundle PPP session to an LNS, although no known implementations of this procedure exist. To do this, the LAC would need to translate the LCP operating over the bundle between the remote system and the LNS because the rules for LCP are slightly different for LCP operating over MP bundles than over other PPP connections.

9.4 Performance

The importance of performance analysis of using L2TP arises from the fact that it is used in place of an alternate solution (that is, direct remote access). The user working from home with a traditional remote access setup dials the number for the NAS at the edge of a corporation to gain access to the private network. The time it takes to access resources on the private network depends on the speed of the user's connection to the NAS, how busy the NAS is, the speed and load of the private network, and the load on the resource on the private network that the user is accessing. Packet loss on the connection between the user's access equipment and the NAS is probably extremely low. In contrast consider the user using L2TP to gain access to his or her private network through an LNS on the private network edge. In this scenario the user's access time to resources on the private network is affected by all of the same factors we have just mentioned, but in addition the speed of the connection across the public network and the congestion of the public network are also factors. Also packet loss (possibly magnified by fragmentation) and packet reordering or duplication may occur.

Another scenario is the user at home accessing the corporate network through L2TP using a modem. For this user, the comparative situation is access to the Internet itself through the cable modem (because there isn't an alternate way for the user to access the corporate network through the cable modem except through some connection over the public network).

The following sections discuss different network characteristics and L2TP behavior and how performance may be affected.

9.4.1 Round-Trip Time

One area that affects overall performance of the tunneled traffic is the Round-Trip Time (RTT) between the remote PPP system and the resource on the private network being accessed. The importance of RTT to the user depends on the type of application being used. As noted in RFC1144, referencing [*Designing the User Interface,* Addison-Wesley 1987], from a user's perspective the response time for trafficking in simple interactive data (for example, Telnet) is considered to be bad if it is greater than 100 to 200 milliseconds (ms) (that is, RTT >100 or 200 ms). On the other hand, for a bulk data transfer, the RTT is almost irrelevant since TCP can expand the window so that the path delay is not the bottleneck. The difference between trafficking in interactive data and bulk transfer data has been blurred through the use of HTTP browsers and complex Web pages with graphics. This new type of traffic is a type of complex pseudo-interactive data that does not have the freedom of general bulk transfer but does have an expanded response acceptability for delay of perhaps (for argument's sake) 3 to 5 seconds (perhaps longer depending on past conditioning). The larger the RTT the longer the transfer of data over TCP will take. In many ways, much of HTTP traffic is bulk transfer, such as large graphics or sound files. On the other hand, this bulk traffic is expected to arrive quickly and is prompted by user feedback. The bottom line is that RTT is likely to matter to the average user because of the effect it has on TCP transfers, particularly if the user has previous experience with which to compare performance (such as previously having used direct remote access to the private network).

Consider an LNS and an NAS both of which are located at the edge of a private network. It is obvious that the RTT for traffic over a connection between a remote system and a private network resource will be different depending on whether the NAS or the LNS is being used to access the private network. As noted above, the difference is that the connection through the LNS travels through the public network in addition to the other portions of the path used by the NAS scenario in which the traffic travels directly between the peers. What is not obvious is, all other things held equal, whether or not the extra path delay introduced by the public network in the LNS scenario affects the performance bottom line. Unfortunately, we will have to stop short of fully investigating whether or not there is a difference in performance. There are simply too many variables to adequately cover the subject in this context. Whether or not a difference will be noticed would depend on the speed of the physical connection to the LAC or the NAS, the performance of the private network (that is, what percentage of the RTT reflects delays caused by the public network), and the actual performance on the public network. Of course, ultimately, even if there is a difference between LNS and NAS there is the question of whether a gain in performance is worth the investment.

From a protocol standpoint, the answer to this question doesn't matter because there is nothing that L2TP can do from a protocol standpoint to affect the performance of the public network. There are undoubtedly many specific paths on the Internet today that would yield terrible tunneled remote access performance. Luckily there seem to be a greater number of paths that are sufficient for the job. The ability to contract Service Level Agreements (SLAs) with ISPs will also help to ensure that the public network will provide an adequate transport for the L2TP tunneled PPP sessions if the traffic stays on the network to which the SLA applies.

9.4.2 Packet Loss and PPP Protocols with History

Probably the biggest degradation of performance is associated with the loss of packets when a PPP protocol with history is being used. The way protocols with history work is that each packet generally can carry both regular information and also information with which to update the history. The best example is a compression protocol where tokens that represent compressed data, uncompressed data, and information on what tokens are equivalent to what data are transferred with each packet. These protocols operate to ensure that the history on both ends remains synchronized. If a packet is lost, the histories are resynchronized (reset on either end to an initial state) so that the data can be decompressed faithfully.

A non-negligible probability of packet loss wreaks havoc on such a protocol because in order to resynchronize histories the receiver that detects that it missed a packet must inform the sending peer that it missed a packet and that the histories have to be reset. Meanwhile, until the receiver is informed that the peer has reset its history, the receiver has to drop received compressed packets. As a result, a single dropped packet can result in many dropped packets while histories are being reset. Unfortunately the base specification of L2TP does not have a mechanism for reducing this effect. Generally to reduce the effects of this problem a windowing scheme is used to limit the number of packets in transit at any one time. Originally L2TP had a flow control (or rate-pacing) mechanism designed for this purpose, but this function was removed from the specification because of problems in its technical specification.[2]

9.4.3 Packet Loss and Packet Reordering Trade-off

The simultaneous possibility of data message loss and data message reordering on the transport carrying the tunnel creates a problem for implementations. The problem is that on an IP or similar network when a message is dropped there is no notification to indicate that the message was dropped as opposed to misordered. Conversely, when a message is misordered there is no notification that it was misordered as opposed to dropped until the late-arriving message is received.

Two examples of implementations that compound the problems of data loss and data message reordering will highlight the boundary conditions of handling these two events and how they depend on each other. For the first example take an implementation that assumes that

---

2. Nonetheless, many interoperable implementations exist that make use of the flow control specified in L2TP as of draft-ietf-pppext-l2tp-12.txt. The specification of L2TP flow control has been moved to a separate document that will become an RFC separately. This topic will be covered in the last chapter, on future directions and extensions in progress to L2TP.

no messages will be lost but that messages received out of order will be reordered. When this implementation detects an early-arriving message, it assumes that the missing message(s) will be received at some future point. The receiving end therefore can queue up early-arriving messages until the late-arriving messages come in and the messages can be decapsulated up to the PPP layer in the proper order. Of course, the drawback of such an implementation is that if a message really is lost, then the receiver will wait forever for a data message that will never come. The second implementation takes the opposite approach. Whenever it receives an early-arriving message it assumes that the late-arriving message will never arrive; every message is assumed to be dropped if a later message is received first. The drawback of this implementation is the opposite of that of the implementation that drops messages needlessly, since when a message is not received in order it is given up on and if it is received later it must be dropped—otherwise order will not be preserved.

Where the compromise between these two implementations can be made is the crux of the trade-off between handling reordering of messages and assuming messages have been silently lost in the underlying network. The basic step taken to resolve the two approaches is to add a timer. The implementation then waits for a finite period of time for a late-arriving message before assuming that the message has been lost.

If only a simple timer is used, there will be a negative affect on performance if messages are getting lost all the time, because each lost message (or group of consecutive messages that are lost) will cause the receiver to wait for the timer to expire before giving up on the lost messages. Fortunately, an implementation can be set up to detect that it is receiving misordered messages even if it has previously given up on the misordered messages. Even though messages that have been given up on must be silently discarded, the implementation can note that a misordered message was received and can modify its receive state accordingly. For instance, the implementation could start by assuming that all missing messages were silently lost messages. If misordered messages are subsequently received, the implementation could change the mode of its receiver instead to wait for missing messages with a timeout.

Certainly, a variety of even more advanced steps could be taken. For instance, an implementation could measure the amount of time it took for misordered messages to be received and then decide whether they are worth waiting for, and if they are, how long to wait for such messages. Also an implementation could attempt to react smoothly to changing networking conditions where message reordering may be prevalent for a time followed by a period of prevalent message dropping.

9.4.4 The Trade-offs in Performance

In this section we have discussed four situations that affect performance. It is important to recognize that all of these situations interact with each other and produce trade-offs (such as the packet loss handling/reordering trade-off described in the previous subsection). These four things are RTT, packet loss with protocols that operate using history, packet loss, and packet reordering.

In general practice, increasing the RTT for a path above a certain limit decreases even the TCP performance of bulk transfers on the path since there is a (configurable) cap on the window size for TCP connections on implementations. This has the general effect of causing underutilization of the path bandwidth. So, for example, an implementation may try to play it too safe by waiting for misordered messages with a timeout when in fact all of the delayed messages were really lost. In this case the average RTT of the path for user data going through the L2TP tunnel is being needlessly increased (of course, the packet loss will probably also reduce performance).

There are trade-offs to be made in curbing lost packets. Lost packets also generally lower performance. This is especially true of TCP connections, which react to lost packets as signs of congestion. The interaction between data message loss and PPP protocols with history becomes very important in this case. The problem is that if one message being dropped on the network causes multiple messages to be dropped while history resynchronization is taking place, then the real packet loss rate as seen by a TCP connection may be much higher than the real loss rate on the network. The dropping of packets can cause protocols such as TCP to improperly interpret the problem as a congestion condition, which it is not. This in turn can cause the TCP to adjust the data transfer rate lower than it really needs to be based on the characteristics of the network itself.

The trade-off between reordering packets and treating packets received out of order as lost should lean toward the treat-as-lost approach. A change in the order of packets on an IP network is the result of errors or misconfigurations and should not happen in general. Packets received out of order on a TCP session reduce performance, and therefore most IP networking equipment is designed not to do this. On the other hand, packet loss is a much more common effect on IP networks, arising from simple line errors or congestion conditions on the network. Implementations should therefore probably allow configuration of a mode where packet reordering is performed, but default the behavior to treating delayed packets as dropped.

VJ Compression should be avoided on tunneled PPP sessions where the LAC is not doing stateful inspection. Efficient operation of VJ is predicated on the rarity of packet loss. Since the frequency of lost packets will frequently be greater in L2TP over non–point-to-point networks than on a real point-to-point link, the model that VJ was designed for no longer really applies.

9.5 Comparing L2TP to L2F and PPTP

The data handling functions performed by L2F and PPTP are both very similar to the actions performed in L2TP. The main difference is that with PPTP controlling the flow of data is mandatory; whereas in L2F or the base specification of L2TP there is no control of the flow of data. While L2TP was advancing through the draft stages it defined modes of operation relative to sequence number handling that constituted a superset of the features offered by L2F and PPTP. It was possible for no sequence numbers to be used for data messages, a facility that is provided by L2F as well. A mode of operation where sequence numbers were present for detecting packet loss and message reordering but there was no sliding window for controlling the flow of data (that is, there were no data message acknowledgments) was provided as well, which, again, is a mode provided in L2F. Finally, L2TP data sessions were able to signal during call establishment that the flow of data for a given session was to be controlled. This last mode of operation was parallel to the mode of operation for data handling provided in PPTP.

As L2TP is defined in the base specification, the PPTP-style data handling with flow control was removed. This decision was made late in the L2TP draft stage because the definition for how the flow control mechanism was to operate was incomplete. Of course, the other two

L2F-style modes of operation remain in L2TP. The major drawback for L2TP is that its base specification does not adequately provide a mechanism for reconciling the tunneling of PPP protocols with history in the face of non-negligible message loss.

The operation of flow control for L2TP has not been abandoned altogether because of its importance. Instead, it has moved to a separate specification where it can be focused on and developed individually.

For the frame-by-frame handling of PPP, L2TP, L2F, and PPTP behave the same. They all assume PPP-over-HDLC, so the equivalent of the LNS for all of them makes the same assumptions and behaves the same. One major difference, however, is that in the case of PPTP if the PPTP equivalent to the LAC negotiates LCP with the remote system, there is no mechanism for the LAC to inform the LNS equivalent of the LCP options that have been negotiated. But PPTP does have the benefit, unlike L2F, of being able to indicate the framing type (synchronous or asynchronous) during the establishment of a session, a feature that is available in L2TP and discussed earlier in this chapter.

9.6 Implementation Tips

9.6.1 VJ Compression and Silent Packet Loss Is Bad

Silent packet loss with VJ Compression undermines one of the key features of TCP. The purpose of TCP is to provide for the reliable delivery of data. VJ Compression bypasses the sending of the TCP checksum and other values in order to compress them out of the TCP header. The VJ Compression protocol then relies on the fact that packets will not get reordered on a point-to-point link and that packet losses will be detected. Only when these two things are true can VJ Compression correctly recover the original TCP/IP packets reliably.

Obviously L2TP can handle the issue of packet reordering. For VJ Compression packets coming from the remote system toward the LAC and then the LNS, the VJ packets will not get reordered on the actual point-to-point connection between the remote system and the LAC, and the LNS can detect any message reordering between the LAC and the LNS. For VJ packets coming from the LNS and heading toward the LAC and ultimately to the remote system, the situation is the same. The LAC can detect any misordered messages between the LNS and the LAC, and once the proper order is established that order will be maintained on the point-to-point link between the LAC and the remote system.

Packet loss is not as easily handled by L2TP, however. For messages lost between the LAC and the LNS, the LNS as the receiver can act simply. L2TP can detect if messages are lost using L2TP sequence numbering and can signal to the PPP layer whenever messages are lost. There are two conditions of packet loss that L2TP cannot handle so easily. First there is the case where an L2TP data message is lost in transit, destined for the LAC from the LNS. In this case the LAC is aware that the message is lost. The problem is that unless the LAC and remote system PPP reside in the same place (as they do in an L2TP client implementation), the LAC has no method to easily notify the remote system that a packet has been lost. The notification can be done. For example, the LAC could send a frame with improper FCS on the point-to-point connection to the remote system. The remote system would then receive the bad FCS and treat it as a lost frame. In the second case a frame is lost (that is, the frame is received with bad FCS) that has been sent from the remote system on the point-to-point link to the LAC. The LAC detects that the remote system has sent a frame that has been subsequently lost, but the LAC has no elegant way to notify the LNS of this situation. The LAC can notify the LNS of such an event by incrementing the sequence number of the next data message it sends to the LNS. When this good frame being sent in a data message is received by LNS, LNS interprets it as an unexpected message (remember, LNS is expecting the sequence number that was skipped). The LNS can then signal to its PPP layer that a message was dropped and the VJ engine can enter the correct state.

Given all of this, VJ TCP/IP header compression is not worth the trouble. A condition that may obviate this conclusion is that it is the LAC that must take the special steps in two of the cases, and it is the LNS PPP that negotiates VJ with the remote system. Because the extra steps noted in this section are not part of the behavior of LAC defined as part of the L2TP protocol, the LNS cannot assume that the LAC will take these steps. Because of this the LNS may decide not to negotiate VJ in order to be safe.

It should also be kept in mind that VJ Compression is essentially a protocol with history. When packet loss does occur, the VJ engine drops packets until a retransmitted packet is detected. In the face of packet loss, therefore, performance may be decreased more than the improvement created by not transmitting TCP/IP headers.

Operation of VJ should be made configurable on the LNS if available at all, and should default to not be done. That way installations that value the performance improvement to be had by compressing TCP/IP headers more than the statistical possibility of improper TCP data delivery have the freedom to make that decision.

9.6.2 Endpoint Discriminator with Coincidentally Tunneled MP

As mentioned above, there are basically two choices for a peer to make when requesting an MP ED at the LNS PPP. If a bundle already exists on the LNS for the MP ED that the PPP peer is requesting from the LNS PPP, then the MP ED used for the LNS's bundle should be used. Otherwise, for a new remote MP ED being requested by a remote system, the LNS can choose its MP ED according to the situation. If the LAC did not take part in LCP negotiation, then the LNS is free to choose its own MP ED. If, however, the LAC did go through LCP negotiation with the remote system, then the LNS can find itself in one of a few different conditions. The most trivial is the case where the LAC negotiated LCP with the remote system but did not include any information on what was negotiated when establishing the data session. In this case the LNS has no choice but to assign its own MP ED to identify itself to the remote system. If the LAC does send the LNS information on the LCP negotiation between the LAC and the remote system, then the LNS has a choice to make. The LNS can decide to use its own MP ED anyway. The problem with this is that there may be some implementations that will balk at a change to the MP ED and tear down the connection. The other choice is for the LNS to use the MP ED value that the LAC negotiated, the advantage being that the MP ED negotiated with the remote system is not changed so there is no potential for creating confusion. The downside of this approach is that it pushes the responsibility of providing uniform MP ED values to remote systems operating across separate MP links from the LNS to the LAC equipment.

It is possible to make the MP ED behavior a configurable behavior. For example, there could be a per-LAC configuration on the LNS as to whether to use the MP ED values negotiated by that LAC or use a value chosen by the LNS. MP ED assignment could also simply be a global configuration item as well, either always to accept the LAC-negotiated MP ED if known, or otherwise to use the LNS's own value for the MP ED.

9.6.3 Backward Compatibility with Draft 12 Data Flow Control

Up through draft 12 of the L2TP specification, L2TP included a data session flow control mechanism that was the same as the one specified for use with PPTP. Draft 13 of the L2TP specification was a major overhaul of the draft 12 version, with the only functional change being the removal of data session flow control. Unfortunately, because so much time was spent developing the base specification of L2TP there are many implementations that make use of the data session flow control mechanism provided in previous draft versions.

Data session flow control has not been completely abandoned, because it is important. A separate document is under development that will define the data session flow control mechanism based on the mechanism present in L2TP up to draft 13. Meanwhile, newer implementations will have to decide how to interoperate with implementations based on draft 12 or before.

Draft implementations before draft 13 can optionally signal the use of data session flow control when data sessions are being established by including the Receive Window Size AVP in the call establishment messages (ICRP, ICCN, OCRQ, and OCCN). Data session flow control is signaled independently in each direction, so it is possible to do data flow control in one direction but not in the other. When data flow control is being used, the Nr field of the data message header has the same meaning as the Nr field with control messages (of course, data messages are not retransmitted, but their rate is limited).

In draft 12 the Receive Window Size AVP in the call setup messages was specified to have the M Bit set in the AVP. It was also required that if this AVP was received by a draft 12 implementation, then rate limiting must be set according to the received window size.

New implementations can decide how to handle data session flow control. There are a few different scenarios that can arise. The simplest scenario involves an older implementation that doesn't include the Receive Window Size AVP at all during call establishment. If a newer implementation doesn't support data session flow control but is working with an older implementation that does, the data session will not be established. This is because the Receive Window Size AVP will have the M Bit set, and the newer implementation will have to treat it as an unrecognized AVP.

As of the time of this writing, work on the separate specification for data session flow control had not been written. The stated intent, however, is that the specification will be based on the specifications present in draft 12. Thus a robust implementation based on the newer L2TP specification will include data session flow control as defined in draft 12. This will allow interoperability between subsequent implementations and older implementations.

Because IETF Internet Drafts have a set lifetime of six months, the data session flow control specifications taken from draft-ietf-pppext-l2tp-12.txt are presented in the Appendix and annotated. This Appendix can serve as a guide to newer implementations to understand the behavior and requirements for interoperability with draft 12 implementations of data flow control.

10

Security

This chapter covers the various security issues related to L2TP. There are two different levels of security we need to be concerned with. The first is the security provided by PPP to the data that is carried within the L2TP data messages. The second level would be security provided by the L2TP itself or by a transport that L2TP can run on top of.

In many cases, even if there is security provided at the level of the tunnel PPP session, this security by itself does not protect against many simple attacks. Because the weakness of security provided by PPP is recognized, the use of the IP Security (IPSEC) protocol is recommended for protection against those security problems that are not covered by PPP security (draft-ietf-pppext-l2tp-security-02.txt). Security issues are handled by either Transport Mode IPSEC protection of the L2TP tunnel (covering control and all data sessions) or the transport that L2TP is running over. For example, work is being done to add security to Frame Relay in general, and when one is running L2TP over Frame Relay, the use of native Frame Relay security measures could be used.

Throughout this chapter we will concentrate on specific aspects of security. But first we describe the terminology that we will be using.

The first concept is *connection authentication*. Connection authentication refers to the act of authenticating an entity when a connection is first made. This is the type of authentication provided by PPP authentication protocols such as PAP and CHAP.

Another type of authentication that is possible is *message authentication*. This type of authentication goes beyond connection authentication and authenticates each message sent on the connection to ensure that every single message is coming from the entity that originally was allowed to connect after a successful connection authentication.

An authentication method that is very close to that of message authentication is *message integrity*. If a message has integrity, that means that the message received has the same contents as the message that was originally sent. In order for this method to work you have to be able to tell that the sender of the message was the proper sender, and that is why message authentication and message integrity generally go hand in hand.

The most common security concept is that of *data hiding*, which is also called encryption. Data is encrypted with the intent that only the desired entities will be able to decrypt the message to get the original data back. Data encryption is done via mathematical manipulation. The concept of encryption "strength" has to do with the amount of mathematical work an entity that is not meant to be privy to the original data has to do in order to figure out the contents of the original data message.

The final security concept we will consider is *replay protection*. If a system only had connection authentication, message authentication, and message integrity there would still be the problem of a malicious party playing back messages from previous connections. This security feature is only useful when message integrity and message authentication is being provided.

Other security concepts that the reader should be aware of are *Denial of Service (DoS)*, *Man in the Middle*, and *Oracle attacks*. A DoS attack is any attack that prevents the system under attack from providing service or the intended level of service. For example, a system can be subjected to so much traffic by an attacker that the system can't process the traffic that it is meant to process. A Man in the Middle attack involves a malicious system butting in between communicating systems and withholding or modifying information sent between the systems in order to compromise the security between the two. An Oracle attack is one in which an attacked system is used to gain information on one connection used to compromise security on another connection to the attacked system.

Security is an area that is rich in content and very actively under research. It is well outside the scope of the current material to give exhaustive in-depth analysis of very specific security aspects in detail. Instead, this chapter will investigate security issues and L2TP at the level of the concepts we have just described to explain at a more general level what security weaknesses or coverage L2TP has under different conditions.

10.1 Control Channel Security

The first architectural piece of L2TP for which security is needed is the L2TP control channel. Clearly all of the security considerations we have described thus far would be desirable for the control of L2TP tunnels. For the L2TP control channel, aspects of two of these security concepts are addressed.

When L2TP peers establish a tunnel, part of the tunnel establishment process is an optional tunnel authentication. Chapter 5 gave the procedure used for tunnel authentication during tunnel establishment. A CHAP-like method is used with a single shared secret for authenticating each end of the tunnel with the other end. Either end can request that the peer authenticate itself. Although the mechanism described is indeed a method for (mutual) authentication of a connection, the security provided by this form of authentication is doubtful. The major weakness is that the basis of the authentication is a long-lived shared secret. Shared-secret authentication is considered to be the weakest of the authentication credential methods. The shared secret is prone to discovery through other means. For example, the shared secret may be simple, such as *password* or *secret*. Or the shared secret may be available in a configuration file that can be easily obtained, or the shared secret may have been sent in the clear in an email, or perhaps the shared secret may be known to someone who used to administer the box but has now moved on to another company.

Aside from the security weakness of using a shared secret, this method of authentication has another major drawback. The use of shared secrets does not scale well, and configuration is required on both ends if the shared secret is to be changed. Because of the drawbacks of shared secrets, other more secure approaches to connection authentication have been created, such as onetime password or token authentication and Digital Certificates.

Also part of the L2TP protocol is the ability to hide AVP value fields in control messages. This is a method of encryption in which the tunnel shared secret is used as the encryption/decryption key. The main problem with this method of encryption is that the encryption key is long lived (because it is also the tunnel shared secret). As a result, it is very important to keep the tunnel secret secure because once it is discovered, it can also be used to decrypt the hidden data in control messages. Chapter 6 gave the details of how AVP hiding in control messages works. Fortunately, the requirement that a random vector be used as part of the AVP hiding makes decrypting the AVP value without knowing the shared secret more difficult. If a random vector were not included, then it would be easier for patterns in the encryption to be discovered and analyzed to produce the original unhidden information.

Beyond these two security measures, no other security is provided for the L2TP control channel. If other security precautions are not taken, it is reasonably possible for falsified control messages to be sent to a tunnel endpoint from an attacker as if they had been sent from a peer. Falsified control messages can be used by an attacker to deny service to an LAC or LNS, the denial of service constituting the attack. The only step necessary would be to forge a CDN or StopCCN message to the LAC or LNS to drop either a call or a tunnel, depending on how much the malicious entity wanted to disrupt service. L2TP provides a weak protection against this mode of attack (it is less a protocol feature and more an implementation feature). The mechanism was noted back in Chapter 6 when we introduced the Tunnel ID and Session ID fields in the L2TP header structure. The protective measure involves picking Tunnel ID and Session ID values randomly so that a malicious attacker who does not have access to inspect traffic for a tunnel cannot guess the values. This countermeasure, combined with the attacker's not knowing the correct sequence number to send (which changes as the window moves), makes it more difficult for such an attacker to mount such a simple attack. But these measures should not be considered sufficient to thwart such an attacker. It should not be assumed that an attacker will not be able to inspect the real tunnel traffic. From a security standpoint it is always best to assume that an attacker has all the tools to make attacking as easy as possible and that real cryptographic methods are necessary to thwart the attacks.

10.2 PPP Security

Although L2TP provides connection authentication and hiding of AVP values in control messages, there are no security protection mechanisms in L2TP for the PPP data being tunneled. Unless the L2TP tunnel is secured by the transport being used (IPSEC being an example), PPP provides the only user data security mechanisms (note that PPP security does not cover control protocols in PPP). Note also that IP user data within a tunnel session can be protected by IPSEC between the remote system and private network hosts.

10.2.1 Authentication

PPP provides for connection authentication of point-to-point connections in its authentication phase. The PPP authentication types are PAP and CHAP, with MSCHAP being a derivative of CHAP. RFC 2284 defines the PPP Extensible Authentication Protocol (EAP), which can be considered a meta-authentication type. During LCP negotiation, EAP can be negotiated as the authentication type. Once the authentication phase is entered, different methods of authentication can be negotiated within EAP. RFC 2284 defines an MD5-challenge type of authentication (a CHAP-like mechanism), onetime password, and generic token card authentication. There are also several works in progress for other authentication mechanisms available within EAP, such as the use of Digital Certificates. So, in theory, connection authentication methods such as Digital Certificates could be possible in PPP and therefore within L2TP data sessions. The problem, of course, is that for years to come there will be several machines around that continue to support only PAP and CHAP.

PAP authentication over a tunneled connection with no encryption provided by the transport running beneath L2TP provides unencrypted passwords, which are forwarded through the tunnel. But once the password for a user is known, then access to the private network by an attacker cannot be far behind.

CHAP authentication does not transfer the password between peers like PAP does. But it has the same problem that was brought up in connection with L2TP tunnel authentication (the similarity is not surprising since L2TP tunnel authentication is CHAP-like). With both PAP and CHAP authentication the connection authentication credential is a shared secret. Even with CHAP this can be a problem. The more times a challenge/response value pair is obtained for a given password, the easier it is to crack the hashing and recover the password, especially given that shared secrets tend to be long-lived. Again, there is also the scalability problem associated with shared secrets. For each user a different shared secret is required, and when the password needs to be changed, both ends must be changed in lockstep.

10.2.2 Encryption

The biggest criticism of encryption done at the level of PPP is that it does not encrypt the PPP control protocols. Therefore LCP negotiation, IPCP negotiation of IP addresses, and so forth are never encrypted. Even the unhidden negotiation of an IP address is seen as a security problem for many installations, since it exposes information (the address space used) about the private network.

There are two flavors of encryption used in PPP. The first is the method developed within the IETF as a Standards Track protocol suite consisting of a control protocol for negotiating encryption and the use of encryption algorithms to do the actual encryption. RFC 1968 is the specification for the PPP Encryption Control Protocol (ECP), and RFC 1969 specifies the use of the Data Encryption Standard (DES) encryption in PPP. Since then the use of Triple DES has also been specified for use in PPP, in RFC 2420. There is currently no definition for dynamic negotiation of keys in ECP, which means that the encryption keys are preshared keys (analogous to the preshared secret of authentication).

The other popular encryption method is a proprietary product developed by Microsoft. This is called the Microsoft Point-to-Point Encryption (MPPE) protocol. MPPE defines the negotiation of the use of encryption not in ECP but within the Compression Control Protocol (CCP) as part of an extension made for another proprietary Microsoft development, the Microsoft Point-to-Point Compression (MPPC) protocol. MPPC is defined in Informational RFC 2118, and CCP is defined in the Standards Track RFC 1962. The use of MPPE also depends on MSCHAP having been used in the PPP Authentication Phase. Unlike in ECP, which uses DES encryption, the MPPE encryption keys are derived from random information in the MSCHAP authentication along with the authentication password. The MPPE keys also change periodically, with subsequent keys being derived from the initial key information. Since MPPE key generation is completely deterministic once the authentication shared secret is known, the efficacy of the encryption rests wholly on the shared secret remaining a secret. The RSA RC4 stream cipher is used to do the actual encryption.

MPPE also runs in either a stateful or a stateless mode. When it is run in the stateful mode there is also the concern about the effect of packet loss on performance, as discussed in Chapter 9.

10.3 L2TP Security Summary

In terms of the security provided by L2TP directly, as we have seen, there is little. The only protocol features of L2TP that provide some security coverage are connection authentication for tunnels and the hiding of AVP values in L2TP control messages. This leaves security for the PPP sessions up to the PPP protocol security features, which can cause scaling issues, for example with MPPE. MPPE uses a 16KB history in one direction, and an 8KB history in the other direction, for a total of 24KB required per connection under stateful MPPE.

The following sections highlight the shortcomings of the combination of L2TP and PPP security measures.

10.3.1 Weak Connection Authentication

Compared to other technical alternatives, the authentication provided by standard PPP authentication mechanisms is weak. First, PAP and CHAP generally rely on a preshared secret for authentication. Since the password is static, it is prone to discovery through other methods. Certainly PAP used with preshared keys is extremely vulnerable because it exposes the preshared secret in unencrypted form. As has been noted already, the use of preshared secrets doesn't scale well because both ends of the connection have to be reconfigured if the password changes.

It is possible not to use preshared secrets with PAP and CHAP but instead to use a onetime password or token authentication. Doing this, however, requires that implementations on both ends understand how the authentication is being done. The use of PPP EAP is also promising for improving the PPP authentication options, but legacy PPP authentication will likely be extremely popular for some time to come simply because of the large installed base of PPP software.

10.3.2 Limited Encryption Scope

Before discussing the specific properties of PPP encryption in the next subsection, it is important to note that the scope of the traffic that gets encrypted when PPP encryption is used does not include the PPP control protocols. A popular example of this drawback is that IPCP will not be protected and the IP address(es) negotiated will be present as clear text. There are other drawbacks as well, such as the fact that the type of authentication done will be visible and the authentication itself will also be in clear text. This latter fact is obviously bad if PAP with preshared secret is being used.

10.3.3 Poor Encryption Key Management

Both DES with ECP and RC4 with MPPE provide strong encryption, but both of these approaches suffer from poor encryption key management.

In the case of ECP-based encryption, the keys are statically defined on either end and do not change (that is, the keys are preshared) unless manually reconfigured. That means that the same encryption keys could be used across multiple sessions and throughout each session in its entirety. The more a key is used (or the longer the key lifetime) the easier it becomes to do a brute-force cryptographic attack to break the encryption, so the use of static keys is a serious weakness.

For MPPE-based encryption, key management is slightly better, although it centers on the agreement of a preshared secret (that is, the password from MSCHAP authentication). The reason that MPPE key management is better than key management in ECP-based systems is that it is not directly as prone to brute-force attacks. This is because the encryption keys used for each session are different, and because the encryption keys also change during the session. Different keys are used for each session because the value of the keys depends both on the password from the MSCHAP authentication as well as random information from each instance of MSCHAP authentication. MPPE also defines two modes of operation for changing keys. In one mode keys are recalculated after every message is processed, and in the other mode keys are recalculated after every 256 packets. It should be noted that the key changes done in MPPE aid in preventing brute-force attacks but they do not limit the amount of data that can be decrypted if the preshared secret is discovered. This is because MPPE key changes do not have the security property called *Perfect Forward Secrecy* (PFS). In systems with PFS, subsequent encryption keys for a session do not depend on the value of the previous encryption keys. In contrast, MPPE keys can be calculated simply if the preshared secret from MSCHAP is discovered, because MPPE does not have the property of PFS.

10.3.4 No Message Authentication

In L2TP and in PPP no message authentication is performed. That means that a received message is implicitly trusted as having come from the expected source. Unfortunately, it is not that difficult to forge messages if no other security is provided to protect data sessions.

PPP was largely developed in the context of connections over dedicated links where the injection of packets is next to impossible (for example, modem connections). But in unprotected L2TP, however, it is easy to inject PPP control messages into a session, or even IP packets through the session and to the remote system or to the private network behind the LNS.

10.3.5 No Message Integrity

The issue of message integrity is similar to the message authentication weakness problem we have already discussed. But through this weakness an attacker would not be forging his or her own packets, but instead would be able to modify actual messages sent from the expected peer. This particular breach of security points to the difference in the security provided by message authentication versus message integrity. If message authentication were provided but message integrity were not, an attacker would not be able to forge his or her own messages but would be able to modify messages that were sent from a trusted source. The absence of message integrity also implies that protection from Man in the Middle attacks is not provided.

10.3.6 No Replay Protection

Replay protection is really only useful when message authentication and message integrity are provided. So by default there is no replay protection in L2TP.

10.4 Transport Mode IPSEC

When L2TP is run over an IP network, the suggested method for getting security features not provided by L2TP or PPP is to use the IP Security (IPSEC) protocol. IPSEC was introduced in Chapter 3, where both Transport mode and Tunnel mode operation of IPSEC were summarized. Figure 3-9 illustrates how an IP datagram is transformed into an IPSEC transport mode protected datagram for a TCP packet. Figure 10-1 shows an L2TP message running over UDP/IP without IPSEC protection and the transformation to the equivalent L2TP message with IPSEC transport mode protection. The portions of the packet that were previously in the clear but are potentially encrypted after IPSEC application are shown in italics.

It would not be possible here to go into detail about how IPSEC provides the security services it does while giving the descriptions proper justice. The area of IPSEC development is one that is rich in features and also one that is necessarily complex. What is important here is how IPSEC behaves from a bird's-eye point of view.

10.4.1 Security Associations

IPSEC operates by establishing security associations (SAs) between end systems. A security association defines security policy for a specific traffic profile. The specification of a traffic profile is generally based on IP addresses and layer 4 port information (that is, UDP and TCP ports).

For example, an SA may be defined between two systems such that any traffic initiated to TCP port 23 (Telnet port) has Digital Certificate connection authentication, DES encryption, and SHA (Secure Hash Algorithm) packet authentication. Of course, we are specifically concerned here with SAs established to protect traffic associated with UDP port 1701. Note that if L2TP were configured on a system to run on a port other than 1701, then the security policy would simply reflect the relevant port number.

Like L2TP, IPSEC has control traffic and data traffic. The control traffic is exchanged within a temporary SA established between two

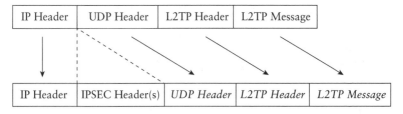

Figure 10-1 *L2TP/UDP/IP with IPSEC transport mode*

systems in order to negotiate the properties of the SA that will be used for the data. The Internet Key Exchange (IKE) protocol (RFC 2409) has been defined for the purpose of establishing transport mode SAs and tunnel mode SAs. The temporary SA set up in order to perform connection authentication, encryption, and packet integrity/authentication is called the IKE SA. The transport mode or tunnel mode SA established to handle the actual IP traffic that is to be secured is generally called the IPSEC SA.

Within the IKE SA, keying material and properties for the IPSEC SAs are established. Keys are dynamically generated and are valid for the lifetime of the SA. In IPSEC, when keys need to change, a new SA with the new keying material is established and the traffic stops using the old SA and moves on to use the new SA. After a period of time sufficient for the transition, the old SA is then removed. An SA can be defined to last a specific amount of time or until a specific amount of data has been secured by the SA. Re-keys occur when such limits are reached. An important attribute of IPSEC re-keying is that perfect forward secrecy (PFS) can be maintained by keeping the derivation of subsequent keying material wholly independent of past keying material.

10.4.2 Connection Authentication

A great method of connection authentication available with IPSEC is the use of X.509 Certificates (that is, Digital Certificates, as included in RFC 2459). Certificates give cryptographically strong assurance that the authenticating party is who it says it is, and they have the advantage of being easier to manage and scale compared to other authentication schemes (such as preshared secrets).

Digital Certificates work by using a public key methodology. In public key methodologies there is a key pair, with one key held privately and the other key made available publicly. When the holder of a private key sends a message, the message can be hashed (that is, signed) using the private key. Anyone with the public key can then verify the hash (signature) of the message. If the message is hashed (signed) correctly using the public key, then it is assured that the sender of the message possessed the private key.

Digital Certificates are managed centrally by an entity called a Certificate Authority (CA). When CA is used, authentication is done without the need to configure any passwords. A Digital Certificate issued by the CA is all that is required. The method involves the use of two public/private key pairs. To start with, the public key of the CA has to be known by the authenticator. The authenticatee is in possession of a Digital Certificate signed by the CA and identifying the authenticatee and providing the public key of the authenticatee. When a connection attempt is made, the authenticatee sends the Digital Certificate to the authenticator. The authenticator can then verify that the Digital Certificate is really from the CA by checking the signature of the certificate using the CA's public key. The authenticator still has to make sure that the sender of the certificate also has the private key associated with the identity provided in the certificate. To do this, some unique information (akin to a challenge) is sent to the authenticatee, who then has to sign the private key of the authenticatee, and the signature is returned to the authenticator. The authenticator then verifies that this signature of the "challenge" is correct using the authenticatee's public key as contained in the Digital Certificate. This sequence of events establishes that the authenticatee holds both a valid certificate from the CA and the private key associated with the identity provided in the certificate.

Notice that the only information required by the authenticator before the connection attempt is the public key of the CA, as well a list of the identities that the authenticator will allow to connect. Digital Certificates are a very scalable solution since password lists do not have to be maintained by the authenticator. Digital Certificates are generally not prone to the security attacks that are possible with password-based mechanisms, such as dictionary attacks.

It should also be noted that the private key is configured on the end being authenticated. If this private key is compromised, then certificate authentication is compromised. Certificates can be revoked and kept in a Certificate Revocation List (CRL) in the CA and accessible to authenticators.

10.4.3 Encryption

Within the IKE SA, the keying material used to encrypt traffic in the IPSEC SA can be derived. When encryption is being used in an IPSEC SA, the "IPSEC Header" shown in Figure 10-1 is in actuality an Encapsulating Security Payload (ESP) header.

Using keys that the two sides have agreed on within the IKE to be used for the IPSEC SA provides secure encryption. The secrecy of the keys ensures that only the two ends involved in the communication will be able to decipher the contents of a message that has been encrypted. When a sender has a datagram to be sent on the SA, it encrypts the data using the agreed upon encryption algorithm and the negotiated encryption key. The message is then sent out. When the receiver receives a datagram on a given SA, it uses the negotiated decryption key and the agreed upon encryption algorithm to recover the original contents of the message. Note that there are no assurances that the message will be decrypted correctly, but the decryption can only fail if the datagram was tampered with. To protect against tampering, ESP can also provide authentication/integrity checking of the encrypted data to ensure that the datagram is received as it was sent.

10.4.4 Authentication/Integrity

Authentication and integrity are provided in one of two ways. Originally, authentication and integrity required the use of an Authentication Header (AH) in the place of an "IPSEC Header," as shown in Figure 10-1. Although now anachronistic, it was once specified that AH and ESP could be used together if a user wanted to employ both encryption and authentication/integrity together. Today encryption, authentication, and integrity can all be provided while using only an ESP header.

Authentication and integrity can be provided together if the parties to the communication use keying material that is negotiated in the IKE SA. Only the parties on either end of the IKE SA are privy to the actual value of the keys used, and the secrecy of the keys is what provides the security. When a packet is sent out, a hash function is performed over the packet based on the contents of the packet and the keying material. The result of the hash is included in the packet in the relevant IPSEC header (AH or ESP). The receiver then performs the same hash function over the packet and checks the results with the hash included in the IPSEC header. The hash will fail under two circumstances. If the packet has been modified between the time the sender performed the hash and the receiver checked it, the hash can fail (like any other checksum). The hash can also fail if the originating peer was not privy to the correct keying material, which is the case of a forged packet. This single hashing check therefore achieves the two goals of making sure data is authenticated and making sure that it is the data that the sender originally sent.

There is one important difference between authentication/integrity checking with AH and with ESP of which one needs to be aware. When AH is used, the hashing function is performed over the entire packet, including the IP header (excluding fields that are allowed to change in transit: TTL and IP header checksum). Therefore when AH is used, the contents of the IP header cannot be changed between sender and receiver. When ESP provides authentication/integrity however, the IP header is not included, and the hash is performed starting at (and including) the ESP header and the contents that follow it.

10.4.5 Replay Protection

Replay protection is provided in conjunction with authentication/integrity checking. The mechanism behind this mode of protection is simple. The IPSEC header contains a field whose value is monotonically increasing by 1 for each datagram. For a given key being used for authentication/integrity checking, the value is not allowed to wrap. The receiver can then check to make sure that it receives no data with the same replay counter field already received. When the replay counter maximum value is almost reached, a new SA is established to replace the old SA, and the new SA has its own replay counter that begins at 1 again. RFC 2085 specifies how this replay prevention is to work when HMAC-MD5 authentication using AH is being performed. The replay protection method is now used with other AH hash functions and with the ESP authentication/integrity hash functions.

The replay counter can easily guarantee protection without forcing dropped datagrams if datagrams are guaranteed not to be misordered in transit. The receiver simply has to check that each received datagram has a replay counter value that is higher than that of the previously received datagram. If datagrams can be misordered over the network, however, it is untenable to guarantee that no forced drops will occur. In theory the receiver could keep a mask of every datagram received so that it could check if a datagram has already been received or not. In this case, even if datagram 2 were not received until after datagram 102, datagram 2 could still be processed. This is not a realistic possibility (RFC 2085 specifies a 64-bit replay counter), but a receiver is allowed to keep a window of a size specifying how many "older" datagrams it will allow to come in. Within the window, however, the receiver still checks that each datagram has not already been received. So, for example, if datagram 102 has been received and there is a window of size 10, datagram 100 will be allowed to be received if and only if it hasn't already been received, but datagram 2 has lost its chance to be received since it is outside the window.

10.4.6 L2TP-Specific IPSEC Issues

The most important goals of this section on IPSEC are to outline what IPSEC has to offer to L2TP traffic and what L2TP-specific issues exist with regard to IPSEC implementation.

The most important thing to realize is that IPSEC provides protection based on layer 4 protocol and port information. In the case of L2TP that is UDP with a port of 1701 (or a configured alternate to port 1701). IPSEC does not differentiate L2TP control from L2TP data, so both are protected equally. It is also important to note that all L2TP data sessions will be protected equally. That means that if an IPSEC SA is established for an L2TP tunnel and a PPP session is being tunneled, then all of the PPP traffic will be given the same level of protection as the L2TP data. In contrast, with PPP encryption, PPP control traffic is not encrypted.

Another consequence of using IPSEC with L2TP is that operation of the tunnel through Network Address Translation (NAT) is hindered. One of the reasons that L2TP uses UDP instead of a GRE header such as that used with PPTP is that NAT will work with UDP applications. When IPSEC is used to provide security, all but the most trivial forms of NAT are no longer easily possible[1] because the UDP header is encrypted and hidden from the NAT device's view.

One performance problem encountered with IPSEC is that there may be security provided both at the tunneled PPP level and also on the tunnel via IPSEC (that is, both PPP encryption and IPSEC encryption are provided). Yet another layer of problem to be aware of is that the PPP session may be carrying data that is on an IPSEC SA into the private network. In this case it is possible that three levels of encryption would be done (by the IPSEC carried by the PPP session, by the

---

1. The expression "IPSEC breaks NAT" is generally found whenever IPSEC and traditional NAT are found in the same sentence. Under limiting assumptions, NAT can be made to work with IPSEC, but in the general (and very practical) sense, IPSEC does break NAT (or does NAT really break IPSEC?).

PPP session, and then by the IPSEC SA for the tunnel). These multiple levels of security are shown in Figure 10-2.

It is obvious that IPSEC adds some security features that are not present in L2TP. Message authentication, message integrity, and replay protection services can be provided to L2TP by IPSEC. IPSEC also overcomes two other security shortcomings of PPP running on L2TP: limited encryption scope and poor encryption key management. The encryption scope issue is handled because IPSEC will protect all of the PPP data, even the PPP control traffic. IPSEC is not prey to the poor encryption key management problem that plagues PPP. IPSEC generates keys dynamically and can provide perfect forward secrecy to subsequent re-keys, unlike PPP key handling. IPSEC also determines lifetimes for keys so that they are not used long enough to be cryptographically vulnerable.

The last area that IPSEC improves is L2TP's weak connection authentication. For connection authentication of the tunnel, IPSEC makes the best improvement. Instead of the preshared secret mechanism built into L2TP (or perhaps used in parallel with it), IPSEC can offer stronger authentication such as with Digital Certificates. Unfortunately, IPSEC cannot directly improve the connection authentication for the tunneled PPP sessions (this is not an issue for the L2TP client model). Tunneled PPP sessions still have to be authenticated using PPP authentication mechanisms, which fundamentally retain all of their weaknesses. Where IPSEC does assist in this area is when encryption is used for the tunnel. With the help of IPSEC encryption, the PPP authentication cannot be snooped within the tunnel. This protects against some methods of breaking PPP authentication passwords, such as snooping PAP passwords or trying to break CHAP authentication cryptographically.

10.5 L2TP Components and Security Overview

Security concerns in L2TP apply not only to the operation of the protocol itself, but also to the components that are used during the life of an L2TP tunnel. Figure 10-2 shows the typical components of an L2TP tunnel secured with IPSEC.

Figure 10-2 shows the components involved in L2TP tunneling and provisioning. All of the components shown are used to ensure a secure L2TP service. Some implementations may involve even more compo-

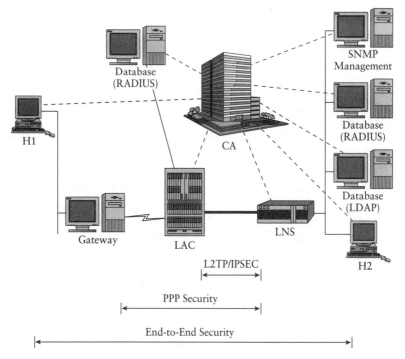

Figure 10-2 *Security components of an L2TP tunnel secured with IPSEC*

nents, such as a serial port management or a Telnet management interface. The dotted line connections between components and the CA represent the configuration of each of the components with a Digital Certificate assigned by the CA.

The bottom of the figure shows the extent of security protection offered for an IP flow from host H1 behind the gateway dialing into the LAC, and host H2 on the private network and behind the LNS. Any of the three security components may be present or not. If both H1 and H2 trust the private networks that lie behind the gateway and behind the LNS, then they may not do end-to-end security and instead rely on either PPP or L2TP/IPSEC security to protect the traffic while the connection runs on the public network. But any real security must be configured end-to-end.

Figure 10-2 shows a connection between the LAC and a RADIUS server. RADIUS provides security through a shared secret. The RADIUS server that the LAC connects to in this instance would contain information for L2TP tunnel authentication and possibly information on how to map PPP authentication user domain names to LNSs. To truly protect access to the RADIUS server, the connection between the LAC and its RADIUS server can be IPSEC protected.

Also shown in Figure 10-2 are a RADIUS server, a Lightweight Directory Access Protocol (LDAP) server, and a Simple Network Management Protocol (SNMP) management station. All of these entities can be used as part of the L2TP service provided by the LNS. The LNS can use either the LDAP or the RADIUS server for session and tunnel authentication. The SNMP management station can be used for monitoring and configuring L2TP on the LNS. All three of these entities typically use a shared secret to protect access. True security can again be provided to any or all of these three by protecting the connections with IPSEC.

One final note on end-to-end security: IPSEC can be used, but application or other transport security can be used as well. For example, the connection between H1 and H2 may be made over a Secure Socket Layer (SSL) connection. Some applications also provide security, in which case the end-to-end security could be nested, involving a connection protected by IPSEC that was carrying an application providing its own security mechanisms.

10.6 The LAC/LNS Trust Relationship

We have seen that it is possible through external security mechanisms (such as IPSEC) to provide comprehensive security services for an L2TP tunnel, including strong connection authentication, message authentication, message integrity, replay protection, encryption, and even perfect forward secrecy of encryption keys. With such protection mechanisms in place it is easy to believe that the security of the tunnel is ensured.

An important concept to security is the trust relationship (often called the trust model) that exists between entities. The trust model is generally centered on an entity and is an enumeration of all the security policies that entity practices relating to communication with other entities.

There is at least one case in which the trust relationship between an LAC and an LNS from the perspective of the LNS is of the utmost importance. It centers on the use of proxy authentication between the LAC and the LNS for incoming call sessions, specifically when CHAP authentication has been done. The use of proxy authentication is useful because it helps the PPP session to be brought up quickly if LCP negotiation between the LAC and the remote system is acceptable to the LNS. Even if LCP is renegotiated between the LNS PPP and the remote system, the proxy authentication can be used by the LNS so it can know the identity of the remote system PPP. Proxy authentication is obviously useful in the case where the identity provided by the remote system PPP is unknown. In this case the PPP session can be terminated right away instead of renegotiating LCP then entering authentication again only to find that the session is going to be dropped. Even such treatment, however, could prove useful to a hacker. By treating known and unknown usernames differently, a search for valid usernames can be done separately from searching for valid passwords. Once a valid username is found, then a search for the password for that username can be undergone. Making this a two-step process cuts down on the number of combinations that the hacker would have to try in order to break in with a combination of username and password and so should be avoided.

The decision that has to be made as part of the LAC/LNS trust relationship is whether or not to trust the proxy CHAP challenge provided by the LAC to the LNS. The principle behind the challenge/response mechanism in CHAP is that the authenticator provides a random challenge that the authenticatee must respond to. The authenticatee is obviously not allowed to provide both the challenge and the response to the authenticator. The authenticator's choice of the challenge is the central feature of CHAP. The operation of proxy CHAP modifies this feature a little bit. With proxy CHAP the LAC has provided a challenge to the remote system, and the remote system provides a response. The challenge and response are then forwarded to the LNS. From the perspective of the LNS, this is an important change in the authentication model. The LNS has to understand its trust relationship with the LAC to decide if it will accept this behavior. If the administrator of the LNS trusts the administrator of the LAC that it will not behave in a malicious manner to gain access to the private network behind the LNS and the LNS can adequately verify the identity of the LAC, then the proxy CHAP challenge can be used. Otherwise, the LNS should reissue its own CHAP challenge to the remote system before PPP connection authentication is deemed successful. The issuance of CHAP challenges by the LNS PPP is the only way that the LNS can guarantee that the remote system PPP really knows the CHAP preshared secret.

The issue of proxy CHAP challenges is even more important if L2TP connection authentication, message authentication, message integrity, or replay protection is not provided between the L2TP peers. In these cases a fourth party (that is, something other than the LAC, remote system, or LNS) could potentially leverage the weak security model of the LNS to gain access to the private network behind the LNS.

10.7 Comparing L2TP to L2F and PPTP

The security of tunneled sessions is the same for L2F, PPTP, and L2TP. All three rely on the security provided by PPP to protect user data.

For control of the tunnels themselves, L2TP inherits its tunnel authentication procedure from L2F (although in L2F it is mandatory, and in L2TP it is optional). L2F does not have a mechanism for hiding information in control messages, so the only thing the two protocols have in common is tunnel connection authentication. In contrast, PPTP does not have tunnel connection authentication or control message encryption options.

Since PPTP assumes operation over an IP network by using TCP/IP for the tunnel control connection, it is conceivable that transport mode IPSEC could be used to offer a secure PPTP service. Since L2F is defined to run over UDP as L2TP is, and thus it can use IPSEC as well, it is notable that because PPTP uses a TCP/IP control channel and carries data over GRE it is possible to offer different policies for securing PPTP control and data packets. For example, it is possible that only PPTP control messages could be IPSEC protected, while tunneled data would not be. It is also possible to have IPSEC protection policies that differ for control messages versus data, such as authentication for control traffic and authentication and encryption for data traffic.

10.8 Implementation Tips

Security is central to the deployment of L2TP as a VPN technology. Because L2TP is used as a technology to access a private network, the consumers of the L2TP service desire a level of security at least as good as their existing solution (PSTN, Frame Relay). Given the importance of security with L2TP, it is worth repeating or clarifying some issues.

10.8.1 Avoid or Adjust for PAP

Given that PAP sends clear text passwords, it seems like simple advice to avoid tunneling PAP for username/password logins (PAP can still be used securely with Onetime Passwords (OTPs), that is, token authentication). There is a potential area for PAP to expose username/password logins if the username/password is not specific to an authentication method. Take for instance an NAS that serves both as an LAC and as a traditional means of establishing dial-up sessions that will involve accessing the public network. For this example we'll say that the NAS decides to tunnel a session based on the authentication information, and also that the NAS wants to allow some of the users who will be accessing the public network to authenticate using PAP.

So when this NAS receives a call from a system that is to be tunneled, the NAS can negotiate PAP authentication. Once in the authentication phase, the NAS receives the PAP Auth Request packet with the username, and NAS figures out that the user is to be tunneled. One decision the LAC can make is whether or not to send the proxy authentication information with the PAP information, and if it does, whether or not to encrypt the AVP containing the PAP proxy authentication information. It is probably obvious that it is a good idea to encrypt the PAP proxy authentication information, or if there is no shared secret between the tunnel peers, not to include the PAP proxy authentication information. This is in fact what RFCl2tp suggests.

Assuming that the proxy PAP authentication information is safe either because it is not included in L2TP control messages or because its values are hidden in the control message, there is still a problem: the remote system PPP is still in the Authentication Phase. Because of this, it may retransmit the PAP Auth Request packet if it does not receive a PAP Auth Response or an LCP Config Request, sending the PPP state machine back into the LCP phase, quick enough.

Take, for example, the case where the remote system sends the PAP Auth Request to the NAS, which then decides that the session is to be tunneled. Now assume that LNS PPP wants to do MSCHAP so that MPPE encryption can be used. The LNS is going to restart into the

LCP phase by sending an LCP Config Request to the remote system. Unfortunately it is possible that the LCP Config Request to the remote system will be lost. In this case the remote system will not receive the LCP Config Request, and it is possible that the remote system will retransmit its PAP Auth Request before the LNS PPP retransmits its LCP Config Request. Once the L2TP session has been established, the LAC is simply passing packets back and forth between the remote system and the LNS, so the retransmitted PAP Auth Request will get tunneled to the LNS. If there is no security on the data messages, the PAP Auth Request is transferred in clear text between the LAC and the LNS—where it is possible that an attacker with access to the network somewhere in between will be able to see it. To be insidious, it is even possible that the attacker was responsible for causing the LCP Config Request from the LNS to be dropped in the first place in order, so as to cause the password to be revealed. But the PAP Config Request could also be dropped by the LAC if the LAC is inspecting the traffic coming from the remote system in order to prevent the PAP password from appearing on the network in the clear.

Obviously it is important to consider timing conditions such as these that can undermine security. Let's look at an example of how a simple condition can cause a major security problem. The administrator of the LNS configured PAP authentication so that it was not allowed, assuming that this meant that the users' passwords would be guaranteed to be protected. But folding in the previous example, loose policy both at the NAS/LAC and the remote system caused a clear text authentication to be negotiated and a password to appear on the network. It should be an established policy that the password used depends on the authentication method being carried out. In this way, the PAP password appearing in the clear will not compromise the secret used for CHAP authentication.

Because it is not possible for the LNS to control what the LAC negotiates during LCP before tunneling to the LNS, the LAC must be responsible for avoiding PAP. Since some L2TP LNS administrators may want to use PAP (for example, for token authentication) but others will want to avoid it (since they just use preshared secrets and want to use CHAP, MSCHAP, or EAP), the LAC may need to accommodate some configuration options to permit some flexibility. The LAC in this case would need to be able to negotiate PAP and discover that the session was to be tunneled to an LNS that didn't allow PAP. The LAC could then renegotiate with the remote system using a different authentication method before beginning to tunnel the session to the LNS.

10.8.2 Trusting Proxy CHAP Challenges

The entire PPP session connection authentication scheme can be compromised by a seemingly innocuous LNS implementation decision involving proxy CHAP. If an LNS implementation were to always blindly trust the CHAP challenge provided in proxy authentication by the LAC, the results would be disastrous. All that would be required to break into the private network of such an LNS would be to have captured the CHAP challenge/response sequence of a successful PPP authentication to the LNS. If an attacker could then establish a tunnel to this LNS,[2] the attacking LAC could then gain access to proxy LCP and proxy CHAP authentication information including the CHAP challenge previously issued by the LNS. Assuming that the proxy LCP information is all agreeable to the LNS, the connection will be allowed by this LNS.

Because of the possibility of such a breach it is recommended that, under normal circumstances, an LNS implementation should never accept proxy CHAP authentication information and always insist on issuing its own challenges. It would be reasonable for an implementation to have configuration options that would allow CHAP challenges in proxy authentication AVPs to be trusted (with a default of not trusting CHAP challenges).

10.8.3 Randomness

The quality of random number generation is always an issue when security is involved. The inclusion of random information is what makes things cryptographically secure. There are a few places where randomness is important when L2TP is used.

The first is in the generation of the value for the Random Vector AVP, which is used when other AVPs are going to have their Value field hidden. The quality of the random number generation for this AVP

---

2. This is trivial in most cases, since to support L2TP client implementations tunnels with no tunnel authentication are generally accepted.

protects both the AVPs being hidden as well as the tunnel preshared secret.

The second place where randomness is important is in the generation of challenges for authentication. This is done both in the CHAP-like authentication for the tunnel itself and in any CHAP authentication performed on individual tunneled PPP sessions.

As mentioned earlier, it is also recommended that random numbers be used for the Tunnel ID and Call ID values used in the protocol. Random values can offer protection against simple attacks where the attacker does not have access to inspect tunnel traffic but is able to forge tunnel traffic. The use of random numbers makes it more difficult for an attacker to gain access, although it simply means that the attacker needs to be either lucky or persistent.

10.8.4 Keep "Backdoor" Holes in Mind

With security, it is always necessary to attempt to expect the unexpected. No matter how secure a mechanism is in protecting against the attacks it was designed to protect against, there is always some outside threat that it cannot account for. The most infamous example involves interlopers finding nontechnological ways around security even in the presence of technological security mechanisms. For example, poor procedures or slack adherence to rules at a Network Operations Center can result in an imposter finding out someone's password by posing as the user and claiming to have forgotten the password.

The nature of security problems is such that the possible backdoor security weaknesses cannot be adequately enumerated. It is therefore extremely important that an implementor or user of L2TP attempt to discover possible weaknesses that are present in an implementation given the other features of the product that the implementation is a part of.

One area of concern with regard to security risks that are entirely technological and directly relevant to L2TP is the presence of SNMP management of L2TP. It should be obvious that the IPSEC transport mode's protection against denial of service attacks can do little if the implementation allows weakly protected SNMP management where an L2TP tunnel (or all L2TP tunnels) can be forcefully dropped. The administrators of an implementation should ensure that protection of L2TP is not undermined by inadequate protection of SNMP. The next chapter shows the options that are available through SNMP management of L2TP, and it should be obvious why security of this mechanism is required once one becomes familiar with how much can be done through it.

It is always a good idea to create diagrams such as the one shown in Figure 10-2 outlining each of the components involved in an implementation. Mapping out the entities involved and their interrelationships can help in determining what the weak points of a system are. For example, Triple DES encryption of the L2TP tunnel is foiled if the LNS's RADIUS server can be compromised and a username and password can be found that can then be used within an L2TP tunnel.

10.9 Further Reading on IPSEC

This chapter covers only the most general level of introduction to the operation of IPSEC; it should be sufficient to understand what IPSEC protection has to offer to L2TP and how IPSEC can fill the security gaps not covered by the L2TP protocol itself.

For interested readers there is an abundance of technical material available regarding IPSEC and security. For material on security in general, the book *Network Security* by Charles Kaufman, Radia Perlman, and Mike Speciner is a good introduction. A more advanced study is provided in Bruce Schneier's book *Applied Cryptography*.

There are several RFCs that are related to IPSEC. RFC 2401 "Security Architecture for the Internet Protocol" lays out the architecture for IPSEC and is probably the most important place to start for investigating IPSEC in detail. RFC 2407 "The Internet IP Security Domain of Interpretation for ISAKMP" is also important for understanding the operation of IPSEC from a high level. RFC 2408 "Internet Security Association and Key Management Protocol (ISAKMP)" and RFC 2409 "The Internet Key Exchange (IKE)" specify how IPSEC security associations are managed. Several other RFCs from RFC 2402 through RFC 2410 provide the detail for the headers used in IPSEC encapsulation and the mathematical transforms used to provide security with these headers. RFC 2411 "IP Security Document Roadmap" is also invaluable for understanding how the IPSEC-related RFCs are to be navigated.

11

SNMP Management

It is often very illuminating to investigate the management structure that has been defined for a protocol. The management structure can yield clues as to what an implementation should be keeping track of and can make excellent implementation suggestions through its structure and content. The set of Internet Drafts under the name draft-ietf-pppext-l2tp-mib-xx.txt (where xx ranges from 00 to 04) define the SNMP Management Information Base (MIB) for L2TP. The most recent of these drafts, as of this writing draft-ietf-pppext-l2tp-mib-04.txt, was updated after the forty-third IETF in Orlando, after it was decided that data session flow control was to be removed.

Although the SNMP MIB for L2TP is still in draft form, it has followed the development of L2TP long enough to be in a fairly mature state. It has undergone major structural changes since the 00 version of the draft, and the draft is not considered controversial in its current form based on the L2TP mailing list history. It is expected that this draft will become an RFC that is not materially different than the current form found in the 04 draft.

Reviewing the L2TP MIB will provide an excellent summary of the L2TP architecture and can serve to reinforce one's understanding of implementation requirements.

11.1 Interface Layering

The overall architecture of L2TP can be discerned from the interface definitions found in the MIB. The ifStackTable is used to define how protocol interfaces are layered onto a stack. Figure 11-1 (adapted from draft-ietf-pppext-l2tp-mib-04.txt) shows the protocol interface layering

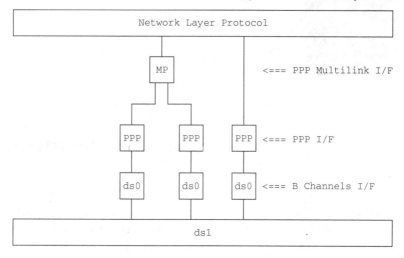

Figure 11-1 *Traditional dial-up protocol interface stack*

for a typical dial-up. Here we have a straightforward breakdown of the interface layering for a dial-up system. The DS-0 channels inside the DS-1 are generally regarded as the physical layer (layer 1). PPP (including MP) makes up the datalink layer (or layer 2) interfaces. Above PPP are the network layer (or layer 3) interfaces. Figure 11-2 shows how this picture is modified when the PPP traffic is being tunneled between an LAC and an LNS with L2TP.

Comparing Figures 11-1 and 11-2, it can be seen that the difference is that in Figure 11-2 L2TP tunnel interfaces have been inserted between the DS0 interfaces and the PPP interfaces. This makes logical sense given how the L2TP protocol works. The purpose of L2TP is to carry traffic between the physical connection handled by the LAC (for example, the DS0 interfaces) and the PPP interfaces handled by the LNS. Figure 11-2 shows this function clearly in the two tunnels between the LAC and LNS. It is important to note that the composite stacks of Figure 11-2 do not exist in any one MIB. The MIB for the LNS contains the network layer, MP, PPP, and upper L2TP tunnel interfaces. The LAC MIB contains the lower L2TP tunnel interfaces and the DS0 and DS1 interfaces.

Note that the placement of the L2TP tunnel interface in the stack depends on whether an LAC or an LNS is being described. This

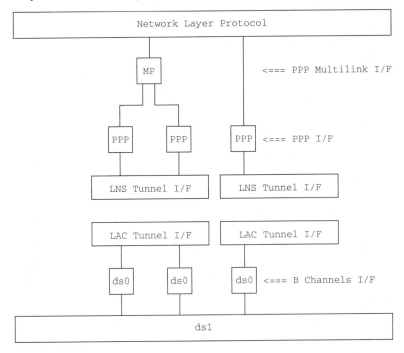

Figure 11-2 *Example LNS (top) and LAC (bottom) composite protocol interface stack*

asymmetric definition is particularly awkward for the LAC if the tunnel is running over another type of interface (for example, Frame Relay). For the LNS this is no problem; the model can just be extended so that the L2TP tunnel interface is stacked on top of a Frame Relay interface. For the LAC this cannot be done, because in the case of the LAC the L2TP tunnel interface is already shown to be over the physical interfaces for the calls (for example, DS0 interfaces). It does not make any sense for the Frame Relay interface that the L2TP tunnel interface is running over to be stacked on top of the L2TP tunnel interface in the MIB.

An obvious question to ask is why the individual L2TP data sessions are not represented in the interface layering model shown in Figure 11-2. One may imagine that an L2TP data session interface entry could be found on the LAC between each DS0 I/F and the appropriate

L2TP Tunnel I/F, and on the LNS between each PPP I/F and the appropriate L2TP Tunnel I/F. Until the 03 version of the L2TP MIB, such an interface layering model did exist. It was removed primarily because it was deemed to be an unnecessary burden on network management applications, and because no special information about the protocol layering was presented by the existence of a session interface. The L2TP data session is really a sub-layering within L2TP and doesn't provide any multiplexing. There is always a one-to-one mapping between the session and another interface. On an LAC the session is mapped directly with a physical connection interface (for example, DS0 in Figure 11-2). On an LNS the session is always mapped directly with a PPP interface as shown in Figure 11-2. Since including the L2TP session interfaces does not add any information on the form of the stack, these interfaces can be safely removed from the ifTable of the resident host without any loss of information. This in turn reduces the size of the ifTable and makes it easier for Network Management Stations to digest the interface structure of the managed system.

11.2 Management Information Base

The L2TP MIB is organized into four main portions: L2TP objects (l2tpObjects), Traps (l2tpTraps), Transports (l2tpTransports), and Compliance (l2tpCompliance). There is little of interest in any of these branches except for in the l2tpObjects branch. The only trap defined under l2tpTraps is a trap for when tunnel authentication fails. The l2tpCompliance branch is interesting when it comes to actually implementing the MIB, but it doesn't shed any light on features of the protocol because it really just provides grouping of SNMP objects found primarily under the l2tpObjects branch of the MIB. The l2tpTransports branch is potentially interesting, but only UDP/IP transport is defined for use in the MIB (following the lead of RFCl2tp, of course). For UDP/IP, the only information in the MIB under l2tpTransports is the source and destination UDP port information for tunnels.

Figure 11-3 shows the organization of the MIB under the l2tpObjects branch. There is one branch underneath l2tpObjects, that being l2tpScalar. The l2tpScalar branch is further branched into l2tpConfig and l2tpStats branches. Both of these branches contain general information on the instance of the L2TP protocol implementation.

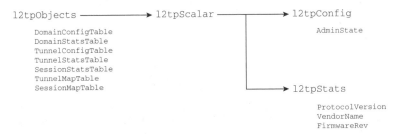

Figure 11-3 *The l2tpObjects branch of the L2TP MIB*

The main part of the L2TP MIB consists of the tables in the l2tpObjects portion of the MIB. These tables are listed in Figure 11-3. The important ones to investigate are those that give the configuration and statistics for tunnels and for tunnel sessions. It is also interesting to note that the MIB shows the possibility of configuring sets of tunnels based on domain information (instead of configuring each tunnel singly). There is a wealth of information in the tables under l2tpObjects, and many of the objects in these tables are straightforward. The following sections summarize the role of these tables in the MIB and point out some of their more interesting aspects.

11.2.1 l2tpTunnelConfigTable

The l2tpTunnelConfigTable contains the definition of some of the objects that should be expected to be configurable. Some of the items that can be configured include the shared secret, the maximum number of retransmission before the control channel is brought down, the type of transport for the tunnel, and so forth. Two configurable items to note are the specification for whether security is required for the tunnel, and the setting of a timeout value for waiting for out-of-order data messages. The first of these, l2tpTunnelConfigSecurity, is interesting because it shows that policy for requiring security of L2TP tunnels with IPSEC is important (which should be obvious from the material on security covered in Chapter 10).

The other object of interest is the l2tpTunnelConfigReassemblyTimeout object. Chapter 8 described the trade-off between waiting for misordered data messages. This object exposes the desirability of providing a configurable item on a tunnel-by-tunnel basis for controlling how long the timeout should be. Setting the value of this object at 0 means that reordering of misordered data messages will not be done and each misordered data message will be treated like a dropped data message.

This l2tpTunnelConfigTable also contains configuration of the transport used for the tunnel. The values currently specified are Other, None, ipUdp, and frameRelay. It is interesting to note that even though ipUdp is specified as the transport in general, there is no configuration in the MIB for what the UDP port or IP address values for the tunnel should be. This means that if a tunnel endpoint is listening for tunnel connections on a port other than 1701, this fact is not reflected in the MIB.

11.2.2 l2tpDomainConfigTable

The l2tpDomainConfigTable contains many of the same configuration items as the l2tpTunnelConfigTable. The differences are that this table also contains an administrative state for the tunnel domain, and this table does not allow specification of the transport used for the tunnels. The index into the table is a full or partial domain name identifying the domain. It is important to differentiate the tunnel domain from the domain name of PPP authentication IDs used by the LAC to determine LNS tunnel termination points.

The purpose of this table is to provide configuration for a tunnel or a set of tunnels based on a full or partial domain name. With this table an entire set of L2TP peers can be configured with one configuration entry. The host name provided by the peer during tunnel establishment can be used to look up configuration in this table for the tunnel being established.

11.2.3 l2tpDomainStatsTable

For a domain of tunnels it is useful to keep track of things such as how many tunnel attempts have failed, how many tunnel authentication attempts have failed, how many tunnels have been successful, and so forth. This table contains just this type of information. In addition, this table keeps track of how many data and control messages and octets have been handled by a tunnel domain.

The index into this table, just as with the l2tpDomainConfigTable, is a full or partial domain name identifying the domain.

11.2.4 l2tpTunnelStatsTable

This table contains statistics for a tunnel. Information about both the control channel and the peer implementation is present. For the control channel this table will yield sequence number state: the last sequence number sent, the last sequence number received, the last sequence number acknowledged, and the last sequence number acknowledged by the peer. The initial control channel receive message window size chosen by the local and remote peers is also given. The local and peer tunnel IDs, the state of the tunnel, and the initiator of the tunnel are also given. The index into the table is the ifTable value for the tunnel used in the interfaces MIB.

The l2tpTunnelStatsTable also contains useful information about the peer implementation. The host name given by the peer, as well as the peer's vendor name, firmware revision, and protocol version are all objects that are listed in this table.

11.2.5 l2tpSessionStatsTable

Although Figure 11-2 shows that the MIB presents no interface entries for L2TP data sessions, it is important to have statistics for individual sessions within an L2TP tunnel. The l2tpSessionStatsTable, indexed by the combination of the ifIndex for the tunnel and the data session ID for the data session, provides statistics for individual L2TP data sessions.

There are plenty of objects in this table, providing everything that would ever want to be known about an L2TP data session. Essentially, there is a one-to-one mapping between the objects in this table and the AVPs that are exchanged during session establishment. Dynamic statistics such as how many messages were received out of order are also present in this table. The table also contains an object that indicates whether or not Proxy LCP was performed by the LAC for a data session.

11.2.6 Mapping Tables

Rounding out the l2tpObjects are two mapping tables. These tables are provided to allow management applications to be able to correctly and efficiently navigate the MIB.

The l2tpTunnelMapTable provides a mapping from local Tunnel ID to the ifIndex used for the tunnel in the interfaces MIB and in other areas of the L2TP MIB. It is natural to identify a tunnel by the local Tunnel ID given the presence of the Tunnel ID in the L2TP protocol. With this table a management application can start with the Tunnel ID for a tunnel and find the ifIndex for the tunnel so that other information for the tunnel can be determined from other parts of the MIB. With this information successful management is possible in the case where the management application starts off knowing only the ifIndex for the tunnel or when it starts off knowing only the local Tunnel ID for the tunnel.

With the l2tpSessionMapTable a management application can identify the L2TP session associated with a given interface identified in the Interfaces MIB. For an LNS the index used would be the ifIndex for the PPP instance associated with the data session. For an LAC the index used would be the ifIndex for the physical interface instance associated with the data session (such as the DS0 instances shown in Figure 11-2). Using the ifIndex of either a PPP instance on an LNS or a physical interface instance on an LAC, a management application can determine the ifIndex for the tunnel and the local data session ID for the associated L2TP data session.

It is important to note that historical tunnel statistics are kept only on a per tunnel domain basis, not on a per tunnel basis (where tunnel would have to be defined as an LAC/LNS pair).

12

Future Direction and Resources

This chapter gives a general summary of L2TP, as well as some forward-looking information on expected areas of future development in L2TP. Useful resources for L2TP developers are also supplied.

12.1 Protocol Summary

L2TP can be best summarized as a protocol that provides for outsourced remote access. The protocol was developed so that devices at the edge of a network (LNSs) providing access to that network would not need to support the various physical methods of remote access. The roles of a traditional remote access device are split into two pieces (LAC and LNS). The job of L2TP is to provide the signaling so that these two types of devices can provide the same service to the remote system that was available when a single device served as the network access point for a remote system.

As has been seen, L2TP handles this service by tunneling PPP between the LAC and the LNS with the PPP session extending from the remote system to the LNS. In this so-called compulsory tunneling mode the LAC acts as a relay agent for the PPP traffic between the remote system and the LNS, and the LAC handles the details of physical framing on the physical connection between the LAC and the remote system.

By collapsing the LAC functionality into the remote system, L2TP has also been used to provide access through an LNS directly from the remote system. This mode of operation is called voluntary tunneling because there is no intermediate L2TP system involved and the decision to encapsulate packets into the tunnel can be made on a per packet basis voluntarily by the remote system. It is important to note that collapsing the LAC functionality into the remote system does not change the nature of the operation of the L2TP protocol between the LAC and LNS. The messages exchanged to establish the tunnel and sessions and to tear down sessions and the tunnel are the same. Some AVPs or AVP values may not apply to the voluntary remote system case, however. Having the voluntary remote system and compulsory tunneling modes behave so similarly from a message exchange standpoint provides the real benefit of making it possible for LNS devices to terminate both types of connections easily.

An important point that has been covered is that L2TP is specified in RFCl2tp such that once a data session has been established between the LAC and the LNS, the LAC blindly forwards PPP frames between the remote system and the LNS. As we saw in Chapters 8 and 9, this blind forwarding of data causes some areas of difficulty in providing some PPP functionality to the remote system (for example, FCS Alternative). But these limitations can be overcome easily by changing the LAC implementation to investigate the PPP traffic it is relaying between the remote system and the LNS. Although this feature is not part of the specification of L2TP, it is also not precluded by it. The stateful inspection of PPP traffic by the LAC was not made part of the L2TP protocol so that the level of complexity of the LAC implementation would be minimized. It is important to understand exactly what is compromised by this choice, however. A more robust LAC implementation will be stateful in order to provide solutions to problems arising from blind LACs. These problems arise from the fact that the LAC is aware of the connection characteristics between the LAC and the remote system, but in contrast the LNS is not fully aware of the characteristics on that connection. The result is a poor split of responsibility between the LAC and LNS for media-dependent LCP options unless the LAC inspects and translates LCP negotiations between the remote system and LNS. Where possible, the LAC could also keep the operation of compression or encryption protocols run over the connection to the remote system only and not extend this functionality over the tunnel.

One problem area of L2TP that cannot be solved by simple stateful inspection and translation of negotiations by the LAC involves the tunneling of PPP sessions that are taking part in the Multilink PPP (MP). The essential problem with multilink is that part of its procedure is for each endpoint to identify itself during LCP negotiation. Because an LAC may be going through LCP negotiation with a remote system before establishing a data session to an LNS for the PPP session, this identification procedure can be a problem. But it is a problem that can conceptually be solved through coordinated configuration between the administrators of the LNS devices and the administrators of the LAC devices. If all of the LAC devices at a POP provide the same endpoint discriminator (ED) value to the remote systems, a consistent value will be used. Then either the LNS devices can be configured with the same ED values, or they can be configured to accept the ED values provided by the LAC devices to the remote systems.

A more complex method can be used by the LAC to greatly improve the operation of MP over L2TP. The MP links can be terminated at the LAC, and then the bundle PPP session can be tunneled to the LNS. If this were to be done, the LNS would not know that MP was being performed. So the LAC would need to make the bundle session look like a regular PPP session to the LNS, while also making sure that the bundle looked like a real bundle from the point of view of the remote system. The reader should understand that this is merely a suggestion and an area for future investigation, and not a feature that is implemented in any known system. This approach is a fairly straightforward marriage of the concept of link aggregation as with the MMP protocol and the concept of a device performing PPP translation.

12.2 Future Direction

Because L2TP is such a new protocol there are several Internet Drafts specifying expansions to it. We'll cover a few of the more important ones.

The most important addition to the main L2TP specification will be the reinstatement of a specification for data flow control. As of the time of this writing the initial Internet Draft specifying data flow control for post–draft 12 implementations was not available.

The specification of IPSEC protection of L2TP is an active L2TP-related Internet Draft. In October 1998 in Binghamton, New York, and in May 1999 in Santa Barbara, California, interoperability bakeoffs were held at which many implementations of L2TP over IPSEC were tested. This draft specifies the use of IPSEC to protect tunnels running over IP and tunnels not running over IP. Originally a separate draft was created for securing L2TP over non-IP without using IPSEC, but this draft has fallen from discussion.

Operation of L2TP over non-IP media types is also under development. Currently draft-ietf-pppext-l2tp-aal5-funi-00.txt for ATM and draft-ietf-pppext-l2tp-fr-01.txt for Frame Relay are under development.

Because L2TP was developed with PPP over HDLC links in mind for the physical connection between the LAC and the remote system, development is under way to ease the accommodation of other physical connection types without adding inspection and translation capabilities at the LAC. The specification draft-ietf-pppext-l2tp-link-00.txt is being developed for this purpose. A popular PPP implementation mechanism for negotiating options is to use state structures for the options wanted, the options allowed, and the options actually negotiated in either direction. These are called the *wantoptions, allowoptions,* and the *gotoptions* and *hisoptions.* The L2TP base specification essentially supports the communication of the gotoptions and hisoptions from the LAC to the LNS if the LAC has performed LCP negotiation before tunneling the PPP session. The draft-ietf-pppext-l2tp-link-00.txt specification essentially adds the wantoptions and allowoptions to be communicated from the LAC to the LNS as well (in fact, these options are usefully communicated even if the LAC hasn't negotiated LCP with the remote system). This mechanism allows the LAC to inform the LNS what link options it supports for negotiation and takes the guesswork out of the LNS. Note that this draft is most useful if the LAC isn't performing stateful inspection of the PPP traffic between the LNS and the remote system. If the LAC is inspecting the traffic between the two, then the LAC can proxy the LCP negotiation between the two so that the correct options are negotiated on the physical connection, even if the LNS doesn't know about them.

12.3 Resources

Because L2TP is in the relatively early stages of its development there are not many resources available for implementers. Information on

L2TP is available almost exclusively through the IETF. L2TP was developed within the PPP Extensions working group of the IETF, although the effort progressed almost as if it were being developed through its own working group. The IETF holds meetings three times a year, and L2TP discussion takes place within the PPP Extensions working group sessions at the IETF meetings.

Bakeoffs are held by the California Broadband Users Group—Cal-BUG (what used to be the California ISDN Users Group, CIUG). Because of the nature of L2TP, testing can also be done privately between willing parties over the Internet for no real cost (compare this to companies joint-testing ISDN for instance, where phone charges would come into play).

12.3.1 Internet Engineering Task Force

The best resources available for L2TP are through the IETF (*http://www.ietf.org*). L2TP is under the PPP Extensions (pppext) working group (*http://www.ietf.org/html.charters/pppext-charter.html*) of the IETF. A separate mailing list from the main pppext mailing list exists for the discussion of L2TP issues and development. The latest information for the L2TP mailing list should be obtained from the pppext charter Web page at the IETF, because it may change. Before sending email to this list asking a question, it is best to consult the mail archive for the list of questions to find out if your question has been asked before (this is likely the case). The archive for the L2TP mailing list through February 1, 1999, can be obtained at *http://bodhi.zendo.com/vandys/l2tp-mail*. The mailing list archive for L2TP after February 1, 1999, can be obtained at *http://www.ipsec.org/email/l2tp*.

Unfortunately there is no Frequently Asked Questions (FAQ) resource yet available for L2TP. When a FAQ for L2TP does become available, a link to it will likely be available on the pppext working group Web page already listed. Mark Townsley, one of the authors of the L2TP RFC, maintains a list of L2TP-related links at *http://www.townsley.net/l2tp.html*.

The IETF Page of Intellectual Property Rights Notices at *http://www.ietf.cnri.reston.va.us/ietf/IPR/* should be consulted for the latest Intellectual Property notices regarding L2TP. The page *http://www.ietf.org/ipr.html* should also be checked for Intellectual Property Rights information.

12.3.2 PPP

For PPP development there are many resources available including free example implementations. Excellent starting points for learning more about PPP are available through the IETF and the book *PPP Design and Debugging* by James Carlson (which also lists a great number of resources available for PPP).

The IETF holds meetings three times a year during which sessions are held in each of the active working groups. Discussion of L2TP takes place in the pppext working group sessions. Consult the IETF Web pages for more information on meetings, meeting times, and so forth.

12.3.3 IPSEC

IPSEC is developed under the Security Area of the IETF under its own working group (*http://www.ietf.org/html.charters/ipsec-charter.html*). This Web page contains the starting point for looking into IPSEC, including information on how to get onto the IPSEC mailing list and how to access the mailing list archives.

12.3.4 Bakeoffs

Interoperability testing of L2TP implementations has been held at events called *bakeoffs,* held by the California Broadband Users Group (CalBUG). The CalBUG originally held bakeoffs as the CIUG to test PPP. Because L2TP tunnels PPP the CalBUG expanded the bakeoffs to include L2TP as well. In the fall of 1998 and the spring of 1999 the CalBUG (then CIUG) held Virtual Private Network interoperability bakeoffs that included testing of L2TP, L2TP secured with IPSEC, and also just IPSEC. Generally the bakeoffs cover new features and do not address established functionality, although tests can be run informally between participants if interested parties can be found. Testing of the base L2TP specification will no longer be considered an item in need of a bakeoff, although various extensions to L2TP will be tested as they are being developed.

For more information about CalBUG and bakeoffs, consult Cal-Bug's Web page at *http://www.ciug.com.*

Appendix: Draft 12 Data Flow Control

As of the time of writing, the data flow control feature was removed from the base L2TP specification to be included in a separate specification. At the same time, this new specification focusing on data message flow control was not yet under way, however, so newer implementations are not able to work with older implementations in this regard.

This appendix contains the information on data channel flow control that was present in draft 12 of the L2TP specification, draft-ietf-pppext-l2tp-12.txt. The motivation for including this information here is because Internet Drafts are temporary documents and are not guaranteed to be maintained by the IETF after a six-month period. Draft 12 has an expiration date of June 1999.

This appendix can be used as a record of the data session flow control implementation specification that was available at the time that L2TP implementations based on draft 12 were being made. By making use of this information, users with newer implementations can work with older implementations that desire or require data channel flow control.

When the new specification concentrating on L2TP data channel flow control becomes available it is expected that it will provide compatibility with the specifications in draft 12. If that becomes the case, then that document, instead of this appendix should be followed. Until such a document becomes available, this appendix should serve as a guide to interoperability with older implementations.

A.1 Summary of Implementations

The next section will give numerous excerpts from draft 12 detailing the specification of data channel flow control. The summary of the differences between an implementation based on draft 13 or later and a draft 12 implementation are given in the following subsections.

A.1.1 Receive Window Size AVP in Call Establishment

Draft 12 specifies the signaling of data channel flow control via the sending of the Receive Window Size AVP (RWS AVP) in call establishment messages. The messages for call establishment that can contain this AVP are OCRQ, OCCN, ICRP, and ICCN.

A.1.2 R Bit in Data Message Header

The data message header defines one of the bits marked as reserved in draft 13 as the Reset-Sr bit (R bit). The transmitting peer uses this bit when it detects the loss of a data message so that it can reset the internal state variable Sr on the receiving peer.

A.1.3 Adaptive Timeouts and Piggybacking

Since the data channel includes acknowledgments, draft 12 defines adaptive timeouts and acknowledgment piggybacking for data messages.

A.2 Draft 12 Specifications

In the following pages we provide excerpts from draft 12 specifying how data message flow control is performed. The following excerpt is necessary to understand some of the discussion. It defines two quantities specified as state variables kept by either end, Ss and Sr.

> Sr represents the value of the next in-sequence message expected to be received for a given session by a peer. Ss represents the sequence number to be placed in the Ns field of the next message sent for a given session by the sending peer. Each state is initialized such that the first message sent and the first message expected to be received for each session has an Ns value of 0. This corresponds to initializing Ss and Sr in both peers to 0 for each new session.

The remainder of this appendix consists of a series of excerpts, occasionally annotated, from draft-ietf-pppext-l2tp-12.txt. Attention is drawn to some of the areas that are important and easier to look over and miss. Section headings are retained because some of the excerpts reference other sections of draft 12. Each of these references should then be found within the excerpts. The notation "[. . .]" is meant to represent text from draft 12 that is not included here because it is not relevant to data message flow control. Annotations will be represented in text type.

4.0 Protocol Overview

[. . .]

As messages are sent for a given session, Nr is set in these messages to reflect one more than the Ns value of the highest (modulo 2**16) in-order message received for that session; if sent before any packet is received Nr will be 0, indicating that the peer expects the next new Ns value received to be 0. When a non-ZLB message is received with an Ns value that matches the session's current Sr value, Sr is incremented by 1 (modulo 2**16). It is important to note that, for both control and payload sessions, Sr is not modified if a message is received with a value of Ns greater than the current Sr value (exceptions to this rule being the permitted handling of out-of-order payload packets by the "simple receiver" discussed in Appendix C and handling of payload packets with the R bit set). For the control session, retransmission of outgoing messages should eventually provide the receiving peer with the expected message. For payload sessions, however, lost messages are never retransmitted so a mechanism involving the use of the "Reset Sr" (R bit) indicator in an outgoing message is used to update the peer's value of Sr to the value of Ns contained in the message. See Sec. 4.2 for details of this mechanism.

The term *ZLB* used in the preceding extract has the same meaning as it does in conjunction with the control channel—a Zero Length Body message. This message is used to send a simple acknowledgment for data messages on a particular session. The message consists entirely of the data message header.

Every time a peer sends a non-ZLB message it increments its corresponding Ss value for that session by 1 (modulo 2**16). This increment takes place after the current Ss value is copied to Ns in the message to be sent. Outgoing messages always include the current value of Sr for the corresponding session in their Nr field.

A message (control or payload) with a zero-length body indicates that the packet is only used to communicate Nr and Ns fields. The Nr and Ns fields are filled in as above, but the sequence number state, Ss, is not incremented. Thus a ZLB message sent after a non-ZLB message will contain a new Ns value while a non-ZLB message sent after a ZLB message will contain the same value of Ns as the preceding zero-length message. Unless the Rbit (Reset Sr) is set, a peer receiving a zero-length message does not update its Sr variable.

Upon receipt of an in-order non-ZLB message, the receiving peer must acknowledge the message by sending back the updated value of Sr in the Nr field of the next outgoing message. This updated Sr value can be piggybacked in the Nr field of any non-ZLB outgoing messages that the peer may happen to send back.

If the peer does not have a message to transmit for a short period of time after receiving a non-ZLB message then it should send a ZLB message containing the latest values of Sr and Ss, as described above. The suggested value for this time interval is 1/4 the receiving peer's value of Round-Trip-Time (RTT - see Appendix A), if it computes RTT, or a maximum of 1/2 of its fixed timeout interval otherwise. This timeout should provide a reasonable opportunity for the receiving peer to obtain a payload message destined for its peer, upon which the ACK of the received message can be piggybacked.

This timeout value should be treated as a suggested maximum; an implementation could make this timeout quite small without adversely affecting the protocol. To provide for better throughput, the receiving peer should skip this timeout entirely and send a ZLB message immediately in the case where its receive window fills and it has no queued data to send for this connection or it can't send queued data because the transmit window is closed.

A suggested implementation of this timer is as follows: Upon receiving a non-ZLB message, the receiver starts a timer that will expire in the recommended time interval. A variable, Lr (Last Nr value sent), is used by the transmitter to store the last value sent in the Nr field of a transmitted payload message for this connection. Upon expiration of this timer, Sr is compared to Lr and, if they are not equal, a ZLB ACK is issued. If they are equal, then no ACK's are outstanding and no action needs to be taken.

This timer should not be reinitialized if a new message is received while it is active since such messages will be acknowledged when the timer expires. This ensures that periodic ACK's are issued with a maximum period equal to the recommended timeout interval. This interval should be short enough to not cause false acknowledgment timeouts at the transmitter when payload messages are being sent in one direction only. Since such ACK's are being sent on what would otherwise be an idle data path, their affect on performance should be small, if not negligible.

See Appendix E for some examples of how sequence numbers progress.

Note that the preceding text references Appendix E in draft 12, which appears later in this appendix.

[. . .]

4.2 Payload Packet Overview
[. . .]

The L2TP header also contains optional acknowledgment and sequencing information that can be used to provide flow control across the underlying medium (which may be an internetwork) as well as congestion control in the network itself (see section 4.3). In this document, these mechanisms will be referred to collectively as "flow control". Control messages are used to determine rate and buffering parameters that are used to regulate the flow of PPP packets for a particular session over the tunnel.

The receiving peer indicates whether flow control is to be performed for payload packets sent to it. If a peer issues a Receive Window Size AVP with a non-zero value during session establishment, then the sending peer MUST abide by the indicated window size value as long as sequence numbers are provided. If a receiving peer does not wish to flow control the payload packets sent to it, it should not issue the Receive Window Size AVP with a non-zero value. Issuing a Receive Window Size AVP with a zero value has special significance. It indicates that the receiver does not want to perform flow-control but it does want the sending peer to provide Ns values in payload packets so that it can detect lost packets or packets received out of order. A peer SHOULD NOT send ZLB ACK's when its advertised Receive Window is zero or not present (flow control is not requested).

Note the importance of the preceding paragraph in terms of the implications for implementations based on draft 13 or later. It says here that if the Receive Window Size AVP is received during call establishment, then the transmitter MUST abide by it. The newer implementation has a choice: either to tear down a call when the RWS AVP is received during call establishment, or to follow the requirements laid out in draft 12 for data flow control.

In the case where neither peer issues a Receive Window Size AVP during session establishment, the optional Nr and Ns fields are absent in all payload packets for that session. In the case where either peer wishes to perform flow-control or to detect out-of-order receive messages (as indicated by the sending of the Receive Window Size AVP with non-zero or zero value, respectively) the Nr and Ns fields MUST be present in payload packets sent by both peers. A proper Ns value starts at 0 and increments by one for each transmitted payload message and a proper Nr value is the current value of the receive sequence number state variable, Sr. See Appendix F for a table detailing when to send sequence numbers with regard to the Receive Window AVP.

Unless the LAC sends the Sequencing Required AVP (see section 6.7 and 6.8) in the ICCN or OCCN message, the LNS has the authority to dynamically enable or disable sending of Ns/Nr and hence controlling the capability of loss detection, reordering and flow control over the link. To disable sequence numbers, the LNS sends a packet with the F bit set to 0 and Ns/Nr fields not present. The LAC, upon receiving such a data packet, MUST process the packet and discontinue inclusion of Ns/Nr fields in any subsequent data packets. Any packets which have been received by L2TP but are being held in queue for reordering SHOULD be flushed without waiting for an ACK from the peer (as if an R bit packet with Ns equal to the current Sr value was received). Ss and Sr should be updated and saved accordingly.

All data packets will continue to be exchanged without sequence numbers until the end of the session or until the LNS resumes sequence numbers by sending a packet with the F bit set and Ns/Nr present. The LAC, upon receiving a packet with the F bit set, MUST resume sending sequence numbers in further packets. In order to properly resume, the LNS and LAC MUST preserve the state of Ss and Sr between periods of disabled sequencing.

While the LNS may initiate disabling of sequencing at any time during the session (including the first data packet sent), it is recommended that for links where reordering or packet loss may occur, sequence numbers always be enabled during the initial negotiation stages of PPP and disabled only when and if the risk is considered acceptable. For instance, if the PPP session being tunneled is not utilizing any stateful compression or encryption protocols and is only carrying IP (as determined by the NCP's that are established), then the LNS might decide to disable sequencing, thus allowing higher level protocols to perform necessary flow control end to end and reducing the per packet L2TP processing burden on the LNS substantially. Further discussion of some of the tradeoffs associated with disabling sequencing over media which may reorder or silently drop packets is given in section 8.2.

Note that no excerpts from section 8.2 of draft 12 are included in this appendix. It so happens that section 8.2 of draft 12 didn't actually discuss the trade-offs mentioned above, they were discussed in section 8.1 instead. But there is no information from these sections that is not in the newer versions of the L2TP specification. In draft 12, section 8.1 was the section on L2TP over UDP/IP.

Special attention should be paid in the following section to how the R bit in the data message header is used during data session flow control. After draft 12, the R bit definition was removed from the data message header because it is used only for data session flow control.

4.3 Flow Control

If a receiving peer offers a non-zero receive window size to a sending peer then the sending peer MUST abide by this window size value as long as sequence numbers are being exchanged (See Appendix F for details of when flow control is enabled in relation to sending of the receive window AVP). The sending peer MUST stop sending payload packets when the window is full; i.e., x consecutive messages have been sent but have not been acknowledged, where x is the value of the Receive Window Size AVP. Implementors should take care to avoid the situation where loss of an ACK by a sending peer with a full transmit window causes a session to hang forever, due to the fact there are no retransmissions of payload packets. Steps must be taken to reopen the transmit window (at least to a value of 1) upon expiration of an ACK wait timeout. See Appendix B for more details.

When sending to a peer that has issued a non-zero receive window size, the sending peer is responsible for resetting the receiver's Sr value when a sent payload message is lost during transmission. When a sent message is lost, the receiving peer's Sr value (and hence the Nr value it sends) will "stick" at the Ns value of the first missing payload message. The "Reset Sr" (R bit) in the payload message header (see Section 5.3) provides a mechanism for the sending peer to indicate to the receiver that it (the sending peer) recognizes that at least one payload message has been lost and that the receiving peer should now reset its Sr value beyond the lost message(s). If the sending peer is performing adaptive window adjustment (see Appendix B.1) then it is this recognition of a lost message that is used to indicate that a window adjustment at the sending peer should be performed.

The sender may use a timer mechanism similar to that used to retransmit lost control messages to determine when transmitted payload packets have been lost. When the timer expires, a payload message (zero or non-zero length) with the R bit set can be issued to indicate to the receiver that it needs to reset its Sr value. Upon receipt of a payload message with the R bit set, the receiver resets Sr to the value of Ns contained in the message, or, if highly congested, to a value between its current value and the value of Ns contained in the message.

Upon receipt of a payload message with R bit set, the receiver takes the following actions: First, the receiver checks for the presence of the R bit in a received payload message before comparing the message's Ns value to its Sr value. If the R bit is set, the receiver will typically set its Sr value equal to that of Ns contained in the message and fall through to normal receive message processing in which Sr will be incremented (modulo $2^{**}16$) if the message is non-ZLB and will remain the same if it is ZLB. However, if the receiver is known to be heavily congested, it MAY choose to not update or set its new Sr value between (modulo $2^{**}16$) the current Sr value and that of Ns contained in the message. This effectively spoofs the transmitter into believing that the R bit packets that have been sent are not being received, ultimately causing the transmitter to backoff more quickly.

In order to prevent an R bit message received out of order from setting Sr to an old value, the receiving peer should compare the value of Ns in an R bit message to its current value of Sr. The receiving peer should reset its Sr value only if Ns is greater than (modulo $2^{**}16$) its current value of Sr.

The sender of the R bit can decide whether it wishes to advance the receiver's Sr value to the value just past the highest (modulo $2^{**}16$) Nr value received (the Ns value of the message just past that of the first lost message) or to its current value of Ss. Resetting it to that just past the first lost message enables the sender to determine if other messages in the same transmit window were also lost. Setting it to the current Ss value of the sender treats losses of multiple messages in the same window the same as the loss of a single message. An implementation may use either, or a combination of both methods. If the transmitter detects that the receiver is heavily congested, piggybacking the R bit on data packets should be refrained in favor of a ZLB with the R bit set for resetting the receiver's Sr.

It is permissible for a sending peer to set the R bit (and hence reset the transmit window) in all transmitted payload packets as an indication that flow control has been disabled at the transmitter.

Receipt of an R bit is NOT an explicit indication to immediately flush all packets which might be in queue to PPP for processing. There are a number of tradeoffs as to precisely when a receiver should decide to pass packets from L2TP to PPP, many dependent on what protocols are being carried by PPP. In general, packets should be declared lost and passed to PPP in a timely enough manner so as to not cause retransmissions by reliable higher-layer protocols due to packets that are held in queue by l2tp.

L2TP does not specify the particular timeout algorithms to use for flow control. Suggested algorithms for the determination of adaptive timeouts to recover from dropped data or acknowledgments on the tunnel are included in Appendix A of this document. Additional examples for sequencing and flow control are included in Appendix E.

[. . .]

5.3 Payload Message Format
[. . .]

```
 0                   1                   2                   3
 0 1 2 3 4 5 6 7 8 9 0 1 2 3 4 5 6 7 8 9 0 1 2 3 4 5 6 7 8 9 0 1
+-+-+-+-+-+-+-+-+-+-+-+-+-+-+-+-+-+-+-+-+-+-+-+-+-+-+-+-+-+-+-+-+
|T|L|R|0|F|0|S|P|0|0|0|0|0| Ver |          Length (opt)         |
+-+-+-+-+-+-+-+-+-+-+-+-+-+-+-+-+-+-+-+-+-+-+-+-+-+-+-+-+-+-+-+-+
|           Tunnel ID           |            Call ID            |
+-+-+-+-+-+-+-+-+-+-+-+-+-+-+-+-+-+-+-+-+-+-+-+-+-+-+-+-+-+-+-+-+
|            Ns (opt)           |            Nr (opt)           |
+-+-+-+-+-+-+-+-+-+-+-+-+-+-+-+-+-+-+-+-+-+-+-+-+-+-+-+-+-+-+-+-+
|        Offset Size  (opt)     |       Offset pad... (opt)     |
+-+-+-+-+-+-+-+-+-+-+-+-+-+-+-+-+-+-+-+-+-+-+-+-+-+-+-+-+-+-+-+-+
```

The important point here, again, is the addition of the R bit, which was removed in draft 13. The description of the R bit for this diagram is given in the following paragraph.

[. . .]

The R bit, "Reset Sr", is used for flow control and indicates that the receiver SHOULD reset its receive state variable, Sr, for this session to the value contained in the Ns field of this message header. Sr is reset to the value of Ns only if Ns is greater than (modulo $2^{**}16$) the receiver's current value of Sr. Normal receive processing of the message is performed after the value of Sr is reset. Note that if the F bit is not set, then this bit MUST be 0. See section 4.2 for a detailed discussion of the use of this bit for flow control on the data channel. See Appendix E for examples of proper R bit usage.

Although the F bit survives from draft 12 into draft 13 and beyond, the description given in the following two paragraphs does not, and the description in draft 13 is much more terse.

If the F bit is set, both the Nr and Ns fields MUST be present. Ns indicates the sequence number of the packet being sent. The Ns value of a message being transmitted is copied from the current value of the send sequence number state variable, Ss. Ss is incremented by one (modulo $2^{**}16$) after copying to the Ns field only if the message being sent is not a ZLB ACK. Nr indicates the sequence number of the next in-order message sequence number to be received (if the last in-order non-ZLB data packet had Ns set to 1, the Nr sent back would be 2). The value of Nr is copied from the current receive state variable, Sr. Together, Nr and Ns can be used to handle out-of-order packets and, together with the R bit, to provide flow control for the connection.

An L2TP peer setting the F bit, and placing Nr and Ns fields in its messages, MUST have previously received or sent a Receive Window Size AVP during establishment of the session. The Nr and Ns fields are present and updated as described in section 4.0 if either side has specified an intention to do payload flow control.

[. . .]

The following four sections from draft 12 included the optional presence of the Receive Window Size AVP. The descriptions for the Receive Window Size AVP in each of these four messages are essentially the same.

6.6 Outgoing-Call-Request (OCRQ)

6.8 Outgoing-Call-Connected (OCCN)

6.10 Incoming-Call-Reply (ICRP)

6.11 Incoming-Call-Connected (ICCN)

Following is an excerpt of one of those descriptions. The description has been adapted in terms relative to the sender of the AVP and the receiver of the AVP. In draft 12 the wording of each description was based on whether the LAC or the LNS was sending or receiving the message containing the RWS AVP.

Receive Window Size

```
0                   1                   2                   3
0 1 2 3 4 5 6 7 8 9 0 1 2 3 4 5 6 7 8 9 0 1 2 3 4 5 6 7 8 9 0 1
+-+-+-+-+-+-+-+-+-+-+-+-+-+-+-+-+-+-+-+-+-+-+-+-+-+-+-+-+-+-+-+-+
|1|0|0|0|0|0|0|          8          |            0              |
+-+-+-+-+-+-+-+-+-+-+-+-+-+-+-+-+-+-+-+-+-+-+-+-+-+-+-+-+-+-+-+-+
|            10           |              Size                   |
+-+-+-+-+-+-+-+-+-+-+-+-+-+-+-+-+-+-+-+-+-+-+-+-+-+-+-+-+-+-+-+-+
```

Receive Window Size AVP encodes the window size being offered by the [*AVP Sender*] for this call. The Attribute value is 10, Receive Window Size, and is marked mandatory. This AVP is present only if Sequence and Acknowledgment Numbers are to be used in the payload session for this call. The 16-bit Size value indicates the number of received data packets the [*AVP sender*] will buffer for this call, which is also the maximum number of data packets the [*AVP Receiver*] should send before waiting for an acknowledgment.

[. . .]

The countless appendices in draft 12 were replaced by two appendices. This isn't surprising because the appendices in draft 12 all had to do with control and data flow control. The following appendix excerpts are relevant to data flow control. Note that the procedures for calculating timeout values given in these excerpts were recommended but not required in draft 12.

Appendix A: Acknowledgment Timeouts

L2TP uses sliding windows and timeouts to provide session and control flow-control across the underlying medium (which may be an internetwork) and to perform efficient data buffering to keep the LAC-LNS data channels full without causing receive buffer overflow. L2TP requires that a timeout be used to recover from dropped data or acknowledgment packets for both control and data messages. The only real difference between the flow-control mechanism used for the two message types is that control messages are retransmitted upon expiration of the acknowledgment timeout in order to assure reliable transport while payload messages are never retransmitted. Because payload messages are not retransmitted, the action taken upon expiration of the acknowledgment timeout for each message type also differs.

When the timeout for a control session expires the previously transmitted control message with Ns value equal to the highest in-sequence value of Nr received from the peer is retransmitted. The receiving peer does not advance its value for the receive sequence number state, Sr, for either a control session or payload session until it receives a message with Ns equal to its current value of Sr (except for the simple receiver described in Appendix C and payload packets with the R bit set). This rule assures that all subsequent acknowledgments for this session will contain an Nr value equal to the Ns value of the first missing message until a message with the missing Ns value is received. This rule also assures that when a payload message is lost anywhere within the current transmit window, the payload session acknowledgment timeout will expire, allowing the transmitter to adjust transmission parameters such as those suggested in this appendix.

According to the above rule for updating of the receiving peer's Sr value, the loss of a transmitted payload message (due to non-retransmission of payload messages) will cause Sr to remain at the value of the first lost payload message. In order to cause the receiving peer to advance its value of Sr beyond that of a lost message's Ns value, upon expiration of a payload session acknowledgment timeout, the sending peer MUST transmit a payload message with R bit set and Ns value greater than or equal to Ns of the lost message. Refer to Section 4 for more details on the use of the R bit.

The exact implementation of the acknowledgment timeout is vendor-specific. It is suggested that an adaptive timeout be implemented with backoff for flow control. The timeout mechanism proposed here has the following properties:

> Independent timeouts for each session. A device (LAC or LNS) will have to maintain and calculate timeouts for every active session.

> An administrator-adjustable maximum timeout, MaxTime-Out, unique to each device.

> An adaptive timeout mechanism that compensates for changing throughput. To reduce packet processing overhead, vendors may choose not to recompute the adaptive timeout for every received acknowledgment. The result of this overhead reduction is that the timeout will not respond as quickly to rapid network changes.

> Timer backoff on timeout to reduce congestion. The backed-off timer value is limited by the configurable maximum timeout value. Timer backoff is done every time an acknowledgment timeout occurs.

In general, this mechanism has the desirable behavior of quickly backing off upon a timeout and of slowly decreasing the timeout value as packets are delivered without timeouts.

Some definitions:

> Packet Processing Delay, "PPD", is the amount of time required for each peer to process the maximum amount of data buffered in its offered receive packet window. The PPD is the value exchanged between the LAC and LNS when a call is established. For the LNS, this number should be small. For an LAC supporting modem connections, this number could be significant.

"Sample" is the actual amount of time incurred receiving an acknowledgment for a packet. The Sample is measured, not calculated.

Round-Trip Time, "RTT", is the estimated round-trip time for an Acknowledgment to be received for a given transmitted packet. When the network link is a local network, this delay will be minimal (if not zero). When the network link is the Internet, this delay could be substantial and vary widely. RTT is adaptive: it will adjust to include the PPD and whatever shifting network delays contribute to the time between a packet being transmitted and receiving its acknowledgment.

Adaptive Timeout, "ATO", is the time that must elapse before an acknowledgment is considered lost. After a timeout, the sliding window is partially closed and the ATO is backed off.

Packet Processing Delay (PPD)
The PPD parameter is a 16-bit time value exchanged during the Call Control phase expressed in units of tenths of a second (64 means 6.4 seconds). The protocol only specifies that the parameter is exchanged, it does not specify how it is calculated. The way values for ATO are calculated is implementation-dependent and need not be variable (static timeouts are allowed). If adaptive timeouts are to be used then the PPD should be exchanged in the call connect sequences. A possible way to calculate the PPD is:

```
PPD = ((PPP_MAX_DATA_MTU - Header) * WindowSize *
    8) / ConnectRate + LACFudge (for an LAC)
```

or

```
PPD = ((PPP_MAX_DATA_MTU - Header) * WindowSize *
    8) / AvePathRate + LNSFudge (for an LNS)
```

Header is the total size of the L2TP and media dependent headers. MTU is the overall MTU for the link between the LAC and LNS. WindowSize represents the number of packets in the sliding window, and is implementation-dependent. The latency of the underlying connection path between the LAC and LNS could be used to pick a window size sufficient to keep the current session's pipe full. The constant 8 converts octets to bits (assuming ConnectRate is in bits per second). LACFudge and LNSFudge are not required but can be used to take overall processing overhead of the LAC or LNS into account.

In the case of the computed PPD for an LNS, AvePathRate is the average bit rate of the path between the LNS and LAC. Given that this number is probably very large and WindowSize is relatively small, LNSFudge will be the dominant factor in the computation of PPD. It is recommended that the minimum value of PPD be on the order of 0.5 second.

The value of PPD is used to seed the adaptive algorithm with the initial RTT[n-1] value.

A.1 Calculating Adaptive Acknowledgment Timeout
We still must decide how much time to allow for acknowledgments to return. If the timeout is set too high, we may wait an unnecessarily long time for dropped packets. If the timeout is too short, we may time out just before the acknowledgment arrives. The acknowledgment timeout should also be reasonable and responsive to changing network conditions.

The suggested adaptive algorithm detailed below is based on the TCP 1989 implementation and is explained in Richard Steven's book TCP/IP Illustrated, Volume 1 (page 300). 'n' means this iteration of the calculation, and 'n-1' refers to values from the last calculation.

```
DIFF[n] = SAMPLE[n] - RTT[n-1]
DEV[n] = DEV[n-1] + (beta * (|DIFF[n]| - DEV[n-
   1]))
RTT[n] = RTT[n-1] + (alpha * DIFF[n])
ATO[n] = MIN (RTT[n] + (chi * DEV[n]),
   MaxTimeOut)
```

DIFF represents the error between the last estimated round-trip time and the measured time. DIFF is calculated on each iteration.

DEV is the estimated mean deviation. This approximates the standard deviation. DEV is calculated on each iteration and stored for use in the next iteration. Initially, it is set to 0.

RTT is the estimated round-trip time of an average packet. RTT is calculated on each iteration and stored for use in the next iteration. Initially, it is set to PPD.

ATO is the adaptive timeout for the next transmitted packet. ATO is calculated on each iteration. Its value is limited, by the MIN function, to be a maximum of the configured MaxTime-Out value.

Alpha is the gain for the round trip estimate error and is typically 1/8 (0.125).

Beta is the gain for the deviation and is typically 1/4 (0.250).

Chi is the gain for the timeout and is typically set to 4.

To eliminate division operations for fractional gain elements, the entire set of equations can be scaled. With the suggested gain constants, they should be scaled by 8 to eliminate all division. To simplify calculations, all gain values are kept to powers of two so that shift operations can be used in place of multiplication or division. The above calculations are carried out each time an acknowledgment is received for a packet that was not retransmitted (no timeout occurs).

A.2 Flow Control: Adjusting for Timeout

This section describes how the calculation of ATO is modified in the case where a timeout does occur. When a timeout occurs, the timeout value should be adjusted rapidly upward. Although L2TP payload packets are not retransmitted when a timeout occurs, the timeout should be adjusted up toward a maximum limit. To compensate for shifting internetwork time delays, a strategy must be employed to increase the timeout when it expires. A simple formula called Karn's Algorithm is used in TCP implementations and may be used in implementing the backoff timers for the LNS or the LAC. Notice that in addition to increasing the timeout, we also shrink the size of the window as described in the next section.

Karn's timer backoff algorithm, as used in TCP, is:

```
NewTIMEOUT = delta * TIMEOUT
```

Adapted to our timeout calculations, for an interval in which a timeout occurs, the new timeout interval ATO is calculated as:

```
RTT[n] = delta * RTT[n-1]
DEV[n] = DEV[n-1]
ATO[n] = MIN (RTT[n] + (chi * DEV[n]),
  MaxTimeOut)
```

In this modified calculation of ATO, only the two values that contribute to ATO and that are stored for the next iteration are calculated. RTT is scaled by delta, and DEV is unmodified. DIFF is not carried forward and is not used in this scenario. A value of 2 for Delta, the timeout gain factor for RTT, is suggested.

Appendix B: Acknowledgment Timeout and Window Adjustment

B.1 Initial Window Size

Although each side has indicated the maximum size of its receive window, it is recommended that a slow start method be used to begin transmitting data. The initial maximum window size on the transmitter is set to half the maximum size the receiver requested, with a minimum size of one packet. The transmitter stops sending packets when the number of packets awaiting acknowledgment is equal to the current maximum window size. As the receiver successfully digests each window, the maximum window size on the transmitter is bumped up by one packet until the maximum specified by the receiver is reached. This method prevents a system from flooding an already congested network because no history has been established.

When for any reason an LAC or LNS receives more data than it can queue for the tunnel, a packet must be discarded. In this case, it is recommended that a "random early discard" algorithm [6] be used rather than the obvious "drop last" algorithm.

B.2 Closing the Window

When a timeout does occur on a packet, the sender adjusts the size of the transmit window down to one half its maximum value when it failed. Fractions are rounded up, and the minimum window size is one.

B.3 Opening the Window

With every successful transmission of a window's worth of packets without a timeout, the maximum transmit window size is increased by one packet until it reaches the maximum window size that was sent by its peer when the call was connected. As stated earlier, no retransmission is done on a timeout. After a timeout, transmission resumes with the maximum transmit window starting at one half the size of the maximum transmit window when the timeout occurred (with a minimum window size of 1) and adjusting upward by one each time the current maximum transmit window is filled with packets that are all acknowledged without timeouts.

B.4 Window Overflow

When a receiver's window overflows with too many incoming packets, excess packets are thrown away. This situation should not arise if the sliding window procedures are being properly followed by the transmitter and receiver. It is assumed that, on the transmit side, packets are buffered for transmission and are no longer accepted from the packet source when the transmit buffer fills.

Appendix C: Handling of Out-of-Order Packets

When the Sequence Number and Acknowledgment Number fields are present in payload packets, they are used to manage packet rate. In addition, they may be used to handle out-of-order arrival of packets. A simple L2TP receiver may choose to skip the test for the Ns value of a received message being equal to Sr, simply updating Sr if Ns is greater than the current value of Sr. For example, if packets 1, 2, 3 arrived as 1, 3, 2, this simple implementation would silently discard packet 2 without informing the sender in any way that packet 2 was discarded. Even though packet 2 is dropped by the receiver, the transmitter will perceive all transmitted packets as being received without loss by its peer.

Such behavior does not affect the L2TP protocol itself, but significantly improved throughput in such environments may be attained by queuing and reordering packets when they arrive out of order. The number of packets to be queued is a function of memory resources on the L2TP implementation, but should never be more than 1/4 of the total sequence number space (i.e., 16384 packets), to avoid the possibility of sequence number aliasing.

It is suggested that receiving peer implementations implement the Sr state variable for payload sessions and that they update Sr only when receiving the next in-sequence Ns value or when receiving a message with the R bit set. Doing so allows a mechanism for reporting of lost payload messages to the transmitter, which is necessary for the transmitter to implement algorithms such as those suggested in Appendix A and B.

Note that while payload messages received out-of-order may either be queued, discarded, or delivered out-of-order, queuing is preferred. PPP does not expect to receive packets out-of-order so, if queuing is not provided by a receiver, it is preferable for it to discard out-of-order packets rather than deliver them to PPP.

[. . .]

Appendix E: Examples of L2TP Sequence Numbering

Although sequence numbers serve distinct purposes for control and data messages, both types of messages use identical techniques for assigning sequence numbers. This appendix shows several common scenarios, and illustrates how sequence number state progresses and is interpreted.

[. . .]

E.4 Lost Payload Packet with ZLB Flow Control

In this example, a packet sent from Peer A to Peer B is lost. Peer B's receive window is 4, so after Peer A realizes that it has filled Peer B's window, it waits. After timing out, Peer A sends a ZLB with the

R bit set to reset Peer B, telling it to give up on 3001. If performing window adjustment, Peer A should now reduce its effective transmit window size until a full window is digested by Peer B.

```
Peer A                         Peer B (RW = 4)
   ->      Payload Packet
           Nr: 7000, Ns: 3000
                               Payload Packet   <-
                               Nr: 3001, Ns: 7000
   ->      Payload packet      (packet lost)
           Nr: 7001, Ns: 3001
                               Payload Packet   <-
                               Nr: 3001, Ns: 7001
   ->  Payload packet
       Nr: 7002, Ns: 3002
   ->  Payload packet
       Nr: 7002, Ns: 3003
   ->  Payload packet
       Nr: 7002, Ns: 3004
       (window full, waiting)
   ->  Timeout, send ZLB w/R bit set
       Nr: 7002 Ns: 3005
                               Payload Packet   <-
                               Nr: 3005 Ns: 7002
```

Note that the ZLB sent with the R bit set could have been any value greater than that of the lost packet, 3001, and the current Ss value plus one. Thus, a ZLB with the R bit set to 3002, 3003, or 3004 instead of 3005 would have had effectively the same result given that peer B received and queued the out-of-order packets.

E.5 Lost Payload Packet with Piggyback Flow Control
In this example, two packets sent from Peer A to Peer B are lost. Peer B's receive window is 4, so after Peer A realizes that it has filled Peer B's window, it waits. After timing out, Peer A sends a payload packet with the R bit set to reset Peer B, telling it to give up on 3001 and 3002. If performing window adjustment, Peer A should now reduce its effective transmit window size until a full

window is digested by Peer B. Note that in this scenario Peer A has no way of knowing that more than one packet was lost.

```
Peer A                             Peer B (RW = 4)
        ->      Payload Packet
                Nr: 7000, Ns: 3000
                               Payload Packet     <-
                               Nr: 3001, Ns: 7000
        ->      Payload packet      (packet lost)
                Nr: 7001, Ns: 3001
        ->      Payload packet      (packet lost)
                Nr: 7001, Ns: 3002
                               Payload Packet  <-
                               Nr: 3001, Ns: 7001
        ->      Payload packet
                Nr: 7002, Ns: 3003
        ->      Payload packet
                Nr: 7002, Ns: 3004
     (window full, waiting)
        ->      Timeout, send Payload w/R bit set
                Nr: 7002 Ns: 3005
                               Payload Packet   <-
                               Nr: 3006 Ns: 7002
```

The draft 12 Appendix F, following, is useful because it makes clear how sequence number and flow-control negotiation is done. Note that the big difference is the Receive Window (RW) sent in the RWS AVP. After draft 12, the base specification keeps the Sequencing Required AVP, which is also present in draft 12, and the ability of the LNS to start and stop sequence numbers if the Sequencing Required AVP (also present in draft 12) is not sent by the LAC.

Appendix F: Flow Control and Sequencing Negotiation

This section provides a table of when sequence numbers are expected and when flow control is enabled on data packets. Note that this does not consider the case of dynamic disabling/enabling of sequencing by the LNS (see section 4.2).

"Peer A" and "Peer B" columns contain the value of the Receive Window (RW) sent by the corresponding peer (e.g. if RW=0 appears in the "Peer A" column, then Peer A sent a RW of 0 to peer B). "RW>0" refers to all possible Receive Window values greater than 0, "no RW" means that the Receive Window AVP was not present in the message sent.

Peer A	Peer B	Action
no RW	no RW	Sequence numbers are absent, no flow control
RW=0	RW=0	Sequence numbers are present, no flow control
RW=0	no RW	Sequence numbers are present, no flow control
no RW	RW=0	Sequence numbers are present, no flow control
RW>0 RW>0	RW=0 no RW	Sequence numbers are present, Peer B flow controls packets sent to Peer A
RW=0 no RW	RW>0 RW>0	Sequence numbers are present, Peer A flow controls packets sent to Peer B
RW>0	RW>0	Sequence numbers are present, Peer A and B flow packets to respective Peer

Glossary

ACCM (Asynchronous Control Character Map) A value representing the octet values to be escaped over a PPP connection

ACFC (Address and Control Field Compression) State of a PPP connection that is allowed to leave off the address and control of PPP frames

ADSL (Asymmetric Digital Subscriber Line) A technology for high-speed data communication over standard copper telephone lines

AH (Authentication Header) A header used on IPSEC packets that are providing authentication and other security services, without providing encryption

AHDLC Asynchronous HDLC

ATM (Asynchronous Transfer Mode) A cell-switching based data link protocol

AVP (Attribute Value Pair) The construct found in L2TP control messages to encode values. L2TP uses AVPs instead of static message fields

BGP (Border Gateway Protocol) An IP routing protocol used at the edge of IP networks

Bundle A PPP session run over aggregated PPP sessions via Multilink PPP

CA (Certificate Authority) An entity responsible for distribution and maintenance of Digital Certificates

Call A connection between a Remote System and LAC over which PPP is run

CCP (Compression Control Protocol) A control protocol of PPP used to negotiate the use of compression

CDN (Call Disconnect Notify) The L2TP message signaling the teardown of an L2TP data session

CHAP (Challenge Authentication Protocol) An authentication protocol of PPP where a challenge and challenge response are exchanged for authentication

DES (Data Encryption Standard) An encryption algorithm used with IPSEC

DoS (Denial of Service) A type of network attack that results in loss of service to legitimate users

EAP (Extensible Authentication Protocol) An authentication protocol in PPP used to provide different types of authentication

ECP (Encryption Control Protocol) A control protocol of PPP used to negotiate the use of encryption

ED (See Multilink PPP Endpoint Discriminator)

ESP (Encapsulating Security Payload) A header used on IPSEC packets that are providing encryption and other security services

FCS (Frame Check Sequence) A value used to verify the integrity of the contents of a frame in PPP

GRE (Generic Routing Encapsulation) The encapsulation defined in RFC1701 for encapsulating network layer protocols

HDLC (High-level data link control)

Home Gateway The L2F equivalent of the L2TP LNS

IANA (Internet Assigned Number Authority)

ICCN (Incoming Call Connected) The L2TP message from an LAC to an LNS to complete the establishment of an L2TP data session for an incoming call

ICRP (Incoming Call Reply) The L2TP message from an LNS to an LAC in response to an ICRQ in order to establish an L2TP data session for an incoming call

ICRQ (Incoming Call Request) The L2TP message used by an LAC to request an L2TP data session to an LNS for tunneling a PPP session as a result of an incoming call to the LAC

IETF (Internet Engineering Task Force)

IKE (Internet Key Exchange) A protocol used in concert with IPSEC used to establish IPSEC security associations dynamically

Incoming Call A PPP connection between a Remote System and LAC initiated by the Remote System

IPCP (Internet Protocol Control Protocol) The Network Control Protocol (NCP) of PPP responsible for negotiation of Internet Protocol parameters over the PPP connection

IPSEC (Internet Protocol Security) A set of protocols defining a method of providing security services to IP traffic

IPXCP (Internet Package Exchange (IPX) Control Protocol) The Network Control Protocol (NCP) of PPP responsible for negotiation of IPX parameters over the PPP connection

ISP (Internet Service Provider) An entity providing access to the Internet for a body of users

L2F (Layer 2 Forwarding) An IETF Historic protocol for tunneling layer 2 protocols such as PPP and SLIP over non-point-to-point networks

L2TP (Layer 2 Tunneling Protocol) An IETF Standards Track protocol for tunneling PPP sessions over non-point-to-point networks

LAC (L2TP Access Concentrator) Device terminating calls to remote systems and tunneling PPP sessions between remote systems and an LNS

LCP (Link Control Protocol) A subprotocol of PPP used to negotiate link parameters for the PPP connection

LDAP (Lightweight Directory Access Protocol) A protocol used to access databases

LNS (L2TP Network Server) A device able to terminate L2TP tunnels from an LAC and terminate PPP sessions to remote systems through L2TP data sessions

MAC (Medium Access Control) The portion of the data link layer responsible for medium-dependent interaction with the physical layer

MD5 (Message Digest 5) The algorithm defined in RFC1321 for producing a hash value of data

MMP (Multilink Multinode PPP Bundle Discovery Protocol) A protocol (Internet draft) that uses L2TP to tunnel multilink PPP link sessions to a single NAS so the MP bundle can aggregate links from multiple devices

MP (See Multilink PPP)

MPED (See Multilink PPP End-point Discriminator)

MPPC (Microsoft Point-to-Point Compression) A protocol developed by Microsoft for PPP compression

MPPE (Microsoft Point-to-Point Encryption) A protocol developed by Microsoft for PPP encryption

MRRU (Maximum Receive Reconstructed Unit) The value of the maximum reconstructed frame size that can be received on an MP bundle. Presence of the MRRU option in LCP negotiations indicates the use of MP

MRU (Maximum Receive Unit) The value of the maximum PPP frame size that can be received on a PPP connection

MSCHAP (Microsoft Challenge Authentication Protocol) The proprietary Microsoft extension to CHAP

MSCHAPv2 (Microsoft Challenge Authentication Protocol Version 2) Version 2 of the proprietary Microsoft extension to CHAP

MTU (Maximum Transmission Unit) A value representing the largest size packet that can be sent on a data link

Multilink PPP (MP) Protocol where PPP sessions are used to carry fragmented data to be aggregated for a higher-level PPP session (bundle)

Multilink PPP End-point Discriminator (MPED) The LCP option used to identify a system in order to aggregate PPP sessions for operation of MP

NAS (Network Access Server) A device for terminating connections over point-to-point connections for access to packet-switched networks. In L2F, the L2F equivalent to the LAC in L2TP is also simply referred to as the NAS

NAT (Network Address Translation) The operation of changing IP header address fields while forwarding

NCP (Network Control Protocol) In PPP, a protocol for negotiating parameters for the operation of a network layer protocol on a PPP data link

OCCN (Outgoing Call Connected) The L2TP message from an LAC to an LNS to complete the establishment of an L2TP data session for an outgoing call

OCRP (Outgoing Call Reply) The L2TP message from an LAC to an LNS to respond to an OCRQ and notify the LNS that an outgoing call to a remote system will be attempted

OCRQ (Outgoing Call Request) The L2TP message from an LNS to an LAC to request the placement of an outgoing call from the LAC to a remote system and the establishment of an L2TP data session

OTP (One Time Password) A password system where a given password is valid only once

Outgoing Call A PPP connection between a Remote System and LAC initiated by the LAC

PAC (PPTP Access Concentrator) In PPTP the PAC is the equivalent of the LAC in L2TP

PAP (Password Authentication Protocol) An authentication protocol of PPP where the username and password are sent in cleartext to the authenticator for authentication

PFC (Protocol Field Compression) The state of a PPP connection that is allowed to compress the two octets of PPP protocol ID in the PPP frame to a single octet when the first octet has the value zero

PNS (PPTP Network Server) In the PPTP Protocol, the PNS is the equivalent of the LNS in L2TP

POP (Point of Presence) An access point for users to an Internet Service Provider's network

PPP (Point-to-Point Protocol) The IETF Standard protocol for communicating over point-to-point connections

PPTP (Point-to-Point Tunneling Protocol) An IETF Informational protocol for tunneling PPP sessions over non–point-to-point networks

PSTN (Public Switched Telephone Network)

QoS (Quality of Service)

Remote System A system connecting through a call to an LAC and ultimately to a network behind an LNS through an L2TP tunnel

SA (Security Association) In IPSEC, an established security policy between two IP systems for a specific set of traffic

SCCCN (Start Control Connection Connected) The L2TP message used to complete the establishment of an L2TP control connection

SCCRP (Start Control Connection Reply) The L2TP message used to reply to an SCCRQ in order to establish an L2TP control connection

SCCRQ (Start Control Connection Request) The L2TP message used to request the establishment of an L2TP control connection

SDP (Self-Describing Padding) A padding mechanism used by PPP to increase the size of PPP packets

SG (Security Gateway) In IPSEC, an IP system that forwards IP packets over IPSEC tunnels to other similar IP systems

SLA (Service Level Agreement) An agreement between a subscriber and a service provider describing the QoS provided by the service provider for the subscriber's traffic

SLI (Set Link Info) The L2TP message from an LNS to an LAC to inform the LAC of link properties negotiated between the LNS and the Remote System during LCP

SNMP (Simple Network Management Protocol) A protocol used for the management of systems connected to IP networks

TCP (Transmission Control Protocol) A reliable transport protocol defined to run over IP networks

UDP (User Datagram Protocol) An unreliable transport protocol defined to run over IP networks

VJ (Van Jacobson) Protocol A protocol used in PPP to compress TCP/IP headers

VPN (Virtual Private Network)

WAN (Wide Area Network)

WEN (Wan Error Notify) The L2TP message from an LAC to an LNS to inform the LNS of errors on the call between the LAC and Remote System

XOR The exclusive logical OR operation

ZLB (Zero Length Body) An L2TP control message sent as an acknowledgment on the L2TP control channel

Bibliography

Carlson, James. *PPP Design and Debugging.* Reading, Mass.: Addison Wesley Longman, 1997.

Kaufman, Charles, Radia Perlman, and Mike Speciner. *Network Security: Private Communication in a Public World.* Englewood Cliffs, N.J.: Prentice Hall, 1995.

Schneiderman, B. *Designing the User Interface.* Reading, Mass.: Addison-Wesley, 1987.

Schneier, Bruce. *Applied Cryptography.* 2e. New York: John Wiley and Sons, 1996.

Index

A

ACCM. *See* Asynchronous Control Character Map
ACCM values
  in SLI message, 132
ACFC. *See* Address and Control Field Compression
Ack Event for Sender action, 115–116, 122, 123, 125
ACK wait timeout, 238
Acknowledgment Number field
  in payload packets, 249
Acknowledgment timeouts, 243–245
  calculating, 246
  and window adjustment, 248–249
Acknowledgments
  and Round-Trip Time, 245
Adaptive acknowledgment timeout
  calculating, 246–247
Adaptive timeout (ATO), 244, 245, 247, 248
Address and Control Field Compression (ACFC), 158–159, 170
Address headers
  HDLC, 13
Addressing
  and layer 2 protocol, 12
  with layer 3 of PPP, 14
AdminClose, 65, 69
ADSL. *See* Asymmetric Digital Subscriber Line
ADSL Forum, 44
AH. *See* Authentication Header
AH hash functions
  and replay protection, 204
AHDLC. *See* Asynchronous HDLC

AHDLC-based calls, 170
Algorithms
  AVP unhiding with no separate storage area, 97–98
  for hiding AVP value, 91
  Karn's, 247, 248
  "random early discard", 248
  for unhiding AVP data, 94–97
Aliasing
  sequence number, 250
allowoptions, 228
Alpha, 247
American National Standards Institute (ANSI), 44
AppleTalk, 7, 46, 50
Applied Cryptography (Schneier), 215
Assigned Tunnel ID AVP
  restrictions on, 99
  of SCCRQ, 79, 80
Asymmetric Digital Subscriber Line (ADSL), ix, x, 43–45
Asynchronous Control Character Map (ACCM), 43, 140, 150, 154–156, 170, 172
Asynchronous framing
  vs. synchronous framing, 170
Asynchronous HDLC (AHDLC), 12, 154
Asynchronous Transfer Model (ATM), 7, 8
ATM AAL5, 12, 151, 152
ATO. *See* Adaptive Timeout
Attribute field
  for AVP instance, 90
Attribute Value Pair (AVP) hiding
  algorithm, 90–94

⋏ THE ADDISON–WESLEY NETWORKING BASICS SERIES

Focused and Concise Hands-On Guides for Networking Professionals

The Addison-Wesley Networking Basics Series is a set of concise, hands-on guides to today's key computer networking technologies and protocols. Each volume in the series covers a focused topic, presenting the steps required to implement and work with specific technologies and tools in network programming, administration, and security. Providing practical, problem-solving information, these books are written by practicing professionals who have mastered complex network challenges.

Please visit our Web site at
http://www.awl.com/cseng/networkingbasics/
for more information on these titles.

Addison-Wesley Computer and Engineering Publishing Group

How to Interact with Us

1. Visit our Web site

http://www.awl.com/cseng

When you think you've read enough, there's always more content for you at Addison-Wesley's web site. Our web site contains a directory of complete product information including:

- Chapters
- Exclusive author interviews
- Links to authors' pages
- Tables of contents
- Source code

You can also discover what tradeshows and conferences Addison-Wesley will be attending, read what others are saying about our titles, and find out where and when you can meet our authors and have them sign your book.

2. Subscribe to Our Email Mailing Lists

Subscribe to our electronic mailing lists and be the first to know when new books are publishing. Here's how it works: Sign up for our electronic mailing at **http://www.awl.com/cseng/mailinglists.html**. Just select the subject areas that interest you and you will receive notification via email when we publish a book in that area.

3. Contact Us via Email

cepubprof@awl.com
Ask general questions about our books.
Sign up for our electronic mailing lists.
Submit corrections for our web site.

bexpress@awl.com
Request an Addison-Wesley catalog.
Get answers to questions regarding your order or our products.

innovations@awl.com
Request a current Innovations Newsletter.

webmaster@awl.com
Send comments about our web site.

cepubeditors@awl.com
Submit a book proposal.
Send errata for an Addison-Wesley book.

cepubpublicity@awl.com
Request a review copy for a member of the media interested in reviewing new Addison-Wesley titles.

We encourage you to patronize the many fine retailers who stock Addison-Wesley titles. Visit our online directory to find stores near you or visit our online store: **http://store.awl.com/** or call **800-824-7799**.

Addison Wesley Longman
Computer and Engineering Publishing Group
One Jacob Way, Reading, Massachusetts 01867 USA
TEL 781-944-3700 • FAX 781-942-3076